CHOCTAW BY BLOOD

ENROLLMENT CARDS

1898-1914

VOLUME XIII

TRANSCRIBED BY

JEFF BOWEN

NATIVE STUDY
Gallipolis, Ohio
USA

Originally published:
Baltimore, Maryland
2016

Reprinted by:

Native Study LLC
Gallipolis, OH
www.nativestudy.com

Library of Congress Control Number: 2020911767

ISBN: 978-1-64968-016-7

Made in the United States of America.

Other Books and Series by Jeff Bowen

1901-1907 Native American Census Seneca, Eastern Shawnee, Miami, Modoc, Ottawa, Peoria, Quapaw, and Wyandotte Indians (Under Seneca School, Indian Territory)

1932 Census of The Standing Rock Sioux Reservation with Births And Deaths 1924-1932

Census of The Blackfeet, Montana, 1897- 1901 Expanded Edition

Eastern Cherokee by Blood, 1906-1910, Volumes I thru XIII

Choctaw of Mississippi Indian Census 1929-1932 with Births and Deaths 1924-1931 Volume I

Choctaw of Mississippi Indian Census 1933, 1934 & 1937, Supplemental Rolls to 1934 & 1935 with Births and Deaths 1932-1938, and Marriages 1936-1938 Volume II

Eastern Cherokee Census Cherokee, North Carolina 1930-1939 Census 1930-1931 with Births And Deaths 1924-1931 Taken By Agent L. W. Page Volume I

Eastern Cherokee Census Cherokee, North Carolina 1930-1939 Census 1932-1933 with Births And Deaths 1930-1932 Taken By Agent R. L. Spalsbury Volume II

Eastern Cherokee Census Cherokee, North Carolina 1930-1939 Census 1934-1937 with Births and Deaths 1925-1938 and Marriages 1936 & 1938 Taken by Agents R. L. Spalsbury And Harold W. Foght Volume III

Seminole of Florida Indian Census, 1930-1940 with Birth and Death Records, 1930-1938

Texas Cherokees 1820-1839 A Document For Litigation 1921

Choctaw By Blood Enrollment Cards 1898-1914 Volumes I thru XII

Visit our website at **www.nativestudy.com** to learn more about these and other books and series by Jeff Bowen

This series is dedicated to
Mike Marchi,
who keeps my spirits up.

CREEK CENSUS.

SECOND NOTICE.

Members of the Dawes Commission will be present at the following times and places for the purpose of enrolling Creek citizens, as required by Act of Congress of June 10, 1896:

At Muskogee, Nov. 8 to 30, 1897, inclusive.
At Wagoner, Nov. 8 to 13, " inclusive.
At Eufaula, Nov. 8 to 13, " inclusive.
At Sapulpa, Nov. 15 to 20, " inclusive.
At Wetumpka, Nov. 15 to 20, " inclusive.
At Okmulgee, Nov. 22 to 30, " inclusive.

All persons who have not heretofore enrolled before the Dawes Commission should appear and enroll. Parents and guardians can enroll their families and wards.

TAMS BIXBY,
FRANK C. ARMSTRONG,
A. S. McKENNON,
THOS. B. NEEDLES,
Commissioners.

The above illustration is similar in nature to what was found throughout Indian Territory for different tribes as far as postings on bulletin boards, public centers, or wherever they could be read so people would be notified of where and when they needed to be for enrollment with the Dawes Commission.

v

This is a picture of the Dawes Commission at Camp Jones in Stonewall, Indian Territory on September 8, 1898.

The images below are of two of the original cards given on the microfilm. The cards given in this book have been formatted to fit on one page and still give all the information found on the original cards.

Choctaw Nation   Choctaw Roll

Choctaw Nation   Choctaw Roll

Introduction

This series of Choctaw Enrollment Cards for the Five Civilized Tribes 1898-1914 has been transcribed from National Archive Film M-1186 Rolls 39-46.

The series contains more than 6100 Choctaw enrollment cards. All of the cards list age, sex and degree of blood, the parties' Dawes Roll Numbers, and date of enrollment by the Secretary of Interior for each person. The contents also give the enrollee's parents' names as well as miscellaneous notes pertaining to the enrollee's circumstances, when needed. Most entries indicate whether or not a spouse is an Intermarried White, with the initials I.W.

Enrollment wasn't as simple a process as most would think just by going through these pages. The relationships between the Five Tribes and the Dawes Commission were weak at best. There were political battles going on between the tribes and the U.S. Government as it was, but the struggles didn't stop there. Each tribe had its own political factions pulling it from every direction. On top of everything else, people from every corner of the United States were trying to figure how to get in on the spoils (Money and Land Allotment) by means of political favor. Kent Carter, author of *The Dawes Commission*, describes the continuous effort required to enroll the different tribes and the pressure the Commission incurred from people all over the country who tried to insinuate themselves into the equation:

"In May 1896 the Dawes Commission Returned To Indian Territory for its third visit, establishing its headquarters at Vinita in the Cherokee Nation. It now had to process applications for citizenship in addition to negotiating allotment agreements; these circumstances make the narrative of events more confusing because the commission attempted the two tasks concurrently. The commissioners resumed making their usual speeches to tribal officials and public gatherings to promote negotiations, but now they inevitably had to respond to questions about how the application process for citizenship would work. They also began receiving letters from people all over the United States asking how they could 'get on the rolls' so they could 'get Indian land'."[1]

For the actual process of Choctaw enrollment, "A commission was appointed in each county of the Choctaw Nation under an act of September 18 to make separate rolls of citizens by blood, by intermarriage, and freedmen; it was to deliver them to recently elected Chief Green McCurtain by October 20, but he rejected them even before they were completed because of charges that people were being left off for political reasons. On October 30, the National Council authorized establishment of a five-member

---

[1] *The Dawes Commission* by Kent Carter, page 15, para. 1

commission to revise the rolls within ten days and then directed McCurtain to turn them over to the Dawes Commission on November 11, 1896. The Choctaws hired the law firm of Stuart, Gordon, and Hailey, of South McAlester to represent the tribe at all proceedings held by the Dawes Commission,"[2] another indication that throughout the Commission's efforts there was always controversy between the tribes and the negotiators.

When completed, this multi-volume series will contain thousands of names, all of them accounted for in the indexes carefully prepared by the author. Hopefully this work will help many researchers find their ancestors and satisfy the questions that so many have had about their Native American heritage.

Jeff Bowen
Gallipolis, Ohio
NativeStudy.com

---

[2] *The Dawes Commission* by Kent Carter, page 16, para. 5

Choctaw By Blood Enrollment Cards 1898-1914

RESIDENCE: Jackson   COUNTY. **Choctaw Nation**   **Choctaw Roll**   CARD NO.

POST OFFICE: Jackson, I.T.   *(Not Including Freedmen)*   FIELD NO. 3601

Dawes' Roll No.	NAME	Relationship to Person	AGE	SEX	BLOOD	Year	County	No.
10173	1 LeFlore, Sophia 27	First Named	24	F	Full	1896	Jackson	8120
10174	2 " Minerva 7	Dau	4	"	1/2	1896	"	8121
10175	3 " Earnestine 5	"	2	"	1/2			
10176	4 " Geneva 2	"	4mo	"	1/2			
	5							
	6							
	7							
	8							
	9							
	10							
	11							
	12							
	13							
	14							
	15							
	16							
	17							

ENROLLMENT
OF NOS. 1,2,3 and 4   HEREON
APPROVED BY THE SECRETARY
OF INTERIOR   FEB 4 1903

TRIBAL ENROLLMENT OF PARENTS

	Name of Father	Year	County	Name of Mother	Year	County
1	Hayes	Dead	Jackson	Liza A Hayes	Dead	Jackson
2	Michael W LeFlore		Chickasaw	No 1		
3	" " "		"	No 1		
4	" " "		"	No 1		
5						
6						
7	No 2 on 1896 roll is Jiney LeFlore					
8	Nos 3-4 Affidavits of birth to					
9	be supplied: Affidavit for No3 recd					
10	Oct 7/99. As to No4 filed Nov 2/99					
11	Husband of No.1 and father of children hereon is Michael W LeFlore on					
12	Choctaw Card #5448					
13	For child of No1 see NB (Apr 26-06) Card #332					
14						
15						
16				Date of Application for Enrollment.	Aug 21/99	
17						

1

Choctaw By Blood Enrollment Cards 1898-1914

RESIDENCE: Jackson COUNTY.
POST OFFICE: Mayhew I.T.

Choctaw Nation

Choctaw Roll *(Not Including Freedmen)*

CARD NO.
FIELD NO. 3602

Dawes' Roll No.	NAME		Relationship to Person	AGE	SEX	BLOOD	TRIBAL ENROLLMENT		
							Year	County	No.
10177	1 Bench, Daniel	29	First Named	26	M	1/2	1896	Jackson	1492
I.W. 974	2 " Katie	22	Wife	19	F	IW	1896	"	14321
10178	3 " Emmett C	3	Son	3mo	M	1/4			
10179	4 " Agnes Alma	1	Dau	5mo	F	1/4			
	5								
	6								
	7	ENROLLMENT OF NOS. 1,3 and 4 HEREON APPROVED BY THE SECRETARY OF INTERIOR FEB 4 1903							
	8								
	9								
	10								
	11	ENROLLMENT OF NOS. ~ 2 ~ HEREON APPROVED BY THE SECRETARY OF INTERIOR SEP 22 1904							
	12								
	13								
	14								
	15								
	16								
	17								

TRIBAL ENROLLMENT OF PARENTS

	Name of Father	Year	County	Name of Mother	Year	County
1	Chris Bench	Dead	Jackson	Nancy Bench	Dead	Jackson
2	Henry Stephens	"	Non Citz	Rudy Stephens	"	Non Citz
3	No1			No2		
4	Nº1			Nº2		
5						
6						
7	No2 See Decision of July 19 '04					
8	No2 as to marriage, see testimony					
9	of No1					
10	No3 Affidavit of birth to be supplied. Filed Nov 2/99					
11	Nº4 Born Dec 31, 1901: enrolled June 3, 1902					
12	For child of Nos 1&2 see NB (Apr 26-06) Card #826					
13	" " " " " " (Mar 3-05) " #1142					
14						
15				#1 to 3		
16				Date of Application for Enrollment	Aug 21/99	
17						

2

Choctaw By Blood Enrollment Cards 1898-1914

RESIDENCE: Blue   COUNTY. **Choctaw Nation**   **Choctaw Roll** (Not Including Freedmen)   CARD NO.

POST OFFICE: Albany, I.T.   FIELD NO. 3603

Dawes' Roll No.	NAME	Relationship to Person	AGE	SEX	BLOOD	TRIBAL ENROLLMENT		
						Year	County	No.
10180	1 Harris, Jincy 57	First Named	54	F	3/8	1896	Blue	10914
	2							
	3							
	4							
	5	ENROLLMENT OF NOS. 1 HEREON APPROVED BY THE SECRETARY OF INTERIOR FEB 4 1903						
	6							
	7							
	8							
	9							
	10							
	11							
	12							
	13							
	14							
	15							
	16							
	17							

TRIBAL ENROLLMENT OF PARENTS

	Name of Father	Year	County	Name of Mother	Year	County
1	David Mackey	Dead	Blue	Sealey Mackey	Dead	Blue
2						
3						
4						
5						
6	On 1896 roll as Jincy Richardson					
7	Nº1 also on 1896 Choctaw census roll page 271 #10626 Chickasaw district as Jincy Peter					
8	This woman appeared before the Commission this Nov 19, 1902, and stated that it is her sister, Isabella Bully, on Choc #3377, who is dead.					
9						
10						
11						
12						
13						
14						
15					Date of Application for Enrollment.	
16					Aug 21/99	
17						

Choctaw By Blood Enrollment Cards 1898-1914

RESIDENCE: Jackson   COUNTY.   **Choctaw Nation**   **Choctaw Roll**   CARD No.
POST OFFICE: Jackson, I.T.   *(Not Including Freedmen)*   FIELD No. 3604

Dawes' Roll No.	NAME		Relationship to Person	AGE	SEX	BLOOD	TRIBAL ENROLLMENT		
							Year	County	No.
10181	1 Dwight, Edwin	30	First Named	27	M	Full	1896	Jackson	3498
10182	2 " Emma	29	Wife	26	F	1/2	1896	"	3499
10183	3 " Thomas L	6	Son	3	M	3/4	1896	"	3500
10184	4 " Simon	4	"	1	"	3/4			
DEAD	5 " ~~Ethel~~ DEAD 3		~~Dau~~	1 mo	F	3/4			
10185	6 " Edwin B	2	Son	1 mo	M	3/4			
DEAD	7 " ~~Norris~~ DEAD 1		~~Son~~	1 mo	M	3/4			
	8								
	9								
	10	ENROLLMENT							
	11	OF NOS.1,2,3,4 and 6 HEREON APPROVED BY THE SECRETARY							
	12	OF INTERIOR FEB 4 1903							
	13	No. 5 and 7 HEREON DISMISSED UNDER							
	14	ORDER OF THE COMMISSION TO THE FIVE							
	15	CIVILIZED TRIBES OF MARCH 31, 1905.							
	16								
	17								

TRIBAL ENROLLMENT OF PARENTS

	Name of Father	Year	County	Name of Mother	Year	County
1	Timothy Dwight	Dead	Jackson	Minerva Dwight		Jackson
2	Ben Hunter	"	"	Tennessee Hunter		Non Citz
3	No1			No2		
4	No1			No2		
5	~~No1~~			~~No2~~		
6	No.1			No.2		
7	~~Nº1~~			~~Nº2~~		
8	No1 on 1896 roll as Edward Dwight					
9						
10	No2 As to marriage of parents of No2					
11	see enrollment of mother Tennessee Hunter					
	No 6 Enrolled Sept. 22d, 1900					
12	Nº7 Born April 17, 1902: enrolled June 3, 1901					
13	No5 died March 3, 1900; proof of death filed Dec 5 1902					#1 to 5 inc
14	No7 " August 18, 1902; " " " " 5 1902				Date of Application for Enrollment.	
15	For child of Nos 1&2 see NB (Mar 3-05) Card #248				Aug 21/99	
16						
17	PO Boswell IT 3/25/25[sic]					

4

Choctaw By Blood Enrollment Cards 1898-1914

RESIDENCE:	Jackson	COUNTY.	**Choctaw Nation**	**Choctaw Roll**	CARD NO.
POST OFFICE:	Jackson, I.T.			*(Not Including Freedmen)*	FIELD NO. 3605

Dawes' Roll No.	NAME		Relationship to Person First Named	AGE	SEX	BLOOD	TRIBAL ENROLLMENT		
							Year	County	No.
10186	₁ Dwight, Minerva	58	Named	55	F	Full	1896	Jackson	3501
10187	₂ " Jeremiah	25	Son	22	M	"	1896	"	3503
DEAD	₃ " Annie	19	Dau	16	F	"	1896	"	3504
	₄								
	₅								
	₆								
	₇								
	₈								
	₉	ENROLLMENT OF NOS. 1 and 2 HEREON APPROVED BY THE SECRETARY OF INTERIOR FEB 4 1903							
	₁₀								
	₁₁	No. 3 HEREON DISMISSED UNDER ORDER OF THE COMMISSION TO THE FIVE CIVILIZED TRIBES OF MARCH 31, 1905.							
	₁₂								
	₁₃								
	₁₄								
	₁₅								
	₁₆								
	₁₇								

TRIBAL ENROLLMENT OF PARENTS

	Name of Father	Year	County	Name of Mother	Year	County
₁	Wa-ka-yah	Dead	Jackson	Ho-ta-le-ma	Dead	Jackson
₂	Timothy Dwight	"	"	No 1		
₃	" "	"	"	No 1		
₄						
₅						
₆	No 3 died June 20, 1900; proof of death filed Dec 5, 1902					
₇						
₈						
₉						
₁₀						
₁₁						
₁₂						
₁₃						
₁₄						
₁₅						
₁₆				Date of Application for Enrollment.	Aug 21/99	
₁₇						

5

Choctaw By Blood Enrollment Cards 1898-1914

RESIDENCE: Blue
POST OFFICE: Caddo, I.T

COUNTY. **Choctaw Nation**

Choctaw Roll
(Not Including Freedmen)

CARD NO.
FIELD NO. 3606

Dawes' Roll No.	NAME		Relationship to Person	AGE	SEX	BLOOD	TRIBAL ENROLLMENT		
							Year	County	No.
10188	1 Damron, Amanda	21	First Named	18	F	1/8	1896	Blue	3551
10189	2 " Lola	4	Dau	5mo	"	1/16			
10190	3 " Lula	1	Dau	2mo	"	1/16			
	4								
	5								
	6	ENROLLMENT							
	7	OF NOS. 1, 2 and 3 HEREON APPROVED BY THE SECRETARY							
	8	OF INTERIOR FEB 4 1903							
	9								
	10								
	11								
	12								
	13								
	14								
	15								
	16								
	17								

TRIBAL ENROLLMENT OF PARENTS

	Name of Father	Year	County	Name of Mother	Year	County
1	Geo. Davis	Dead	Blue	Mary Davis		Non Citz
2	Wm Damron		Non Citz	No1		
3	" "		" "	No1		
4						
5						
6	No1 on 1896 roll as Amanda Davis					
7						
8	No1 – As to marriage of parents, see enrollment of brother; Alfred Davis					
9	No2 Affidavit of birth to be					
10	supplied:-					
11	No.3 Born September 5, 1901: Enrolled November 1, 1901					
12						
13	See testimony filed in 3610					
14					Date of Application for Enrollment.	
15	For child of No1 see NB (Mar 3-1905) Card #243				Aug 21/99	
16						
17						

Choctaw By Blood Enrollment Cards 1898-1914

RESIDENCE: Blue	COUNTY:				Choctaw Roll	CARD No.	
POST OFFICE: Caddo, I.T.	**Choctaw Nation**				(Not Including Freedmen)	FIELD No. **3607**	

Dawes' Roll No.	NAME	Relationship to Person First Named	AGE	SEX	BLOOD	TRIBAL ENROLLMENT Year	County	No.
15265	1 Booker, Lizzie 40	First Named	37	F	1/16	1893	Kiamitia	111
15266	2 Carroll, Homer 20	Son	17	M	1/32	1893	"	113
15267	3 " Birdie 18	Dau	15	F	1/32	1893	"	114
15268	4 " Byron 16	Son	13	M	1/32	1893	"	115
15269	5 " Bessie 14	Dau	11	F	1/32	1893	"	116
15270	6 Booker Carroll 6	Son	3	M	1/32			
I.W. 1124	7 " William P 59	Husband	59	M	I.W.			

8

9 ENROLLMENT OF NOS. 1,2,3,4,5 and 6 HEREON APPROVED BY THE SECRETARY

10 OF INTERIOR May 9 1904

11

12 ENROLLMENT OF NOS. ~~~ 7 ~~~ HEREON APPROVED BY THE SECRETARY

13 OF INTERIOR Nov 16 1904

14 No.1 is granddaughter of John Null,

15 who was admitted by decision of

16 Supreme Court of Choctaw Nation in October, 1872.

17

TRIBAL ENROLLMENT OF PARENTS

	Name of Father	Year	County	Name of Mother	Year	County
1	Jas Null	Dead	Blue	Martha Null	Dead	Non-Citz
2	Geo. Carroll	"	Non Citz	No1		
3	" " "	"	" "	No1		
4	" " "	"	" "	No1		
5	" " "	"	" "	No1		
6	W. P. Booker		Intermarried	No1		
7	George Booker	dead	non-citizen	Frances Booker	dead	non-citizen

8

9 No1 on 1893 Pay roll, Page 121, No 111, Kiamitia Co, as Lizzie Carroll

10 No2 " 1893 " " 121, " 113 " " " Homer Carroll

11 No3 " 1893 " " 121, " 114 " " " Birdie "

No4 " 1893 " " 121, " 115 " " " Byron "

12 No5 " 1893 " " 121, " 116 " " " Bessie "

13 No6 Affidavit of birth to be supplied. Recd Oct 7/99

14 No1 Evidence as to marriage of parents to be supplied

No6 Admitted by Dawes Commission in 1896. Choctaw Case #924

15 W P. Booker father of above children in TD 340

16 No7 transferred from Choctaw Card #D-340 Oct 31, 1904: See decision of Oct 15,1904

17 For child of No3 see NB (March 3, 1905) #1164

		Date of Application for Enrollment.
		Aug 21/99

No7 P.O. Waupanucka[sic] I.T. 11/18/02

Choctaw By Blood Enrollment Cards 1898-1914

| RESIDENCE: Blue | COUNTY. | **Choctaw Nation** | Choctaw Roll | CARD NO. 3608 |
| POST OFFICE: Caddo, I.T. | | | (Not Including Freedmen) | FIELD NO. 360_ |

Dawes' Roll No.		NAME	Relationship to Person First Named	AGE	SEX	BLOOD	TRIBAL ENROLLMENT Year	County	No.
DEAD.	1	Robinson, Calvin	72	M	1/4	1896	Blue	10932
10191	2	" Clisto C 20	Son	17	"	1/8	1896	"	10934
15856	3	" Mary E	Wife	63	F	3/8	1896	"	10933
15857	4	Trice Mary A	S.Dau	29	"	3/16	1896	"	12430
	5								
	6								
	7	ENROLLMENT OF NOS. 2 HEREON APPROVED BY THE SECRETARY OF INTERIOR FEB 4 1903							
	8								
	9								
	10	No. 1 HEREON DISMISSED UNDER ORDER OF THE COMMISSION TO THE FIVE CIVILIZED TRIBES OF MARCH 31, 1905.							
	11								
	12								
	13	ENROLLMENT OF NOS. ~ 3 and 4 ~ HEREON APPROVED BY THE SECRETARY OF INTERIOR JUN 12 1905							
	14								
	15								
	16	For child of No4 see NB (Apr 26-06) Card #376							
	17								

TRIBAL ENROLLMENT OF PARENTS

	Name of Father	Year	County	Name of Mother	Year	County
1	Emziah Robinson	Dead	Non Citz	Emily Folsom	Dead	Eagle
2	No1			Mary E Robinson		Non Citz
3	John Patterson	dead	Skullyville	Mary Patterson	dead	Skullyville
4	Jas J Trice	"	Non Citz	No.3		
5						
6						
7	Enrollment of Nos 3 and 4 cancelled by Department March 4, 1904					
8	Nos 3 and 4 restored to roll by Departmental authority of January 19, 1909 (File 5-51)					
9	No2 on 1896 roll as Christie C. Robinson					
	Nº1 Died Sept 15,1902: proof of death filed Oct 2 1902					
10	No.3 on 1885 Choc Census Roll, Blue Co, No 637 as Mary E Robinson					
11	No.4 " " " " " 639 " Mary Ann Trial					
12	No.3 denied by Dawes Commission in 1896; Choctaw case #661: no appeal					
	No.4 " " " " " " " " " "					
13	Nos 3 and 4 originally listed for enrollment on Choc cards Nos D-363 and D-364 respectively					
14	Aug 24/99: transferred to this card May 15, 1905. See					
15	decision of March 28, 1905					
16					Date of Application for Enrollment.	Aug 21/99
17						

8

Choctaw By Blood Enrollment Cards 1898-1914

RESIDENCE:	Jackson	COUNTY.							
POST OFFICE:	Mayhew, I.T.	**Choctaw Nation**					**Choctaw Roll** *(Not Including Freedmen)*	CARD NO. FIELD NO.	3609

Dawes' Roll No.	NAME		Relationship to Person	AGE	SEX	BLOOD	TRIBAL ENROLLMENT		
							Year	County	No.
10192	1 Sanders, William	31	First Named	28	M	1/4	1896	Jackson	11549
I.W. 336	2 " Ada	26	Wife	23	F	I.W	1896	"	15053
10193	3 " George	11	Son	8	M	1/8	1896	"	11550
10194	4 " Rhoda	9	Dau	6	F	1/8	1896	"	11551
10195	5 " Dot	5	"	2	"	1/8			
10196	6 " Amy	3	Dau	9mo	F	1/8			
10197	7 " Jewel	1	Dau	2mo	F	1/8			
	8								
	9	ENROLLMENT OF NOS. 1,3,4,5,6 and 7 HEREON APPROVED BY THE SECRETARY OF INTERIOR FEB 4 1903							
	10								
	11								
	12								
	13	ENROLLMENT OF NOS. 2 HEREON APPROVED BY THE SECRETARY OF INTERIOR SEP 12 1903							
	14								
	15								
	16								
	17								

TRIBAL ENROLLMENT OF PARENTS

	Name of Father	Year	County	Name of Mother	Year	County
1	James Sanders	Dead	Non Citz	Katie Battiest	Dead	Jackson
2	Weatherford	"	" "	Eliza Weatherford		Non Citz
3	No 1			No 2		
4	No 1			No 2		
5	No 1			No 2		
6	No. 1			No. 2		
7	Nº 1			Nº 2		
8						
9						
10			No5 Affidavit of birth to be			
11			supplied: Rec'd Oct 7/99			
12			No.6 Enrolled November 23rd, 1900			
13			Nº7 Born July 30, 1902, enrolled Sept. 29, 1902			Date of Application for Enrollment.
14			For child of Nos 1&2 see NB (March 3, 1905) #1054			
15						Aug 21/99
16						
17						

9

Choctaw By Blood Enrollment Cards 1898-1914

RESIDENCE: **Blue** COUNTY. **Choctaw Nation** **Choctaw Roll** CARD NO.
POST OFFICE: Caddo, I.T. *(Not Including Freedmen)* FIELD NO. 3610

Dawes' Roll No.	NAME		Relationship to Person First Named	AGE	SEX	BLOOD	TRIBAL ENROLLMENT		
							Year	County	No.
10198	1 Davis, Alfred	24	First Named	21	M	1/8	1896	Blue	3550
I.W. 369	2 " Maggie	19	Wife	16	F	I.W			
10199	3 " Ira Cecil	3	Son	4mo	M	1/16			
10200	4 " Mary E	1	Dau	2wks	F	1/16			
	5								
	6								
	7	ENROLLMENT							
	8	OF NOS. 1,3 and 4 HEREON APPROVED BY THE SECRETARY							
	9	OF INTERIOR FEB 4 1903							
	10								
	11	ENROLLMENT							
	12	OF NOS. ~~~~ 2 ~~~~ HEREON APPROVED BY THE SECRETARY							
	13	OF INTERIOR FEB -8 1904							
	14								
	15								
	16								
	17								

TRIBAL ENROLLMENT OF PARENTS

	Name of Father	Year	County	Name of Mother	Year	County
1	George Davis	Dead	Blue	Mary Davis		Intermarried
2	Winton	"	Non Citz	Mollie Betts	Dead	Non Citz
3	No.1			No.2		
4	Nº1			Nº2		
5						
6						
7						
8						
9			No1 as to marriage of parents see			
10			testimony of Calvin Robinson			
11			For child of Nos 1 and 2 see N.B. (Apr 26 '06) No. 790			
12			" " " " " " " (Mar 3-05) " 242			
13						
14					#1&2	
15			No.3 Enrolled May 24, 1900	Date of Application for Enrollment.	Aug 21/99	
16			Nº4 Born July 14, 1902 enrolled July 26, 1902			
17	Antioch I.T. 7/20/02					

10

Choctaw By Blood Enrollment Cards 1898-1914

RESIDENCE: Jackson	COUNTY.							
POST OFFICE: Jackson, I.T.	**Choctaw Nation**				Choctaw Roll (Not Including Freedmen)		CARD NO. FIELD NO. 3611	

Dawes' Roll No.	NAME	Relationship to Person	AGE	SEX	BLOOD	TRIBAL ENROLLMENT		
						Year	County	No.
10201	1 Crowder, Martin S ⁴⁸	First Named	46	M	1/4	1896	Jackson	2772
10202	2 " Emily ³⁹	Wife	36	F	3/4	1896	"	2773
10203	3 " Perry ²²	Son	19	M	1/2	1896	"	2774
10204	4 " Margaret ¹⁴	Dau	11	F	1/2	1896	"	2775
10205	5 " Sibbey ¹²	"	9	"	1/2	1896	"	2776
10206	6 " Flora ⁹	"	6	"	1/2	1896	"	2777
10207	7 " Sallie ⁷	"	4	"	1/2	1896	"	2778
10208	8 DIED PRIOR TO SEPTEMBER 25,1902 Mary Bell	Dau	6mo	F	1/2			

ENROLLMENT
OF NOS. 1,2,3,4,5,6,7 and 8 HEREON
APPROVED BY THE SECRETARY
OF INTERIOR FEB 4 1903

TRIBAL ENROLLMENT OF PARENTS

	Name of Father	Year	County	Name of Mother	Year	County
1	Louis Crowder		Jackson	Polly Crowder	Dead	Non Citz
2	Silas Ward	Dead	Tobucksy	Betsy Ward	"	Tobucksy
3	No1			No2		
4	No1			No2		
5	No1			No2		
6	No1			No2		
7	No1			No2		
8	No.1			No.2		
9	No1 on 1896 roll as M. S. Crowder					
10	No1 As to marriage of parents					
11	see his testimony which is deemed sufficient					
12	No.8 died Sept - 1900; Enrollment cancelled by Department July 8, 1904					
13	No.8 Enrolled June 30th, 1900					#1 to 7
14	For child of No.3 see NB (Apr 26'06) Card #254					Date of Application for Enrollment.
15	" " " Nos1&2 " " (March3,1905) " #712					Aug 21/99
17	PO Bennington IT 5/7/03					

11

Choctaw By Blood Enrollment Cards 1898-1914

RESIDENCE: Jackson COUNTY. **Choctaw Nation** Choctaw Roll CARD NO.
POST OFFICE: Jackson, I.T. *(Not Inclu...)* FIELD NO. 3612

Dawes' Roll No.	NAME	Relationship to Person First Named	AGE	SEX	BLOOD	TRIBAL ENROLLMENT		
						Year	County	No.
10209	1 Waichebbee, Leir 53	First Named	50	M	Full	1896	Jackson	13799
10210	2 " Ellen 41	Wife	38	F	"	1896	"	13800
	3							
	4							
	5	ENROLLMENT						
	6	OF NOS. 1 and 2 HEREON APPROVED BY THE SECRETARY						
	7	OF INTERIOR FEB 4 1903						
	8							
	9							
	10							
	11							
	12							
	13							
	14							
	15							
	16							
	17							

TRIBAL ENROLLMENT OF PARENTS

Name of Father	Year	County	Name of Mother	Year	County
1 Waichebbee	Dead	...tia	Sealey Durant		Jackson
2 Johnson Dwight	"		Lucy Dwight	Dead	"
3					
4					
5					
6					
7					
8					
9					
10					
11					
12					
13					
14				Date of Application for Enrollment	
15				Aug 21/99	
16					
17 P.O. Mayhew I.T.					

12

Choctaw By Blood Enrollment Cards 1898-1914

RESIDENCE: Blue   COUNTY. **Choctaw Nation**   **Choctaw Roll** CARD NO.
POST OFFICE: Caddo, I.T.   (Not Including Freedmen)   FIELD NO. **3613**

Dawes' Roll No.	NAME	Relationship to Person First Named	AGE	SEX	BLOOD	TRIBAL ENROLLMENT		
						Year	County	No.
10211	1 Nicholas, Rayson 42	First Named	39	M	Full	1896	Blue	9821
10212	2 " Hannah 42	Wife	39	F	"	1896	"	9822
10213	3 Gibson, Wilson 18	Nephew	15	M	"	1896	"	4922
	4							
	5							
	6	ENROLLMENT OF NOS. 1,2 and 3 HEREON APPROVED BY THE SECRETARY						
	7	OF INTERIOR Feb 4 1903						
	8							
	9							
	10							
	11							
	12							
	13							
	14							
	15							
	16							
	17							

TRIBAL ENROLLMENT OF PARENTS

Name of Father	Year	County	Name of Mother	Year	County
1 Adam Nicholas	Dead	Blue	Mulsey Nicholas	Dead	Blue
2 As King	"	"		"	"
3 Cephus Gibson		Atoka	Cillen Gibson	"	"
4					
5					
6					
7					
8 No 1 on 1896 roll as Reason J Nicholas					
9					
10					
11					
12					
13					
14				Date of Application for Enrollment.	
15				Aug 21/99	
16					
17					

13

Choctaw By Blood Enrollment Cards 1898-1914

RESIDENCE: **Blue**   COUNTY. **Choctaw Nation**   **Choctaw Roll**   CARD No.
POST OFFICE: Bok Chito, I.T.   *(Not Including Freedmen)*   FIELD No. **3614**

Dawes' Roll No.	NAME	Relationship to Person First Named	AGE	SEX	BLOOD	TRIBAL ENROLLMENT Year	County	No.
10214	1 Williams, Galloway 52	Named	49	M	Full	1896	Atoka	13899
10215	2 " Lyless 34	Wife	31	F	"	1896	"	14023
10216	3 " George 22	Son	19	M	"	1896	"	13901
10217	4 Carnes, Minnie 7	S.Dau	4	F	"	1896	"	2970
	5							
	6	~~ENROLLMENT~~						
	7	OF NOS. 1,2,3 and 4 HEREON						
	8	APPROVED BY THE SECRETARY ~~OF INTERIOR~~ FEB 4 1903						
	9							
	10							
	11							
	12							
	13							
	14							
	15							
	16							
	17							

TRIBAL ENROLLMENT OF PARENTS

	Name of Father	Year	County	Name of Mother	Year	County
1	Geo Williams	Dead	Blue	Ma-ka-ho-ke	Dead	Blue
2	Rayson Anderson	"	Atoka	Wisey Anderson	"	Atoka
3	No1			Sallie Williams	"	Blue
4	Lyman Carnes		Atoka	No2		
5						
6						
7						
8	(No2 on 1896 roll as Lyless Wright)					
9						
10						
11						
12						
13						
14					Date of Application for Enrollment.	
15					Aug 21/99	
16						
17						

14

Choctaw By Blood Enrollment Cards 1898-1914

RESIDENCE:	Jackson	COUNTY.	**Choctaw Nation**	**Choctaw Roll** (*Not Including Freedmen*)	CARD No.	
POST OFFICE:	Jackson, I.T.				FIELD NO. 3615	

Dawes' Roll No.	NAME	Relationship to Person First Named	AGE	SEX	BLOOD	TRIBAL ENROLLMENT		
						Year	County	No.
1	McGee, Eastman		46	M	Full	1896	Jackson	9405
2								
3								
4								
5								
6								
7								
8								
9								
10								
11								
12								
13	DISMISSED JAN 14 1907							
14								
15								
16								
17								

TRIBAL ENROLLMENT OF PARENTS

	Name of Father	Year	County	Name of Mother	Year	County
1	Sam McGee	Dead	Blue	Melinda McGee	Dead	Blue
2						
3						
4						
5						
6						
7	No1 died January 1, 1902. Proof of death filed January 12 1907					
8						
9						
10						
11						
12						
13						
14					Date of Application for Enrollment.	
15					Aug 21/99	
16						
17						

15

Choctaw By Blood Enrollment Cards 1898-1914

Dawes' Roll No.	NAME	Relationship to Person First Named	AGE	SEX	BLOOD	TRIBAL ENROLLMENT Year	County	No.
10218	1 McGee, Isaac DIED PRIOR TO SEPTEMBER 25, 1902		29	M	Full	1896	Blue	9425
10219	2 Jincey DIED PRIOR TO SEPTEMBER 25, 1902	Wife	30	F	"	1896	"	9426
10220	3 Sampson DIED PRIOR TO SEPTEMBER 25, 1902	Son	1mo	M	"			
10221	4 Frazier, Lizian 17	S.Dau	14	F	"	1893	Jackson	203
10222	5 Hooper, Agnes 11	S.Dau	8	F	"	1896	Jackson	5834
	6							
	7							
	8	ENROLLMENT						
	9	OF NOS. 1,2,3,4 and 5 HEREON						
	10	APPROVED BY THE SECRETARY OF INTERIOR FEB -4 1903						
	11	No.1 died Dec. 27, 1901: No.2 died						
	12	July 24, 1902: No.3 died Dec. 13, 1901:						
	13	Enrollment cancelled by Department Sept. 16, 1904						
	14							
	15							
	16							
	17							

TRIBAL ENROLLMENT OF PARENTS

	Name of Father	Year	County	Name of Mother	Year	County
1	Sam McGee	Dead	Blue	Melinda McGee	Dead	Blue
2	Moses Lapastoya	"	"	Phoebe Lapastoya	"	"
3	No1			No2		
4	Isom Frazier	Dead	Blue	No2		
5	Abel Hooper	"	"	No.2		
6						
7						
8						
9						
10	No5 Enrolled July 29, 1901					
11	No4 on 1893 Pay Roll, Page 24, No 203, Jackson					
12	County as Lizean Frazier					
13	No3 Affidavit of birth to be supplied:- Filed Nov 2/99				#1 to 4	
14	No.4 On 1896 roll as Lizzie Frazier, page				Date of Application for Enrollment.	
15	104, No. 4290, Jackson County.			Feby 15, 1900		
16	No.4 Proper name is Lizian Frazier, see			Aug 21/99		
	letters attached. Feby 23d, 1900					
17	No.5 also on 1896 Choctaw roll: page 144: #5898, as Agnes Harper.					

Choctaw By Blood Enrollment Cards 1898-1914

RESIDENCE:	Blue	COUNTY.					CARD No.		
POST OFFICE:	Blue, I.T.		**Choctaw Nation**			**Choctaw Roll** *(Not Including Freedmen)*	FIELD No. 3617		

Dawes' Roll No.	NAME	Relationship to Person	AGE	SEX	BLOOD	TRIBAL ENROLLMENT		
						Year	County	No.
10223	1 McGee, Solomon	First Named	39	M	Full	1896	Blue	9427
10224	2 " Martha 49	Wife	46	F	"	1896	"	9428
	3							
	4							
	5	ENROLLMENT						
	6	OF NOS. 1 and 2 HEREON APPROVED BY THE SECRETARY						
	7	OF INTERIOR FEB 4 1903						
	8							
	9							
	10							
	11							
	12							
	13							
	14							
	15							
	16							
	17							

DIED PRIOR TO SEPTEMBER 25 1902

TRIBAL ENROLLMENT OF PARENTS

Name of Father	Year	County	Name of Mother	Year	County
1 Sam McGee	Dead	Blue	Melinda McGee	Dead	Blue
2 E-ba-ha-tey	"	Jackson	Susan	"	Jackson
3					
4					
5					
6					
7					
8					
9 No 1 died - - 1901. Enrollment cancelled by Department July 8, 1904					
10					
11					
12					
13					
14				Date of Application for Enrollment.		
15				Aug 21/99		
16					
17					

17

Choctaw By Blood Enrollment Cards 1898-1914

RESIDENCE:	Blue	COUNTY.		CARD No.
POST OFFICE:	Bok Chito, I.T.	**Choctaw Nation** Choctaw Roll *(Not Including Freedmen)*		FIELD No. **3618**

Dawes' Roll No.	NAME	Relationship to Person	AGE	SEX	BLOOD	TRIBAL ENROLLMENT		
						Year	County	No.
10225	1 Payton, Daniel 52	First Named	49	M	Full	1896	Blue	10496
10226	2 " Susan 8	Dau	5	F	"	1896	"	10500
10227	3 Jackson Freenian 16	Ward	13	M	"	1896	Jackson	7092
I.W. 1415	4 Payton Amanda Elizabeth 49	Wife	47	F	I.W.			
	5							
	6							
	7	ENROLLMENT OF NOS. 1, 2 and 3 HEREON APPROVED BY THE SECRETARY OF INTERIOR Feb 4 1903						
	8							
	9							
	10							
	11							
	12	ENROLLMENT OF NOS. ~ 4 ~ HEREON APPROVED BY THE SECRETARY OF INTERIOR Jun 12 1905						
	13							
	14							
	15	See Choc Card #2813						
	16	No4 requested that no further correspondence taken in [remainder illegible]						
	17	No4 P.O. Provence I.T. 5/24/04						

TRIBAL ENROLLMENT OF PARENTS

Name of Father	Year	County	Name of Mother	Year	County
1 Tecumseh Payton	Dead	Blue	Rachael Payton	Dead	Bok Tuklo
2 No1			Sophia Payton	"	Blue
3 David Jackson	Dead	Jackson	Lizzie Jackson	"	Jackson
4 George Sugg	"	non-citizen	Martha J Sugg	"	non-citizen
5					
6					
7		No3 on 1896 roll as Preman[sic] Jackson.			
8					
9					
10		No4 Enrolled June 14, 1900			
11					
12					
13					
14					
15				Date of Application for Enrollment.	Aug 21/99
16					
17		Was not No.1 the husband of Nancy C. Payton on Choc Card #D.338?			

Choctaw By Blood Enrollment Cards 1898-1914

RESIDENCE: Blue   COUNTY. **Choctaw Nation**   Choctaw Roll   CARD NO.
POST OFFICE: Wade I.T.   *(Not Including Freedmen)*   FIELD NO. **3619**

Dawes' Roll No.	NAME		Relationship to Person First Named	AGE	SEX	BLOOD	TRIBAL ENROLLMENT		
							Year	County	No.
DEAD	1 Crawford Tabitha	51	Named	48	F	1/2			
DEAD	2 " Henry DEAD		Son	24	M	1/4			
14369	3 " Gus	23	"	20	"	1/4			
14370	4 " Barnett	20	"	17	"	1/4			
14371	5 " Marvin	16	"	13	"	1/4	ENROLLMENT		
14372	6 " Pearl	14	Dau	11	F	1/4	OF NOS. 10 HEREON APPROVED BY THE SECRETARY		
14373	7 " Alice	11	"	8	"	1/4	OF INTERIOR Mar 15 1905		
14374	8 " Ollie	3	G Dau	2mo	F	1/8			
14375	9 " Flora May	1	Gr Dau	10mo	F	1/8			
15789	10 " George	1	Son of No3	2	M	1/8			

11   ENROLLMENT   For child of No4 see NB(Mar 3,1905) #1484
12   OF NOS. 3,4,5,6,7,8 and 9 HEREON APPROVED BY THE SECRETARY   No8 As to sex see testimony of Gus Crawford
13   OF INTERIOR Apr 11 1903   of Sept 10 1903
   Correction made in accordance with
14 No1 died June 29, 1901: proof of   Departmental letter
15 death filed Dec 9, 1902
Nos 1 and 2 hereon dismissed under order of the
16 Commission to the Five Civilized Tribes March 31,1900
17

TRIBAL ENROLLMENT OF PARENTS

	Name of Father	Year	County	Name of Mother	Year	County
1	John Morris	Dead	Choctaw	Rebecca Morris	Dead	Choctaw
2	George Crawford		Non Citz	No1		
3	" "		" "	No1		
4	" "		" "	No1		
5	" "		" "	No1		
6	" "		" "	No1		
7	" "		" "	No1		
8	No3			Beckie Crawford		white woman
9	No2			Emma Crawford		" "
10	No.3			Becky Crawford		" "
11	Admitted by Dawes Commission Case					
12	No17 No Appeal					
13	As to residence, see testimony of No1					
14	N°2 Died March 3,1902: proof of death filed Aug 22 1902					
15	No8 enrolled subj to receipt of evidence of marriage of parents. Same #1 to 7 inc				Date of Application for Enrollment. Nov.7,1903(G.O.31502) Aug 21/99	
16	requested Filed Jany 4,1900					No8 enrolled Dec 16/99
17	N°2 is now the husband of Emma Crawford evidence of marriage filed Aug 9,1902 No10 Born Aug 13,1901. It is claimed application was made at Caddo I.T. about Oct 8,1901.					
	See affidavits and correspondence No10 Enrolled 5/2/04					

No9 Born Oct 2,1901: enrolled Aug 9,1902. For child of No.4 see NB (March 3,1905) #1090

Choctaw By Blood Enrollment Cards 1898-1914

RESIDENCE:	Blue	COUNTY.	**Choctaw Nation**				**Choctaw Roll**	CARD NO.	
POST OFFICE:	Caddo, I.T.						*(Not Including Freedmen)*	FIELD NO. 3620	

Dawes' Roll No.	NAME		Relationship to Person First Named	AGE	SEX	BLOOD	TRIBAL ENROLLMENT		
							Year	County	No.
10228	1 Homer Soloman J	32	First Named	29	M	1/2	1896	Blue	5847
I.W 666	2 " Blanche E	28	Wife	25	F	I.W			
10229	3 " St Clair	3	Son	2mo	M	1/4			
	4								
	5 DECISION PREPARED Oct 29 03								
	6								
	7 ENROLLMENT OF NOS. 1 and 3 HEREON								
	8 APPROVED BY THE SECRETARY OF INTERIOR FEB 4 1903								
	9								
	10 ENROLLMENT OF NOS. 2 HEREON								
	11 APPROVED BY THE SECRETARY								
	12 OF INTERIOR MAR 26 1904								
	13								
	14								
	15								
	16								
	17								

TRIBAL ENROLLMENT OF PARENTS

	Name of Father	Year	County	Name of Mother	Year	County
1	Jos. S Homer	Dead	Jackson	Mary Attaway		Cherokee
2	Marx		Non-Citz	M. C. Marx		Non Citz
3	No1			No2		
4						
5						
6						
7						
8	No1 As to marriage of parents, see			Jany 10,1901 No1 identified on Cherokee		
9	testimony of Peter Maytubby			Pay Roll for year 1894, page 108, #1403		
10				Delaware Dist as Sol J Homer.		
11	Evidence of marriage to be			Not found on other Cherokee Rolls		
12	supplied: Recd Oct 7/99			No3 enrolled Nov 2/99		
13						
14	Aug 25/99: Examine rolls to see status of					No3 enrolled Nov 2/99
15	enrollment of Mary A Attaway &					Aug 21/99
16	also of Solomon J Homer, also see his testimony.					Date of Application for Enrollment.
17						

20

Choctaw By Blood Enrollment Cards 1898-1914

RESIDENCE:	Jackson	COUNTY:							
POST OFFICE:	Bennington, I.T.	**Choctaw Nation**				**Choctaw Roll** *(Not Including Freedmen)*		CARD No. FIELD No. 3621	

Dawes' Roll No.	NAME		Relationship to Person Named	AGE	SEX	BLOOD	TRIBAL ENROLLMENT		
							Year	County	No.
10230	1 Johnson, Philip	51	First Named	48~~48~~	M	Full	1896	Jackson	7101
10231	2 " Frances	38	Wife	35	F	"	1896	"	7102
10232	3 " Moses	24	Son	21	M	"	1896	"	7103
10233	4 " Mary	6	Dau	3	F	"	1896	"	7106
10234	5 " Henry	5	Son	1	M	"			
10235	6 " Pearl	3	Dau	8mo	F	"			
10236	7 " Missie	2	Dau	2mo	F	"			
	8								
	9	ENROLLMENT							
	10	OF NOS. 1,2,3,4,5,6 and 7 HEREON APPROVED BY THE SECRETARY							
	11	OF INTERIOR FEB 4 1903							
	12								
	13								
	14								
	15								
	16								
	17								

TRIBAL ENROLLMENT OF PARENTS

	Name of Father	Year	County	Name of Mother	Year	County
1	Charles	Dead	Jacks Fork	Sallie	Dead	Jacks Fork
2	Edmond Jones		Atoka	Isabelle Jones	"	Blue
3	No 1			Sarah Johnson	"	Jacks F[sic]
4	No 1			No 2		
5	No 1			No 2		
6	No. 1			No. 2		
7	Nº 1			Nº 2		
8						
9						
10	No 5 Affidavit of birth to be					
11	supplied: Recd Oct 7/99					
12						
13	No.6 Enrolled June 23d. 1900					
14	Nº 7 Born July 13, 1902. Enrolled Sept 25, 1902			#1 to 5		
15				Date of Application for Enrollment.	Aug 21/99	
16						
17						

Choctaw By Blood Enrollment Cards 1898-1914

RESIDENCE: Jackson COUNTY. **Choctaw Nation** Choctaw Roll CARD NO.
POST OFFICE: Bennington, I.T.   *(Not Including Freedmen)* FIELD NO. 3622

Dawes' Roll No.	NAME	Relationship to Person	AGE	SEX	BLOOD	TRIBAL ENROLLMENT		
						Year	County	No.
10237	1 Johnson, Eliza ²²	First Named	19	F	Full	1896	Jackson	7104
10238	2 Ramsey, Ellen ⁷	Dau	4	"	"	1896	"	10868
	3							
	4							
	5	ENROLLMENT						
	6	OF NOS. 1 and 2 HEREON APPROVED BY THE SECRETARY						
	7	OF INTERIOR FEB 4 1903						
	8							
	9							
	10							
	11							
	12							
	13							
	14							
	15							
	16							
	17							

TRIBAL ENROLLMENT OF PARENTS

	Name of Father	Year	County	Name of Mother	Year	County
1	Philip Johnson		Jackson	Sarah Johnson	Dead	Jackson
2	Leas Ramsey	Dead	"	No1		
3						
4						
5						
6						
7						
8						
9						
10						
11						
12						
13						
14					Date of Application for Enrollment.	
15					Aug 21/99	
16						
17						

Choctaw By Blood Enrollment Cards 1898-1914

RESIDENCE:	Jackson	COUNTY.							
POST OFFICE:	Mayhew, I.T.	**Choctaw Nation**				Choctaw Roll *(Not Including Freedmen)*		FIELD NO. 3623	

Dawes' Roll No.	NAME		Relationship to Person Named	AGE	SEX	BLOOD	TRIBAL ENROLLMENT		
							Year	County	No.
10239	1 Battiest, Frank	22	First Named	19	M	1/2	1896	Jackson	1470
I.W.745	2 " Sallie	25	Wife	22	F	I.W.			
10240	3 " Benjamin	3	Son	1 mo	M	1/4			
	4								
	5								
	6								
	7	ENROLLMENT OF NOS. 1 and 3 HEREON							
	8	APPROVED BY THE SECRETARY OF INTERIOR FEB 4 1903							
	9								
	10	ENROLLMENT OF NOS. 2 HEREON							
	11	APPROVED BY THE SECRETARY OF INTERIOR MAY -7 1904							
	12								
	13								
	14								
	15	DECISION PREPARED No2 Nov 27 03							
	16								
	17								

TRIBAL ENROLLMENT OF PARENTS

	Name of Father	Year	County	Name of Mother	Year	County
1	Ben Battiest	Dead	Jackson	Kizzie Battiest		Jackson
2	Glenn	"	Non Citz	Frances Glenn		Non Citz
3	No 1			No 2		
4						
5						
6						
7			No2 See Decision of March 2, 04			
8			No3 Affidavit of birth to be			
9			supplied: Recd Oct 11/99 Evidence of divorce between N°2 and			
10			her former husband filed Oct 7, 1903			
11						
12						
13						
14						
15				Date of Application for Enrollment.		Aug 21/99
16						
17	P.O. Boswell IT 11/15/03					

Choctaw By Blood Enrollment Cards 1898-1914

RESIDENCE: Jackson COUNTY. **Choctaw Nation** **Choctaw Roll** CARD NO.
POST OFFICE: Jackson, I.T. *(Not Including Freedmen)* FIELD NO. 3624

Dawes' Roll No.	NAME	Relationship to Person First Named	AGE	SEX	BLOOD	TRIBAL ENROLLMENT		
						Year	County	No.
10241	1 Frazier, Eliza A 57	First Named	54	F	Full	1893	Jackson	206
10242	2 " Wallace 25	Son	22	M	"	1896	"	4266
10243	3 " Harriet 23	Dau	20	F	"	1896	"	4267
10244	4 " Simon 21	Son	18	M	"	1896	"	4268
	5							
	6							
	7							
	8							
	9							
	10							
	11							
	12							
	13							
	14							
	15							
	16							
	17							

ENROLLMENT
OF NOS. 1-2-3 and 4
APPROVED BY THE SECRETARY HEREON
OF INTERIOR FEB 4 1903

TRIBAL ENROLLMENT OF PARENTS

	Name of Father	Year	County	Name of Mother	Year	County
1	Wa-chubbee	Dead	Kiamitia	Sealey Durant		Jackson
2	Willie Frazier	"	Jackson	No1		
3	" "	"	"	No1		
4	" "	"	"	No1		
5						
6						
7						
8				No1 on 1893 Pay Roll, Page 25, No 206		
9				Jackson Co, as Lizann Frazier		
10				No4 on 1896 roll as Simeon Frazier		
11						
12						
13						
14						Date of Application for Enrollment.
15				Date of application for enrollment		Aug 21/99
16						
17						

24

Choctaw By Blood Enrollment Cards 1898-1914

RESIDENCE: Jackson   COUNTY.   **Choctaw Nation**   **Choctaw Roll**   CARD NO.
POST OFFICE: Jackson, I.T.   *(Not Including Freedmen)*   FIELD NO. 3625

Dawes' Roll No.	NAME	Relationship to Person	AGE	SEX	BLOOD	TRIBAL ENROLLMENT		
						Year	County	No.
10245	1 Durant, Sealey 73	First Named	70	F	Full	1896	Jackson	3473
	2							
	3							
	4							
	5							
	6							
	7							
	8							
	9							
	10							
	11							
	12							
	13							
	14							
	15							
	16							
	17							

ENROLLMENT
OF NOS. 1 HEREON
APPROVED BY THE SECRETARY
OF INTERIOR FEB 4 1903

TRIBAL ENROLLMENT OF PARENTS

Name of Father	Year	County	Name of Mother	Year	County
1 Alick Durant	Dead	in Mississippi	E-la-ho-to-na	Dead	Jackson
2					
3					
4					
5					
6	On 1896 roll as Sallie Durant				
7					
8					
9					
10					
11					
12					
13					
14			Date of Application for Enrollment.		
15			Aug 21/99		
16					
17					

Choctaw By Blood Enrollment Cards 1898-1914

RESIDENCE: **Blue**   COUNTY. **Choctaw Nation**   **Choctaw Roll** *(Not Including Freedmen)*   CARD NO.
POST OFFICE: **Caddo, I.T.**   FIELD NO. **3626**

Dawes' Roll No.	NAME	Relationship to Person First Named	AGE	SEX	BLOOD	TRIBAL ENROLLMENT Year	County	No.
10246	1 Folsom, Loren S.W 79	First Named	76	M	1/8	1896	Blue	4330
I.W. 155	2 " Katie 34	Wife	31	F	I.W.	1896	"	14538
10247	3 " Bessie 7	Dau	4	"	1/16	1896	"	4531
10248	4 " Irene 6	"	3	"	1/16	1896	"	4332
10249	5 " Victor 1	Son	16mo	M	1/16			
	6							
	7							
	8							
	9							
	10							
	11							
	12							
	13							
	14							
	15							
	16							
	17							

ENROLLMENT OF NOS. 1,3,4 and 5 HEREON APPROVED BY THE SECRETARY OF INTERIOR FEB 4 1903

ENROLLMENT OF NOS. 2 ~~~~~ HEREON APPROVED BY THE SECRETARY OF INTERIOR JUN 13 1903

TRIBAL ENROLLMENT OF PARENTS

	Name of Father	Year	County	Name of Mother	Year	County
1	David Folsom	Dead	Red River	Rhoda Folsom	Dead	Red River
2	E. B. Freeman	"	Non Citz	Emeline Freeman	"	Non Citz
3	No1			No2		
4	No1			No2		
5	Nº1			Nº2		
6						
7						
8	No2 was admitted by Dawes Com					
9	Case Bi 462 as an intermarried citizen: no appeal					
10	No2 on 1896 roll Katie Fulsom					
11	Nos 3 and 4 admitted by Dawes Commission in 1896: Choctaw case #440: no appeal					
12	Nº5 Born April 21, 1901: enrolled Aug 19, 1902					
13	For child of Nos 1&2 see NB (March 3 1905) #1013					
14					Date of Application for Enrollment.	
15					Aug 21/99	
16						
17						

RESIDENCE: Jackson   COUNTY. **Choctaw Nation**   **Choctaw Roll**   CARD NO.
POST OFFICE: Jackson, I.T.   *(Not Including Freedmen)*   FIELD NO. 3627

Dawes' Roll No.	NAME		Relationship to Person Named	AGE	SEX	BLOOD	TRIBAL ENROLLMENT		
							Year	County	No.
10250	₁ Paul, Solomon	21	First Named	18	M	Full	1893	Blue	939
10251	₂ " Eliza	23	Wife	20	F	"	1896	"	8132
10252	₃ LeFlore, Moses	6	S.Son	3	M	"	1896	"	8133
	4								
	5								
	6	~~ENROLLMENT~~							
	7	OF NOS. 1,2 and 3 HEREON							
	8	APPROVED BY THE SECRETARY ~~OF INTERIOR~~ FEB 4 1903							
	9								
	10								
	11								
	12								
	13								
	14								
	15								
	16								
	17								

TRIBAL ENROLLMENT OF PARENTS

	Name of Father	Year	County	Name of Mother	Year	County
₁	Sam Paul	Dead	Jackson	Sabile Paul	Dead	Jackson
₂	Charley Scott	"	"	Kizzie Scott	"	"
₃	Joshua LeFlore		"	No2		
4						
5						
6						
7			No1 on 1893 Pay Roll, Page 90, No 939, Blue			
8			Co, as Saul Paul			
9			No2 on 1896 roll as Eliza LeFlore			
10			~~No3 " 1896 " " Narsie "~~			
11			~~No1 " 1896 " " Stall Solomon, Page~~ 298, No 11565, Jackson Co			
12						
13			~~No3 is now ward of James P Dunn Choc D67~~			Date of Application for Enrollment.
14						
15						Aug 21/99
16						
17						

27

Choctaw By Blood Enrollment Cards 1898-1914

RESIDENCE: Jackson   COUNTY. **Choctaw Nation**   **Choctaw Roll** CARD No.
POST OFFICE: Jackson, I.T.   *(Not Including Freedmen)* FIELD No. 3628

Dawes' Roll No.	NAME	Relationship to Person	AGE	SEX	BLOOD	TRIBAL ENROLLMENT		
						Year	County	No.
10253	1 Frazier, Dixon 47	First Named	44	M	Full	1896	Jackson	4270
	2							
	3							
	4							
	5							
	6							
	7							
	8							
	9							
	10							
	11							
	12							
	13							
	14							
	15							
	16							
	17							

ENROLLMENT
OF NOS. 1 HEREON
APPROVED BY THE SECRETARY
OF INTERIOR FEB 4 1903

TRIBAL ENROLLMENT OF PARENTS

	Name of Father	Year	County	Name of Mother	Year	County
1	Tash-ka-nosh	Dead	Jackson	Na-ne-ma	Dead	Jackson
2						
3						
4						
5						
6						
7						
8						
9						
10						
11						
12						
13						
14						
15				Date of Application for Enrollment.	Aug 21/99	
16						
17						

| RESIDENCE: | Jackson | COUNTY. | | | | | |
| POST OFFICE: | Jackson, I.T | | | | | | |

Choctaw Nation

Choctaw Roll (Not Including Freedmen)

CARD NO.

FIELD NO. 3629

Dawes' Roll No.	NAME		Relationship to Person First Named	AGE	SEX	BLOOD	TRIBAL ENROLLMENT		
							Year	County	No.
10254	1 Nicholas, Asias W	54		51	M	Full	1896	Kiamitia	9769
10255	2 " Sealy	59	Wife	56	F	"	1896	"	9770
10256	3 " Isaac	21	Son	18	M	"	1896	"	9779
10257	4 Scott Sampson	22	S.Son	19	"	"	1896	Jackson	11576
	5								
	6								
	7	ENROLLMENT							
	8	OF NOS. 1,2,3 and 4 HEREON APPROVED BY THE SECRETARY							
	9	OF INTERIOR FEB 4 1903							
	10								
	11								
	12								
	13								
	14								
	15								
	16								
	17								

TRIBAL ENROLLMENT OF PARENTS

	Name of Father	Year	County	Name of Mother	Year	County
1	Willis Nicholas	Dead	Blue	Sophia Nicholas	Dead	Blue
2	Ko-cha-hick-ubbee	"	Kiamitia	E-ma-ti-ya	"	Kiamitia
3	No1			Seliney Nicholas	"	Jackson
4	Abner Scott	Dead	Jackson	No2		
5						
6						
7						
8						
9			No1 on 1896 roll as I. W. Nicholas			
10			No2 " 1896 " " Salina "			
11						
12						
13						
14					Date of Application for Enrollment.	
15						Aug 21/99
16						
17						

Choctaw By Blood Enrollment Cards 1898-1914

RESIDENCE: **Blue**   COUNTY. **Choctaw Nation**   **Choctaw Roll** *(Not Including Freedmen)*   CARD NO.
POST OFFICE: **Bennington, I.T.**   FIELD NO. **3630**

Dawes' Roll No.	NAME		Relationship to Person First Named	AGE	SEX	BLOOD	Year	County	No.
10258	1 Risener, Lucy	36	First Named	33	F	Full	1896	Blue	10905
10259	2 " Lizzie	16	Dau	13	"	1/2	1896	"	10906
10260	3 " Elmira	14	"	11	"	1/2	1896	"	10907
10261	4 " George	11	Son	8	M	1/2	1896	"	10909
10262	5 " Eliza	9	Dau	6	F	1/2	1896	"	10908
10263	6 " Henry	6	Son	3	M	1/2	1896	"	10910
10264	7 " Jessie	4	Dau	7mo	F	1/2			
10265	8 " Jack	2	Son	4mo	M	1/2			
I.W. 1629	9 " William		Hus	38	M	I.W.			
	10		ENROLLMENT						
	11		OF NOS. 1,2,3,4,5,6,7 and 8 HEREON						
	12		APPROVED BY THE SECRETARY OF INTERIOR FEB 4 1903						
	13		No9 Transferred from Choctaw card No D721 under						
	14		Departmental instructions of Nov 20 '06 ordering him						
	15		enrolled as an intermarried citizen of the Choctaw Nation ENROLLMENT						
	16		OF NOS. 9 HEREON APPROVED BY THE SECRETARY						
	17		OF INTERIOR FEB 19 1907						

TRIBAL ENROLLMENT OF PARENTS

	Name of Father	Year	County	Name of Mother	Year	County
1	Wilson Webster	Dead	Gaines		Dead	Gaines
2	William Risener		Non Citz	No1		
3	" "		" "	No1		
4	" "		" "	No1		
5	" "		" "	No1		
6	" "		" "	No1		
7	" "		" "	No1		
8	" "		" "	No1		
9	Jack Risener		Non Citz	Elizabeth Risener	Dead	Cherokee
10	No3 on 1896 roll as Emma Risener					
11	No7 Affidavit of birth to be					
12	supplied:- Recd: Oct 7/99					
13	No8 Enrolled May 16, 1901					#1 to 7 inc.
14	Husband of Nº1 and father of the children on this card is					Date of Application for Enrollment.
15	William Risener on Choctaw card #D721					Aug 21/99
16	For child of Nos 1&9 see NB (Mar 3-1905) #606					
17	" " " No 2 " " " " #607					

30

Choctaw By Blood Enrollment Cards 1898-1914

RESIDENCE: Jackson COUNTY.
POST OFFICE: Crowder, I.T.

Choctaw Nation

Choctaw Roll
(Not Including Freedmen)

CARD No.
FIELD No. 3631

Dawes' Roll No.	NAME		Relationship to Person	AGE	SEX	BLOOD	TRIBAL ENROLLMENT		
							Year	County	No.
10266	1 Airington Rufus	30	First Named	27	M	1/8	1896	Tobucksy	134
10267	2 " Pearl	7	Dau	4	F	1/16	1896	"	136
10268	3 " Fred J	9	Son	6	M	1/16	1896	"	135
10269	4 " Dora	2	Dau	10mo	F	1/16			
10270	5 " William Florence	1	Son	7wks	M	1/16			
I.W. 1258	6 " Lillie	25	Wife	25	F	I.W.			
	7								
	8	ENROLLMENT OF NOS 1,2,3,4 and 5 HEREON							
	9	APPROVED BY THE SECRETARY OF INTERIOR Feb 4 1903							
	10								
	11	ENROLLMENT OF NOS ~ 6 ~~~ HEREON							
	12	APPROVED BY THE SECRETARY OF INTERIOR Dec 30 1904							
	13								
	14	No.6 originally listed for enrollment							
	15	December 4,1902 on Choctaw card #D-845:							
	16	transferred to this card Dec. 15, 1904.							
	17	See decision of Nov. 28, 1904.							

TRIBAL ENROLLMENT OF PARENTS

	Name of Father	Year	County	Name of Mother	Year	County
1	Jack Airington		Blue	Sarah Airington	Dead	Non Citz
2	No1			Lillie Airington		" "
3	No1			" "		" "
4	No1			" "		" "
5	No1			" "		" "
6	James Manus			Martha A Manus		non citizen
7						
8						
9						
10	No3 on 1896 roll as Fred Airington					
11	As to marriage of parents of No.1					
12	see testimony of Thomas Ashford					
13	As to marriage of parents of Nos 23					#1 to 3
14	see testimony of Nicholas Goins.			Date of application for		
15	No.4 Enrolled Aug 13, 1901			enrollment		Aug 21/99
16	No5 Born Sept 1, 1902, enrolled Oct 24, 1902					Date of Application for Enrollment.
17	No1 is husband of Lillie Airington on Choctaw card D845					

31

Choctaw By Blood Enrollment Cards 1898-1914

RESIDENCE: Jackson   COUNTY. **Choctaw Nation**   **Choctaw Roll** CARD NO.
POST OFFICE: Bennington, I.T.   *(Not Including Freedmen)* FIELD NO. **3632**

Dawes' Roll No.	NAME	Relationship to Person First Named	AGE	SEX	BLOOD	TRIBAL ENROLLMENT		
						Year	County	No.
10271	1 James, Ben ³⁹	First Named	36	M	1/2	1896	Jackson	7108
10272	2 " Seborn ¹⁷	Son	14	"	1/2	1896	Blue	7180
	3							
	4							
	5							
	6	ENROLLMENT OF NOS. 1 and 2 HEREON						
	7	APPROVED BY THE SECRETARY						
	8	OF INTERIOR Feb 4 1903						
	9							
	10							
	11							
	12							
	13							
	14							
	15							
	16							
	17							

TRIBAL ENROLLMENT OF PARENTS

	Name of Father	Year	County	Name of Mother	Year	County
1	Henry James	1896	Atoka	Malena James	Dead	Jackson
2	No1			Frances Johnson		"
3						
4						
5						
6						
7			No2 on 1896 roll as Seaborn James			
8						
9						
10						
11						
12						
13					Date of Application for Enrollment.	
14						
15					Aug 21/99	
16						
17						

Choctaw By Blood Enrollment Cards 1898-1914

RESIDENCE:	Jackson	COUNTY.							
POST OFFICE:	Crowder, I.T.					Choctaw Roll *(Not Including Freedmen)*	CARD No. FIELD No. 3633		

Choctaw Nation

Dawes' Roll No.	NAME	Relationship to Person	AGE	SEX	BLOOD	TRIBAL ENROLLMENT		
						Year	County	No.
10273	1 Going, Nicholas 27	First Named	24	M	3/4	1896	Jackson	4852
I.W. 337	2 " Lena 25	Wife	22	F	I.W.	1896	"	14574
10274	3 " Ally Modena 1	Dau	2mo	F				
	4							
	5							
	6							
	7	ENROLLMENT						
	8	OF NOS. 1 and 3 HEREON APPROVED BY THE SECRETARY						
	9	OF INTERIOR FEB 4 1903						
	10	ENROLLMENT						
	11	OF NOS. 2 HEREON APPROVED BY THE SECRETARY						
	12	OF INTERIOR SEP 12 1903						
	13							
	14							
	15							
	16							
	17							

TRIBAL ENROLLMENT OF PARENTS

	Name of Father	Year	County	Name of Mother	Year	County
1	Jim Goings		Jackson	Sealey Goings		Jackson
2	Frank Stephens		Non Citz	Mary Stephens		Non Citz
3	Nº 1			Nº 2		
4						
5						
6	No. 2 was admitted by Dawes Commission					
7	in 1896 as an intermarried citizen: case #997:					
8	see original papers					
9						
10	Nº3 Born July 6, 1902, enrolled Sept 24, 1902.					
11	For child of Nos 1&2 see NB (March 3,1905) #722					
12						
13						
14					#1&2	
15				Date of Application for Enrollment.	Aug 21/99	
16						
17	P.O. Boswell I.T. 12/4/02					

Choctaw By Blood Enrollment Cards 1898-1914

RESIDENCE:	Blue	COUNTY.							
POST OFFICE:	Blue, I.T.							CARD NO. FIELD NO. 3634	

Choctaw Nation — Choctaw Roll (Not Including Freedmen)

Dawes' Roll No.	NAME	Relationship to Person First Named	AGE	SEX	BLOOD	TRIBAL ENROLLMENT		
						Year	County	No.
10275	1 Perkins, Eli 13	First Named	10	M	1/2	1896	Blue	10523
	2							
	3							
	4							
	5	ENROLLMENT						
	6	OF NOS. 1 HEREON APPROVED BY THE SECRETARY						
	7	OF INTERIOR FEB 4 1903						
	8							
	9							
	10							
	11							
	12							
	13							
	14							
	15							
	16							
	17							

TRIBAL ENROLLMENT OF PARENTS

Name of Father	Year	County	Name of Mother	Year	County
1 Joel Perkins		Chickasaw	Sillie Johnson		Blue
2					
3					
4					
5					
6					
7					
8					
9					
10					
11					
12					
13					
14					Date of Application for Enrollment
15					Aug 21/99
16					
17					

Choctaw By Blood Enrollment Cards 1898-1914

RESIDENCE: Blue
POST OFFICE: Ego, I.T.

COUNTY. **Choctaw Nation**

Choctaw Roll
(Not Including Freedmen)

Dawes' Roll No.		NAME		Relationship to Person First Named	AGE	SEX	BLOOD	TRIBAL ENROLLMENT		
								Year	County	No.
DEAD.	1	Izard, Sarah A		Named	54	F	1/16	1896	Blue	6306
10276	2	" John C	23	Son	20	M	1/32	1896	"	6307
10277	3	" Sherley B	21	"	18	"	1/32	1896	"	6308
10278	4	Reynolds, Inis U	10	S.Dau	7	F	1/64	1893	"	1013
10279	5	Izard, Biddy C	1	G.Son	3mo	M	1/64			
I.W 1474	6	" Tommie	20	Wife of No2	20	F	IW			
	7			For child of Nos 2&6 see NB (Mar 3-05) #250						
	8									
	9	ENROLLMENT OF NOS. 2,3,4 and 5 HEREON								
	10	APPROVED BY THE SECRETARY OF INTERIOR FEB 4 1903								
	11	No. 1 HEREON DISMISSED UNDER								
	12	ORDER OF THE COMMISSION TO THE FIVE								
	13	CIVILIZED TRIBES OF MARCH 31, 1905.								
	14	ENROLLMENT OF NOS. Six ~~~ HEREON								
	15	APPROVED BY THE SECRETARY								
	16	OF INTERIOR AUG 22 1905								
	17									

TRIBAL ENROLLMENT OF PARENTS

	Name of Father	Year	County	Name of Mother	Year	County
1	C. H. Moran	Dead	Non Citz	Eliz. M. Moran		Blue
2	G. H. Izard	"	" "	No 1		
3	" " "	"	" "	No 1		
4	Jno. W. Reynolds		" "	Georgia A Reynolds	Dead	Blue
5	No.2			Tommie Izard		M.C.R. #66
6	John Penny			Bettie Penny		
7						
8						
9	No1 on 1896 roll as Sarah E. Izard			No6 placed hereon under order of the		
10	No2 " 1896 " " Jno C. "			Commission of April 20, 1905 holding that		
11	No3 " 1896 " " Shirby B. "			application was made for her enrollment		
12	No4 on 1893 Pay Roll, Page 97, No 1013,			within the time provided by Act of Congress		
	Blue Co, as Ular Reynolds			of July 1, 1902.		
13	No.2 is the husband of Tommie Izard on Miss Choc card #R.66					
14	Evidence of marriage filed with Miss Choc #R.66					Date of Application for Enrollment #1 to 4
15	No.5 born July 25, 1901: Enrolled Oct 28th, 1901					Aug 21/99
16	Tommie Izard, the mother of No.5 is an applicant for identification as a Miss Choc, see case #R.66 Evidence of marriage of parents of No.5 on M.C.R. 66					
17	No.5 is a duplicate of No.2 on M.C.R. #66. N°1 Died June 25,1901; proof of death filed Sept. 4,1902					
	No.4 is a female. Sex changed under Departmental authority of Nov. 10, 1906 (I.T.D.22276-1906) DC 50101-1906					

35

Choctaw By Blood Enrollment Cards 1898-1914

RESIDENCE: Blue   COUNTY. **Choctaw Nation**   **Choctaw Roll**   CARD No.
POST OFFICE: Ego, I.T.   *(Not Including Freedmen)*   FIELD No. 3636

Dawes' Roll No.	NAME		Relationship to Person	AGE	SEX	BLOOD	TRIBAL ENROLLMENT		
							Year	County	No.
10280	1 Creecy Ula L	27	First Named	24	F	1/32	1896	Blue	12607
10281	2 Creecy, John Dow	1	Son	1mo	M	1/64			
	3								
	4								
	5								
	6	ENROLLMENT							
	7	OF NOS. 1 and 2 APPROVED BY THE SECRETARY	HEREON						
	8	OF INTERIOR FEB 4 1903							
	9								
	10								
	11								
	12								
	13								
	14								
	15								
	16								
	17								

TRIBAL ENROLLMENT OF PARENTS

	Name of Father	Year	County	Name of Mother	Year	County
1	George Izard	Dead	Non Citz	Sarah Izard		Blue
2	W. C. Creecy		" "	No.1		
3						
4						
5						
6	On 1896 roll Ula Vaughn					
7	No.1 is now the wife of W.C. Creecy, a non-citizen Oct 30, 1901					
8	No.2 born Sept 17, 1901: Enrolled Oct. 30, 1901					
	Evidence of marriage of No.1 to W. C. Creecy filed Nov. 7, 1901					
9	For child of No.1 see N.B. (Apr 26, 1906) Card No. 44					
10	" " " " " (Mar 3-1905) " No 251					
11						
12						
13						
14					Date of Application for Enrollment.	
15					Aug 21/99	
16						
17	P.O. Milburn. I.T. 3/8/05					

36

Choctaw By Blood Enrollment Cards 1898-1914

	RESIDENCE:	Blue							

RESIDENCE: Blue **COUNTY.** **Choctaw Nation** **Choctaw Roll** (Not Including Freedmen) **CARD NO.**
POST OFFICE: Ego, I.T. **FIELD NO.** 3637

Dawes' Roll No.	NAME	Relationship to Person First Named	AGE	SEX	BLOOD	TRIBAL ENROLLMENT Year	County	No.
10282	1 Izard, Silas P 39	First Named	36	M	1/32	1896	Blue	6309
I.W. 156	2 " Mary L 24	Wife	21	F	I.W.	1896	"	14768
10283	3 " Leona P 6	Dau	3	"	1/64	1896	"	6310
10284	4 " Roy P 4	Son	1	M	1/64			
10285	5 " William Leslie 2	Son	2mo	M	1/64			
10286	6 " Sarah Ethel 1	Dau	4mo	F	1/64			
	7							
	8							
	9	ENROLLMENT						
	10	OF NOS. 1,3,4,5 and 6 HEREON APPROVED BY THE SECRETARY						
	11	OF INTERIOR Feb 4 1903						
	12	ENROLLMENT						
	13	OF NOS. 2 ~~~~ HEREON APPROVED BY THE SECRETARY						
	14	OF INTERIOR Jun 13 1903						
	15							
	16							
	17							

TRIBAL ENROLLMENT OF PARENTS

	Name of Father	Year	County	Name of Mother	Year	County
1	George Izard	Dead	Non Citz	Sarah Izard		Blue
2	William Moran		" "	Sallie Moran	Dead	Non Citz
3	No1			No2		
4	No1			No2		
5	No1			No2		
6	Nº1			Nº2		
7						
8						
9	No2 on 1896 roll as Lena P Izord					
10	No3 " 1896 " " Mary M "					
11	No4 Affidavit of birth to be supplied: Recd Oct 7/99					
12	No5 Enrolled December 7th, 1900					
13	Nº6 Born Jany 31, 1902: enrolled May 19, 1902					
14					Date of Application for Enrollment.	
15	For child of Nos 1&2 see NB (Mar 3-05) Card #243				Aug 21/99	
16						
17	P.O. Milburn I.T. 3/16/05					

37

Choctaw By Blood Enrollment Cards 1898-1914

RESIDENCE: Blue COUNTY. **Choctaw Nation** **Choctaw Roll** CARD NO.
POST OFFICE: Caddo, I.T. (Not Including Freedmen) FIELD NO. 3638

Dawes' Roll No.	NAME		Relationship to Person First Named	AGE	SEX	BLOOD	TRIBAL ENROLLMENT		
							Year	County	No.
10287	1 Jones, Jincey	68	First Named	65	F	Full	1896	Blue	7213
	2								
	3								
	4								
	5	ENROLLMENT							
	6	OF NOS. 1 HEREON APPROVED BY THE SECRETARY							
	7	OF INTERIOR FEB 4 1903							
	8								
	9								
	10								
	11								
	12								
	13								
	14								
	15								
	16								
	17								

TRIBAL ENROLLMENT OF PARENTS

	Name of Father	Year	County	Name of Mother	Year	County
1	Robert James	Dead	Towson	Christina James	Dead	Towson
2						
3						
4						
5						
6						
7						
8						
9						
10						
11						
12						
13					Date of Application for Enrollment.	
14						
15					Aug 21/99	
16						
17						

38

Choctaw By Blood Enrollment Cards 1898-1914

RESIDENCE:	Jackson	COUNTY.						
POST OFFICE:	Bennington, I.T.							

Choctaw Nation — Choctaw Roll *(Not Including Freedmen)* CARD NO. FIELD NO. 3639

Dawes' Roll No.	NAME	Relationship to Person Named	AGE	SEX	BLOOD	TRIBAL ENROLLMENT		
						Year	County	No.
10288	1 Starks, Thomas 30	First Named	27	M	1/4	1896	Jackson	11554
10289	2 " Lillie 6	Dau	2	F	1/8			
10290	3 " Robert Ernest 1	Son	1mo	M	1/8			
I.W. 830	4 " Josephine (25)	Wife	25	F	IW			
	5							
	6	ENROLLMENT						
	7	OF NOS. 1-2 and 3 HEREON						
	8	APPROVED BY THE SECRETARY OF INTERIOR FEB 4 1903						
	9							
	10							
	11	ENROLLMENT						
	12	OF NOS. 4 HEREON APPROVED BY THE SECRETARY						
	13	OF INTERIOR MAY 21 1904						
	14							
	15							
	16							
	17							

TRIBAL ENROLLMENT OF PARENTS

	Name of Father	Year	County	Name of Mother	Year	County
1	Thos Starks		Non Citz	Felicity Starks	Dead	Sans Bois
2	No1			Hettie Stout		Non Citz
3	No1			Josephine Stark		" "
4	Stover	Dead	noncitizen	Lizzie Stover		" "
5						
6						
7						
8						
9	No2 Evidence of marriage of parents to be supplied:-					
10	No2 Affidavit of birth to be					
11	supplied:- Recd Oct 7/99					
12	No1 was divorced from his wife Hettie Stark in Aug 1899. Evidence filed Sept 23 1901					
13	No1 is now the husband of Josephine Stark. Certificate of marriage filed Sept 23 1901					
14	No3 Enrolled Sept 23, 1901					
15	No4 transferred from Choctaw card D967 April 15 1904. See decision of March 15, 1904			Date of Application for Enrollment.	Aug 21/99	
16	For child of Nos 1&4 see NB (Mar 3-05) Card #244					
17	" " " " 1&4 " " (April 26,1906) " #248					

39

Choctaw By Blood Enrollment Cards 1898-1914

RESIDENCE: Jackson COUNTY.
POST OFFICE: Mayhew, I.T.
Choctaw Nation
Choctaw Roll (Not Including Freedmen)
CARD NO.
FIELD NO. 3640

Dawes' Roll No.	NAME	Relationship to Person First Named	AGE	SEX	BLOOD	TRIBAL ENROLLMENT		
						Year	County	No.
10291	1 LeFlore, Charles 40	First Named	37	M	Full	1896	Jackson	8148
10292	2 " Susanna 26	Wife	23	F	"	1896	"	10472
10293	3 " Mary 15	Dau	12	"	"	1896	"	8150
10294	4 " Lucy 13	"	10	"	"	1896	"	8151
10295	5 " Jerry 1	Son	10mo	M	"			
	6							
	7	ENROLLMENT OF NOS. 1,2,3,4 and 5 HEREON APPROVED BY THE SECRETARY OF INTERIOR FEB 4 1903						
	8							
	9							
	10							
	11							
	12							
	13							
	14							
	15							
	16							
	17							

TRIBAL ENROLLMENT OF PARENTS

	Name of Father	Year	County	Name of Mother	Year	County
1	Sim LeFlore	Dead	Jackson		Dead	Jackson
2	Nicholas Paxton	"	Jacks Fork	Sibbie	"	Jacks Fork
3	No1			Bickie LeFlore	"	Jackson
4	No1			" "	"	"
5	№ 1			№ 2		
6						
7						
8						
9			No2 on 1896 roll as Susana Patterson			
10			№5 Born Oct 18, 1901: enrolled Aug 16, 1902			
11						
12						
13						
14					#1 to 4 inc	
15				Date of Application for Enrollment.		Aug 21/99
16						
17	P.O. Limestone 11/1/04					

P.O. Bennington I.T. 8/16/02

40

Choctaw By Blood Enrollment Cards 1898-1914

RESIDENCE:	Jackson	COUNTY.							
POST OFFICE:	Bennington, I.T								

Choctaw Nation

Choctaw Roll (Not Including Freedmen)

CARD NO.
FIELD NO. 3641

Dawes' Roll No.	NAME	Relationship to Person	AGE	SEX	BLOOD	TRIBAL ENROLLMENT		
						Year	County	No.
10296	1 McKinney, Sampson C [30]	First Named	27	M	Full	1896	Jackson	9408
10297	2 " Mattie [23]	Wife	20	F	1/2	1896	"	9409
10298	3 " Gladys [4]	Dau	8mo	"	3/4			
10299	4 " Irving [1]	Son	1	M	3/4			
	5							
	6							
	7	ENROLLMENT OF NOS. 1,2,3 and 4 HEREON						
	8	APPROVED BY THE SECRETARY OF INTERIOR FEB 4 1903						
	9							
	10							
	11							
	12							
	13							
	14							
	15							
	16							
	17							

TRIBAL ENROLLMENT OF PARENTS

	Name of Father	Year	County	Name of Mother	Year	County
1	Geo McKinney	Dead	Nashoba		Dead	Nashoba
2	Zachariah Jones		Jackson	Malinda Jones		Non Citz
3	No1			No2		
4						
5						
6						
7			No2. As to marriage of parents see			
8			testimony of James Wesley			
9						
10			No4. Enrolled Nov. 26, 1902			
11						
12						
13						Date of Application for Enrollment.
14						
15						Aug 21/99
16						
17						

41

Choctaw By Blood Enrollment Cards 1898-1914

RESIDENCE: Jackson COUNTY. **Choctaw Nation** Choctaw Roll CARD NO.
POST OFFICE: Bennington, I.T. (Not Including Freedmen) FIELD NO. 3642

Dawes' Roll No.		NAME		Relationship to Person	AGE	SEX	BLOOD	TRIBAL ENROLLMENT		
								Year	County	No.
15464	1	Wesley, James	43	First Named	40	M	Full	1896	Jackson	13805
10300	2	" Lucy	27	Wife	24	F	"	1896	"	13806
10301	3	" Johnson	10	Son	7	M	"	1896	"	13807
10302	4	" Elizabeth	6	Dau	2	F	"			
10303	5	" Willie	3	Son	4mo	M	"			
	6									
	7	ENROLLMENT								
	8	OF NOS. 2,3,4 and 5 HEREON APPROVED BY THE SECRETARY								
	9	OF INTERIOR FEB 4 1903								
	10									
	11	ENROLLMENT								
	12	OF NOS. 1 HEREON APPROVED BY THE SECRETARY								
	13	OF INTERIOR MAY 9 1904								
	14									
	15									
	16									
	17									

TRIBAL ENROLLMENT OF PARENTS

	Name of Father	Year	County	Name of Mother	Year	County
1	Adam Wesley	Dead	Skullyville	Pe-sa-hu-na	Dead	Skullyville
2	Joe Hampton		Jackson	Kizzie Hampton		Red River
3	No1			No2		
4	No1			No2		
5	No1			No2		
6						
7						
8	No1 on 1896 roll as Jimmie Westley					
9	No2 " 1896 " " Lucy "					
10	No3 " 1896 " " Johnson "					
11	Nos 4-5 Affidavits of birth to be supplied:- Filed Nov 2/99					
12						
13						
14	For child of No3 see NB (Apr 26-06) Card #864				Date of Application for Enrollment.	
15					Aug 21/99	
16						
17						

42

Choctaw By Blood Enrollment Cards 1898-1914

RESIDENCE: Jackson COUNTY. **Choctaw Nation**   Choctaw Roll   CARD NO.
POST OFFICE: Mayhew, I.T.   *(Not Including Freedmen)*   FIELD NO. 3643

Dawes' Roll No.	NAME	Relationship to Person	AGE	SEX	BLOOD	TRIBAL ENROLLMENT		
						Year	County	No.
I.W.338	1 Yandell, John M ⁴⁵	First Named	42	M	I.W	1896	Jackson	15210
10304	2 " Dora ²¹	Wife	18	F	1/4	1896	"	14232
10305	3 " John ⁵	Son	8mo	M	1/8			
10306	4 Smallwood, Lena ⁷	S.Dau	4	F	1/8	1896	Jackson	11555
10307	5 Yandell, George William ¹	Son	2mo	M	1/8			
	6							
	7							
	8	ENROLLMENT						
	9	OF NOS. 2,3,4 and 5 HEREON APPROVED BY THE SECRETARY						
	10	OF INTERIOR FEB 4 1903						
	11	ENROLLMENT						
	12	OF NOS. 1 HEREON APPROVED BY THE SECRETARY						
	13	OF INTERIOR SEP 12 1903						
	14							
	15							
	16							
	17							

TRIBAL ENROLLMENT OF PARENTS

	Name of Father	Year	County	Name of Mother	Year	County
1	J. N. Yandell	Dead	Non Citz	Sarah Yandell		Non Citz
2	Ben Olsen	" "		Siney Olsen		Kiamitia
3	No1			No2		
4	Dan Smallwood		Jackson	No2		
5	No1			No2		
6						
7			No1 was admitted by Dawes Com,			
8			Case No 73			
9			No1 on 1896 roll as J. M. Yandel			
10			No3 Affidavit of birth to be supplied:- Filed Nov 2/99			
11			No5 Enrolled February 21, 1901			
12		For child of Nos 1&2 see NB (Apr 26-06) Card #360				
13		" " " " " " (Mar 3-05) " #802			#1 to 4	
14					Date of Application for Enrollment.	
15					Aug 21/99	
16						
17	PO Boswell IT 4/8/0?					

43

Choctaw By Blood Enrollment Cards 1898-1914

RESIDENCE: Blue   COUNTY. **Choctaw Nation**   **Choctaw Roll** CARD NO.
POST OFFICE: Blue, I.T.   *(Not Including Freedmen)*   FIELD NO. 3644

Dawes' Roll No.	NAME	Relationship to Person First Named	AGE	SEX	BLOOD	TRIBAL ENROLLMENT Year	County	No.
10308	1 Nicholas, Amy ⁵³	First Named	50	F	Full	1896	Blue	9797
10309	2 " Lina ²⁰	Dau	17	"	"	1896	"	9799
10310	3 " Wilburn ¹⁷	Son	14	M	"	1896	"	9800
10311	4 " Lucy ¹⁵	Dau	12	F	"	1896	"	9801
10312	5 " Elizabeth ¹¹	"	8	"	"	1896	"	9802
	6							
	7	ENROLLMENT						
	8	OF NOS. 1-2-3-4 and 5 HEREON APPROVED BY THE SECRETARY						
	9	OF INTERIOR FEB 4 1903						
	10							
	11							
	12							
	13							
	14							
	15							
	16							
	17							

TRIBAL ENROLLMENT OF PARENTS

	Name of Father	Year	County	Name of Mother	Year	County
1	Alfred	Dead	Blue	Tik-ba-ho-ya	Dead	Atoka
2	Solomon Nicholas	"	"	No1		
3	" "	"	"	No1		
4	" "	"	"	No1		
5	" "	"	"	No1		
6						
7						
8			No1 on 1896 roll as Annie Nicholas			
9			No2 " 1896 " " Linnie "			
10			No3 " 1896 " " William "			
11						
12			For child of No2 see NB (Apr 26-06) Card #753			
13						
14					Date of Application for Enrollment.	
15					Aug 21/99	
16						
17						

Choctaw By Blood Enrollment Cards 1898-1914

RESIDENCE: Blue	COUNTY.	**Choctaw Nation**	**Choctaw Roll** *(Not Including Freedmen)*	CARD NO.
POST OFFICE: Bok Chito, I.T.				FIELD NO. 3645

Dawes' Roll No.	NAME	Relationship to Person Named	AGE	SEX	BLOOD	Year	County	No.
10313	1 Frazier, Loring W 35	First Named	32	M	Full	1896	Blue	4376
10314	2 " Emma 28	Wife	25	F	7/8	1896	"	4377
10315	3 " Lena 7	Dau	4	"	15/16	1896	"	4378
DEAD.	4 " Willie 5	Son	2	M	15/16			
DEAD.	5 " Ada 2	Dau	6mo	F	15/16			
	6							
	7							

ENROLLMENT OF NOS. 1, 2 and 3 APPROVED BY THE SECRETARY OF INTERIOR FEB 4 1903

No. 4 and 5 HEREON DISMISSED UNDER ORDER OF THE COMMISSION TO THE FIVE CIVILIZED TRIBES OF MARCH 31, 1905.

TRIBAL ENROLLMENT OF PARENTS

Name of Father	Year	County	Name of Mother	Year	County
1 Willie Frazier	Dead	Jackson	Lizann Frazier		Jackson
2 Silas Hunter	"	Blue	Sophie Jones		Blue
3 No1			No2		
4 No1			No2		
5 No1			No2		

No4 Affidavit of birth to be supplied:- Recd Oct 7/99

No.5 Enrolled August 31, 1901

No4 died Nov. 22, 1899, evidence of death filed Nov 26, 1902
No5 " June 27, 1902 " " " " " 26, "

#1 to 4 Date of Application for Enrollment. Aug 21/99

45

Choctaw By Blood Enrollment Cards 1898-1914

RESIDENCE: Blue COUNTY.	**Choctaw Nation**	Choctaw Roll	CARD NO.
POST OFFICE: Bok Chito, I.T		(Not Including Freedmen)	FIELD NO. 3646

Dawes' Roll No.	NAME	Relationship to Person First Named	AGE	SEX	BLOOD	TRIBAL ENROLLMENT		
						Year	County	No.
10316	1 Walker, Malinda 29	First Named	26	F	1/2	1896	Blue	13890
10317	2 " Minnie 4	Dau	1	"	1/4			
10318	3 DIED PRIOR TO SEPTEMBER 25, 1902 Vinnie	"	1	"	1/4			
	4							
	5							
	6	ENROLLMENT						
	7	OF NOS. 1, 2 and 3 HEREON APPROVED BY THE SECRETARY						
	8	OF INTERIOR FEB 4 1903						
	9							
	10							
	11							
	12							
	13							
	14							
	15							
	16							
	17							

TRIBAL ENROLLMENT OF PARENTS

	Name of Father	Year	County	Name of Mother	Year	County
1	Lewis Robinson	Dead	Blue	Phillis Robinson	Dead	Blue
2	Tilden Walker		Non Citz	No1		
3	" "		" "	No1		
4						
5						
6						
7			Nos 2-3 Affidavits of birth to be			
8			supplied:- Recd Oct 7/99			
9			No.3 died Oct 22, 1901. Enrollment cancelled by Department July 8, 1904			
10			For child of No.1 see NB (Apr 26, '06) Card No. 229			
			" " " " " (Mar 3-05) " " 245			
11						
12						
13						Date of Application for Enrollment.
14						
15						Aug 21/99
16	PO Bradley IT 3/22/05					
17	P.O. Chickasha, I.T. 2/16/03					

46

Choctaw By Blood Enrollment Cards 1898-1914

RESIDENCE:	Blue	COUNTY.	**Choctaw Nation**	**Choctaw Roll** *(Not Including Freedmen)*	CARD NO.
POST OFFICE:	Caddo, I.T				FIELD NO. 3647

Dawes' Roll No.	NAME	Relationship to Person First Named	AGE	SEX	BLOOD	TRIBAL ENROLLMENT		
						Year	County	No.
✓ 1	Alexander, Eliza A	Named	34	F	1/4			
✓ 2	" Willie M	Dau	14	"	1/8			
✓ 3	" Charles	Son	11	M	1/8			
✓ 4	" John E	"	9	"	1/8			
✓ 5	" James M	"	6	"	1/8			
✓ × 6	" Henry	"	4	"	1/8			
DP 7	" Dewey E	"	1½	"	1/8			
DP 8	" Mable	Dau	1	F	1/8			
9								
10								
11	Nos 7&8 MAY 27 1904 DISMISSED							
12								
13								
14								
15	Nos 7&8 Dismissed Case #86 April 18, 1904							
16								
17	See Petition # (Illegible)							

TRIBAL ENROLLMENT OF PARENTS

	Name of Father	Year	County	Name of Mother	Year	County
1	David Powers	Dead	Non Citz	Tabitha Powers	Dead	Choctaw
2	Jas. Alexander	" "	No1			
3	" "	" "	No1			
4	" "	" "	No1			
5	" "	" "	No1			
6	" "	" "	No1			
7	" "	" "	No1			
8	" "	" "	No1			
9	Nos 1 to 7 incl now in C C Ct Case #86			Nos 1 to 6 incl denied 96 Case #1122		
10	All but No7 admitted by U.S. Court,			Judgment of U.S. Court admitting Nos 1 to 6 incl vacated		
11	Central Dist, Sept 8/97, Case No 41			and set aside by Decree of C.C.Ct Dec 17/02		
12	No2 was admitted as Willie May Alexander					
13	No4 " " " John Edgan "			No8 born Jany 25, 1902:		
14	No5 " " " James Mimus "			erroneously enrolled on Choctaw		
15	As to residence, see testimony of No1			card #203 March 4, 1902		
16	No7 Affidavit of birth to be			and transferred Aug 21/99		
17	supplied:- Recd Oct 7/99			to this card Nov. 9, 1902		
	For children of No1 see NB #954 (Act Apr 26-'06)					
	P.O. Non I.T. 2/18/06 ; Dec C. 1.06					

DENIED CITIZENSHIP BY THE CHOCTAW AND CHICKASAW CITIZENSHIP COURT

Date of Application for Enrollment. Aug 21/99

Choctaw By Blood Enrollment Cards 1898-1914

RESIDENCE: Blue COUNTY. **Choctaw Nation** Choctaw Roll CARD NO.
POST OFFICE: Caddo, I.T. *(Not Including Freedmen)* FIELD NO. 3648

Dawes' Roll No.	NAME		Relationship to Person First Named	AGE	SEX	BLOOD	TRIBAL ENROLLMENT		
							Year	County	No.
DEAD	1 Myer, Ephrahim		First Named	44	M	Full	1896	Blue	8799
10319	2 " Lucy A	33	Wife	30	F	"	1896	"	8800
10320	3 " Harriet	16	Dau	12	"	"	1896	"	8801
10321	4 " Eleat	13	Son	10	M	"	1896	"	8802
	5								
	6								
	7	ENROLLMENT							
	8	OF NOS. 2-3 and 4 HEREON APPROVED BY THE SECRETARY							
	9	OF INTERIOR FEB 4 1903							
	10	No. 1 HEREON DISMISSED UNDER							
	11	ORDER OF THE COMMISSION TO THE FIVE							
	12	CIVILIZED TRIBES OF MARCH 31, 1905.							
	13								
	14								
	15								
	16								
	17								

TRIBAL ENROLLMENT OF PARENTS

	Name of Father	Year	County	Name of Mother	Year	County
1	Jas. Meyer[sic]	Dead	Blue		Dead	Blue
2	E-la-ho-ta	"	"	Hok-key	"	"
3	No1			No2		
4	No1			No2		
5						
6						
7	No2 on 1896 roll as Lucy Ann Meyer					
8	No4 "	1896	" " Elias	"		
9						
10	No1 died Feb 1, 1899, proof of death filed Nov 26 1902					
11						
12	For child of No3 see NB (Apr 26-06) Card #680					
13						
14					Date of Application for Enrollment.	
15					Aug 21/9ᶜ	
16						
17	No3 P.O. Caney, Okla 1/20/08					

48

Choctaw By Blood Enrollment Cards 1898-1914

RESIDENCE: Blue COUNTY. **Choctaw Nation**   **Choctaw Roll** CARD NO.
POST OFFICE: Bok Chito, I.T.   *(Not Including Freedmen)* FIELD NO. 3649

Dawes' Roll No.	NAME	Relationship to Person Named	AGE	SEX	BLOOD	TRIBAL ENROLLMENT		
						Year	County	No.
10322	1 Hampton, Wilburn W [61]	First Named	58	M	Full	1896	Blue	5858
10323	2 " Susan [57]	Wife	54	F	3/4	1896	"	5859
	3							
	4							
	5	ENROLLMENT						
	6	OF NOS. 1 and 2 HEREON APPROVED BY THE SECRETARY						
	7	OF INTERIOR FEB 4 1903						
	8							
	9							
	10							
	11							
	12							
	13							
	14							
	15							
	16							
	17							

TRIBAL ENROLLMENT OF PARENTS

Name of Father	Year	County	Name of Mother	Year	County
1 Nicholas Hampton	Dead	Blue	Hok-tey	Dead	Gaines
2 Adam LeFlore	"	Towson	Polly LeFlore	"	Jackson
3					
4					
5					
6					
7		No 1 on 1896 roll as W. W. Hampton			
8					
9					
10					
11					
12					
13					
14				Date of Application for Enrollment.	
15				Aug 21/99	
16					
17					

Cards 442 - 3590 - 4642

Choctaw By Blood Enrollment Cards 1898-1914

RESIDENCE: **Blue** COUNTY.
POST OFFICE: **Folsom, I.T.**   **Choctaw Nation**   **Choctaw Roll** (Not Including Freedmen)   CARD NO. FIELD NO. **3650**

Dawes' Roll No.	NAME	Relationship to Person First Named	AGE	SEX	BLOOD	TRIBAL ENROLLMENT Year	County	No.
Denied 1	Mitts, William E		29	M	I.W			
10324 2	Mitts, Lucinda 23	Wife	20	F	1/2	1896	Blue	8783
10325 3	" Dora E 8	Dau	5	"	1/4	1896	"	8784
10326 4	" Dolly M 5	"	2	"	1/4			
DEAD 5	" Jesse E DEAD 3	Son	3mo	M	1/4			
10327 6	" Dovey 2	Dau	4mo	F	1/4			
7								
8								
9	ENROLLMENT OF NOS. 2,3,4 and 6 HEREON APPROVED BY THE SECRETARY OF INTERIOR FEB 4 1903		No. 5 HEREON DISMISSED UNDER ORDER OF THE COMMISSION TO THE FIVE CIVILIZED TRIBES OF MARCH 31, 1905.					
10								
11								
12								
13	Jan 17 1905 Decision of Commission of Dec 15, 1904 denying No1 approved by the Secretary of the Interior (I.T.D. #74 1905) DX 3437-1905							
14								
15								
16								
17								

TRIBAL ENROLLMENT OF PARENTS

	Name of Father	Year	County	Name of Mother	Year	County
1	George Mitts	Dead	Non Citz	Mary Mitts		Non Citz
2	Jas Allen	"	Blue	Mary A Allen	Dead	Blue
3	No1			No2		
4	No1			No2		
5	No1			No2		
6	Wᵐ E Mitts		non-citizen	No.2		
7						
8						
9	No3 on 1896 roll as Dora Mitts					
10	No4 Affidavit of birth to be					
11	supplied:- Recd Oct 7/99					
	No.6 Enrolled June 5th, 1901					
12	No5 died Feb 28, 1900; proof of death filed Nov 26 1902					
13	For children of No.2 see NB (Mar 3'05) #466					#1 to 5
14						Date of Application for Enrollment.
15						Aug 21/99
16	No.1 married under U.S. Law. Enrolled by mistake.					
17						

50

RESIDENCE:	Jackson	COUNTY.							
POST OFFICE:	Jackson, I.T.		**Choctaw Nation** *(Not Including Freedmen)*			Choctaw Roll		CARD NO. FIELD NO. 3651	

Dawes' Roll No.	NAME	Relationship to Person First Named	AGE	SEX	BLOOD	TRIBAL ENROLLMENT		
						Year	County	No.
10328	1 Chubbee, Lamon 47		44	M	Full	1896	Jackson	2781
10329	2 " Isabelle 46	Wife	43	F	"	1896	"	2782
10330	3 " Robert 20	Son	17	M	"	1896	"	2783
10331	4 Frazier, Emily 23	S.Dau	20	F	"	1896	"	4264
	5							
	6							
	7							
	8	ENROLLMENT OF NOS. 1,2,3 and 4 HEREON APPROVED BY THE SECRETARY OF INTERIOR FEB 4 1903						
	9							
	10							
	11							
	12							
	13							
	14							
	15							
	16							
	17							

TRIBAL ENROLLMENT OF PARENTS

	Name of Father	Year	County	Name of Mother	Year	County
1	Jim Chubbee	Dead	Atoka		Dead	Jacks Fork
2	William Frazier	"	Jackson	Na-ne-ma	"	Jackson
3	No1			No2		
4	Charley Fletcher	Dead	Kiamitia	No2		
5						
6						
7						
8						
9						
10						
11						
12						
13						
14						Date of Application for Enrollment.
15						Aug 21/99
16						
17	P.O. Bennington I.T. 3/18/07					

51

RESIDENCE:	Jackson	COUNTY.								

RESIDENCE: Jackson **COUNTY.** **Choctaw Nation** **Choctaw Roll** (Not Including Freedmen) **CARD NO.**
POST OFFICE: Mayhew, I.T **FIELD NO.** 3652

Dawes' Roll No.	NAME		Relationship to Person	AGE	SEX	BLOOD	TRIBAL ENROLLMENT		
							Year	County	No.
10332	1 Battiest, Kizzie	51	First Named	48	F	1/2	1896	Jackson	1467
10333	2 Turley Sissie B	19	Dau	16	"	3/4	1896	"	1469
10334	3 Battiest Turner	17	Son	14	M	3/4	1896	"	1468
10335	4 " Steven	12	"	9	"	3/4	1896	"	1471
10336	5 " Lela	3	G.Dau	2mo	F	3/8			
10337	6 Turley Linsey	1	Son of No2	4m	M	3/8			
I.W. 605	7 Battiest Rachel Lucinda		Wife of No 3	17	F	IW			
	8								
	9	ENROLLMENT							
	10	OF NOS.1,2,3,4,5 and 6 HEREON							
	11	APPROVED BY THE SECRETARY OF INTERIOR FEB 4 1903							
	12	ENROLLMENT							
	13	OF NOS.~~~~7~~~~ HEREON APPROVED BY THE SECRETARY							
	14	OF INTERIOR FEB 12 1907							
	15	No7							
	16	GRANTED NOV -6 1906							
	17								

	TRIBAL ENROLLMENT OF PARENTS					
	Name of Father	Year	County	Name of Mother	Year	County
1	Benj. James	Dead	Bok Tuklo	Mary James	Dead	Blue
2	Ben Battiest	"	Blue	No1		
3	" "	"	"	No1		
4	" "	"	"	No1		
5	Tom Brown		Non Citz	No2		
6	J. D. Turley		"	No2		
7	John Jones		noncitizen	P. J. Story		noncitizen
8						
9						
10	No4 on 1896 roll as Steve Battiest					
11	No.2 is the wife of J. D. Turley non-citizen. Evidence of marriage filed July 7,1902					
12	No.6 Born March 2nd 1902: Enrolled July 16th 1902					
13					#1 to 5 inc	
14	No.7 placed hereon under order of Commissioner to Five Civilized Tribes of				Date of Application for Enrollment	
15	October 19, 1906, holding application was made for her enrollment within the time provided by Act of Congress approved April 26, 1906.				Aug 21/99	
16	(34 Stat. 137) For child of No.2 see NB (March 3,1905) #1240					
17						

Choctaw By Blood Enrollment Cards 1898-1914

| RESIDENCE: | Blue | COUNTY. | **Choctaw Nation** | **Choctaw Roll** | CARD No. |
| POST OFFICE: | Caddo, I.T. | | | *(Not Including Freedmen)* | FIELD No. 3653 |

| Dawes' Roll No. | NAME | Relationship to Person | AGE | SEX | BLOOD | TRIBAL ENROLLMENT | | |
						Year	County	No.
10338	1 Jackson, Andrew	First Named	60	M	Full	1896	Blue	7178
	2							
	3							
	4							
	5							
	6							
	7							
	8							
	9							
	10							
	11							
	12							
	13							
	14							
	15							
	16							
	17							

DIED PRIOR TO SEPTEMBER 25 1902

ENROLLMENT
OF NOS. 1 HEREON
APPROVED BY THE SECRETARY
OF INTERIOR FEB 4 1903

TRIBAL ENROLLMENT OF PARENTS

	Name of Father	Year	County	Name of Mother	Year	County
1	Jackson	Dead	Blue	Elzira Lucas	Dead	Blue
2						
3						
4						
5						
6			Also on 1896 roll, Page 177, No 7206			
7						
8			No. 1 died August 25, 1902; Enrollment cancelled by Department May 2 1906			
9						
10						
11						
12						
13						
14						Date of Application for Enrollment.
15						Aug 21/99
16						
17						

53

Choctaw By Blood Enrollment Cards 1898-1914

RESIDENCE:	Blue		COUNTY.	**Choctaw Nation**				**Choctaw Roll**		CARD No.	
POST OFFICE:	Caddo, I.T.							*(Not Including Freedmen)*		FIELD No. 3654	

Dawes' Roll No.	NAME		Relationship to Person	AGE	SEX	BLOOD	TRIBAL ENROLLMENT			
							Year	County		No.
10339	1 Ellis, Zerena	43	First Named	40	F	Full	1896	Blue		3814
	2									
	3									
	4	ENROLLMENT OF NOS. 1 HEREON APPROVED BY THE SECRETARY OF INTERIOR FEB 4 1903								
	5									
	6									
	7									
	8									
	9									
	10									
	11									
	12									
	13									
	14									
	15									
	16									
	17									

TRIBAL ENROLLMENT OF PARENTS

	Name of Father	Year	County	Name of Mother	Year	County
1	Sime-homma	Dead	Blue	Elzira Lucas	Dead	Blue
2						
3						
4						
5						
6						
7						
8						
9						
10						
11						
12						
13						
14						Date of Application for Enrollment.
15						
16						
17						

Choctaw By Blood Enrollment Cards 1898-1914

RESIDENCE: Jackson
POST OFFICE: Jackson I.T.

COUNTY. **Choctaw Nation**

Choctaw Roll (Not Including Freedmen)

CARD NO.
FIELD NO. **3655**

Dawes' Roll No.	NAME		Relationship to Person First Named	AGE	SEX	BLOOD	TRIBAL ENROLLMENT		
							Year	County	No.
10340	1 Frazier, Jackson	42		39	M	Full	1896	Jackson	4309
15628	2 " Louisa	24	Wife	21	F	"	1896	"	11547
10341	3 " James	13	Son	10	M	"	1896	"	4310
10342	4 Scott, Jeremiah	6	S.Son	3	"	"	1896	"	11548
	5								
	6								
	7								
	8	ENROLLMENT OF NOS. 1,3 and 4 HEREON APPROVED BY THE SECRETARY OF INTERIOR Feb 4 1903							
	9								
	10								
	11								
	12								
	13								
	14	ENROLLMENT OF NOS. 2 HEREON APPROVED BY THE SECRETARY OF INTERIOR Sep 22 1904							
	15								
	16								
	17								

TRIBAL ENROLLMENT OF PARENTS

	Name of Father	Year	County	Name of Mother	Year	County
1	Tobias Frazier	Dead	Jackson	Che-ma-le-hoke	Dead	Jackson
2	Charley Scott	"	"	Kizzie Scott	"	"
3	No1			Lucy Frazier	"	"
4	Robert Barnes		Jackson	No2		
5						
6						
7						
8			No2 on 1896 roll as Louisa Scott			
9			No4 is illegitimate			
10						
11						
12						
13						
14					Date of Application for Enrollment.	
15					Aug 21/99	
16						
17	P.O. Boswell I.T. 7/19/04					

55

Choctaw By Blood Enrollment Cards 1898-1914

RESIDENCE:	Jackson	COUNTY.						
POST OFFICE:	Crowder, I.T.	**Choctaw Nation**				Choctaw Roll *(Not Including Freedmen)*	CARD NO. FIELD NO. **3656**	

Dawes' Roll No.	NAME		Relationship to Person First Named	AGE	SEX	BLOOD	TRIBAL ENROLLMENT		
							Year	County	No.
I.W.1533	1 Crowder, Julia A	36	First Named	33	F	I.W.	1896	Jackson	14415
15921	2 " Eli W	14	Son	11	M	1/8	1896	"	2768
15922	3 " James	12	"	9	"	1/8	1896	"	2769
15923	4 " Katie B	10	Dau	7	F	1/8	1896	"	2770
15924	5 " Pinkie B	7	"	4	"	1/8	1896	"	2771
15925	6 " John A	5	Son	1½	M	1/8			
	7								
	8 #1 is now wife of Eli Crowder Card 1575						No1 Granted Nov 14, 1905		
	9 Nᵒˢ 2 to 6 Inc Granted May 23 1905								
	10								
	11 No.1 on 1885 roll, Kiamitia Co., No 640								
	12 ENROLLMENT								
	13 OF NOS.2,3,4,5 & 6 HEREON APPROVED BY THE SECRETARY								
	14 OF INTERIOR Aug 23 1905								
	15								
	16 Nos 2,3,4,5 & 6 restored to roll by Depart-								
	17 mental authority of January 18, 1909 (File 5-51)								

TRIBAL ENROLLMENT OF PARENTS

	Name of Father	Year	County	Name of Mother	Year	County
1	Asa Taylor	Dead	Non Citz	Abigail Taylor	Dead	Non Citz
2	John Crowder	"	Jackson	No1		
3	" "	"	"	No1		
4	" "	"	"	No1		
5	" "	"	"	No1		
6	" "	"	"	No1		
7						
8						
9						
10	John Crowder, father of children, on 1896 Jackson No. 2767 as Jno A. Crowder					
11	No4 on 1896 roll as Kate Crowder			ENROLLMENT		
12	No5 " 1896 " John A "			OF NOS ~~~ I ~~~ HEREON APPROVED BY THE SECRETARY		
13	No6 Affidavit of birth to be supplied:- Recd Oct 7/99 ~~order of~~			OF INTERIOR Mar 14 1906		
14	~~Enrollment of Nos 2,3,4,5 and 6 cancelled by~~ Department March 4, 1907			Date of Application for Enrollment.		
15	No2 – Dec 6/99 See Dawes Commission record 1896. Case 704			Aug 21/99		
16	No.1 denied by Dawes Commission in 1896: Choctaw Case #704: No appeal					
17	Nos 2 to 5 inclusive were denied by Dawes Commission: Choctaw Case #762: No appeal					

P.O. Boswell I.T. 1/13/05

56

Choctaw By Blood Enrollment Cards 1898-1914

RESIDENCE: Jackson COUNTY.
POST OFFICE: Mayhew, I.T.
Choctaw Nation
Choctaw Roll
(Not Including Freedmen)
CARD No.
FIELD No. **3657**

Dawes' Roll No.	NAME	Relationship to Person First Named	AGE	SEX	BLOOD	TRIBAL ENROLLMENT		
						Year	County	No.
10343	1 Whitten Annie B ²⁴	Named	21	F	3/4	1896	Jackson	3491
10344	2 Duncan Henry ⁸	Son	5	M	3/8	1896	"	3492
10345	3 " Charlie ⁶	"	3	"	3/8	1896	"	3493
	4							
	5							
	6	ENROLLMENT						
	7	OF NOS. 1,2 and 3 HEREON APPROVED BY THE SECRETARY						
	8	OF INTERIOR Feb 4 1903						
	9							
	10							
	11							
	12							
	13							
	14							
	15							
	16							
	17							

TRIBAL ENROLLMENT OF PARENTS

	Name of Father	Year	County	Name of Mother	Year	County
1	Ben Battiest	Dead	Jackson	Kizzie Battiest		Jackson
2	Gavin D. Duncan		white man	No 1		
3	" " "		" "	No 1		
4						
5						
6						
7						
8	No1 on 1896 roll as Annie Durant					
9	No2 " " " " Henry "					
10	No3 " " " " Charlie "					
11	Husband on Card No D343					
12	No.1 divorced from G.D. Duncan and married to a non-					
13	citizen by the name of Whitten. Evidence of marriage					
14	filed Dec. 6, 1902 - No.1 and second husband John Whitten, also separated			Date of Application for Enrollment.		
15				Aug 21/99		
16						
17						

Choctaw By Blood Enrollment Cards 1898-1914

RESIDENCE: Blue   COUNTY.

POST OFFICE: Blue I.T.

Choctaw Nation

Choctaw Roll
(Not Including Freedmen)

CARD No.

FIELD No. **3658**

Dawes' Roll No.	NAME	Relationship to Person First Named	AGE	SEX	BLOOD	TRIBAL ENROLLMENT Year	County	No.
10346	1 Dunn, Jane ²¹	First Named	18	F	Full	1896	Blue	1637
DEAD	2 Dunn Lavenia May	Dau	2wks	F	1/2			
I.W. 667	3 Dunn, James P ³⁶	Hus	36	M	I.W.			
	4							
	5							
	6							
	7							
	8							
	9							
	10							
	11							
	12							
	13							
	14	No. 2 hereon dismissed under order of the Commission to the Five Civilized Tribes of March 31, 1905.						
	15							
	16							
	17							

ENROLLMENT OF NOS. 1 HEREON APPROVED BY THE SECRETARY OF INTERIOR Feb 4 1903

ENROLLMENT OF NOS. 3 HEREON APPROVED BY THE SECRETARY OF INTERIOR Mar 26 1904

TRIBAL ENROLLMENT OF PARENTS

	Name of Father	Year	County	Name of Mother	Year	County
1	Albert Brown	Dead	Blue	Noelsie Brown		Jacks' Fork
2	James P. Dunn		white man	No.1		
3	Absalom Dunn	Dead	non citizen	Sarah C. Dunn		non citizen
4						
5						
6						
7	No.1 is now the wife of James P. Dunn on Choctaw Card #D.671					
8	No.2 born Dec. 10, 1901: Enrolled Dec. 23, 1901					
9	No2 died May 22, 1902: proof of death filed Nov 22 1902					
10						
11	No3 transferred from Choctaw card D671 January 21, 1904. See decision of January 4, 1904.					
12						
13						
14					#1	
15				Date of Application for Enrollment.	Aug 21/99	
16						
17						

Choctaw By Blood Enrollment Cards 1898-1914

RESIDENCE: Blue
POST OFFICE: Caddo, I.T.

COUNTY. **Choctaw Nation**

Choctaw Roll
(Not Including Freedmen)

CARD No.
FIELD No. **3659**

Dawes' Roll No.	NAME		Relationship to Person	AGE	SEX	BLOOD	TRIBAL ENROLLMENT		
							Year	County	No.
10347	1 Byington, Cyrus	32	First Named	29	M	Full	1896	Blue	1633
10348	2 " Sophia	31	Wife	28	F	"	1896	"	1634
10349	3 " Albert	8	Son	5	M	"	1896	"	1635
10350	4 " Zue	6	Dau	3	F	"	1896	"	1636
	5								
	6								
	7	ENROLLMENT OF NOS. 1,2,3 and 4 HEREON							
	8	APPROVED BY THE SECRETARY OF INTERIOR Feb 4 1903							
	9								
	10								
	11								
	12								
	13								
	14								
	15								
	16								
	17								

TRIBAL ENROLLMENT OF PARENTS

	Name of Father	Year	County	Name of Mother	Year	County
1	Henry Byington		Blue	Sallie Byington	Dead	Blue
2	Albert Brown	Dead	Jacks Fork	Eliza Impson	"	Jacks Fork
3	No1			No2		
4	No1			No2		
5						
6						
7						
8						
9						
10						
11						
12						
13						
14				Date of Application for Enrollment.		
15				Aug 21/99		
16						
17						

59

Choctaw By Blood Enrollment Cards 1898-1914

RESIDENCE:	Blue	COUNTY.	**Choctaw Nation**	**Choctaw Roll**	CARD No.	
POST OFFICE:	Blue, I.T			*(Not Including Freedmen)*	FIELD No. 3660	

Dawes' Roll No.	NAME	Relationship to Person First Named	AGE	SEX	BLOOD	TRIBAL ENROLLMENT Year	County	No.
DEAD.	1 King, Alfred		40	M	Full	1896	Blue	7630
10351	2 Houston, Crena ⁴¹	Wife	38	F	"	1896	"	7631
	3							
	4							
	5							
	6							
	7							
	8							
	9							
	10							
	11							
	12							
	13							
	14							
	15							
	16							
	17							

ENROLLMENT
OF NOS. 2 HEREON
APPROVED BY THE SECRETARY
OF INTERIOR FEB 4 1903

No. 1 HEREON DISMISSED UNDER ORDER OF THE COMMISSION TO THE FIVE CIVILIZED TRIBES OF MARCH 31, 1905.

TRIBAL ENROLLMENT OF PARENTS

Name of Father	Year	County	Name of Mother	Year	County
1 Bob King		Blue		Dead	Blue
2 Jack Folsom	Dead	Jackson	Nellie Folsom	"	Jackson
3					
4					
5					
6					
7		No2 on 1896 roll as Cerrena King			
8		No1 Died Dec 3, 1900: proof of death filed Nov 22 1902			
9		No.2 is now wife of Benjamin Houston, Choc. #3372 11/17 '02			
10					
11					
12					
13					
14				Date of Application for Enrollment	
15				Aug 21/99	
16					
17					

Choctaw By Blood Enrollment Cards 1898-1914

RESIDENCE:	Blue	COUNTY:						CARD NO.	
POST OFFICE:	Jackson, I.T.		**Choctaw Nation**			**Choctaw Roll** *(Not Including Freedmen)*		FIELD NO.	3661

Dawes' Roll No.	NAME		Relationship to Person First Named	AGE	SEX	BLOOD	TRIBAL ENROLLMENT		
							Year	County	No.
DEAD.	₁ Barnes, Cornelius	²²		19	M	Full	1896	Blue	1725
10352	₂ Ward Emma	²¹	Wife	18	F	"	1896	Jackson	5832
10353	₃ Ward Mitchell	²	Son of No2	2	M	"			
	₄								
	₅								
	₆								
	₇	ENROLLMENT							
	₈	OF NOS. 2 and 3 HEREON APPROVED BY THE SECRETARY							
	₉	OF INTERIOR FEB 4 1903							
	10								
	11								
	12								
	13	No 1							
	14	DISMISSED							
	15	FEB 28 1907							
	16								
	17								

TRIBAL ENROLLMENT OF PARENTS

Name of Father	Year	County	Name of Mother	Year	County
₁ Jackson Barnes	Dead	Jackson	Eliz. Barnes	Dead	Jackson
₂ Sidney Homer	"	"	Liley Homer		"
₃ Joel M Ward		"	No. 2		
₄					
₅					
₆ No2 on 1896 roll as Emma Homer					
₇ Nº2 is now the wife of Joel Ward on Choctaw Card #3931. See copy of					
₈ letter from Joel M Ward filed Sept 30, 1902					
₉ No3 born Jan 25, 1901. enrolled Dec 11, 1902					
10 Nº1 Died Dec 24, 1901. proof [sic] death filed July 17, 1903. Additional proof					
filed Jan 14, 1907					
11					
12					
13					
14			#1 & 2		
15			Date of Application for Enrollment.	Aug 21/99	
16					
17					

Choctaw By Blood Enrollment Cards 1898-1914

RESIDENCE: Blue COUNTY. **Choctaw Nation** Choctaw Roll CARD No.
POST OFFICE: Caddo, I.T. *(Not Including Freedmen)* FIELD No. 3662

Dawes' Roll No.	NAME	Relationship to Person First Named	AGE	SEX	BLOOD	TRIBAL ENROLLMENT Year	County	No.
10354	1 Bilbo, Charles A 45	First Named	42	M	1/8	1896	Blue	1551
I.W. 339	2 " Ella 32	Wife	28	F	IW	1896	"	14328
10355	3 " Charles C 11	Son	8	M	1/16	1896	"	1552
10356	4 " Cecil A 9	"	6	"	1/16	1896	"	1553
10357	5 " William W 7	"	4	"	1/16	1896	"	1554
DEAD	6 " ~~Czerna~~ DEAD	~~Dau~~	2	F	1/16			
	7							
	8 No. 6 HEREON DISMISSED UNDER ORDER OF THE COMMISSION TO THE FIVE							
	9 CIVILIZED TRIBES OF MARCH 31, 1905.							
	10 No.2 admitted as an intermarried							
	11 citizen by Dawes Commission in 1896							
	12 Choctaw Case #927: No appeal							
	13							
	14 ENROLLMENT							
	15 OF NOS. 1,3,4 and 5 HEREON APPROVED BY THE SECRETARY							
	16 OF INTERIOR FEB 4 1903							
	17							

TRIBAL ENROLLMENT OF PARENTS

	Name of Father	Year	County	Name of Mother	Year	County
1	William Bilbo	Dead	Non Citz	Henrietta Bilbo	Dead	in Mississippi
2	Clay McCoy		" "		"	Non Citz
3	No1			No2		
4	No1			No2		
5	No1			No2		
6	No1			No2		
7						
8						
9						
10					ENROLLMENT	
11	No1 on 1896 roll as C. A. Bilbo			OF NOS. 2 HEREON APPROVED BY THE SECRETARY		
12	No3 " 1896 " " Charlie C.B. Bilbo			OF INTERIOR SEP 12 1903		
13	No5 " 1896 " " Willie W. "					
14	No2 " 1896 " " Ella Bilboe					Date of Application for Enrollment.
15	Nos 102 Marriage certificate exhibited, dated Sept 11/89 in due form, but not in con-					Aug 22/99
16	dition to be filed No6 Affidavit of birth to be					
17	supplied:-					

Proof of death of #6 requested 8/10/05

62

Choctaw By Blood Enrollment Cards 1898-1914

RESIDENCE: Blue		COUNTY. **Choctaw Nation**				**Choctaw Roll** *(Not Including Freedmen)*	CARD No.	
POST OFFICE: Caddo, I.T.							FIELD No. 3663	

Dawes' Roll No.	NAME	Relationship to Person First Named	AGE	SEX	BLOOD	TRIBAL ENROLLMENT		
						Year	County	No.
DEAD.	1 Bates William H		46	M	I.W.			
10358	2 " Christina A ⁵⁰	Wife	47	F	1/2	1896	Blue	1645
	3							
	4							
	5							
	6 ENROLLMENT							
	7 OF NOS. 2 HEREON APPROVED BY THE SECRETARY							
	8 OF INTERIOR FEB 4 1903							
	9							
	10 No. 1 HEREON DISMISSED UNDER							
	11 ORDER OF THE COMMISSION TO THE FIVE							
	12 CIVILIZED TRIBES OF MARCH 31, 1905.							
	13							
	14							
	15							
	16							
	17							

TRIBAL ENROLLMENT OF PARENTS

Name of Father	Year	County	Name of Mother	Year	County
1 W. M. Bates	Dead	Non Citz	Sarah Bates	Dead	Non Citz
2 Israel Folsom	"	Blue	Christina Folsom	"	Blue
3					
4					
5					
6		No 1 was admitted by Dawes Com, No 629			
7		as W. H. Bates			
8		No 1 died Aug 17, 1901: proof of death filed Nov 22 1902			
9					
10					
11					
12					
13					
14				Date of Application for Enrollment.	
15				Aug 22/99	
16					
17					

Choctaw By Blood Enrollment Cards 1898-1914

RESIDENCE: Blue   COUNTY. **Choctaw Nation**   **Choctaw Roll**   CARD NO.
POST OFFICE: Caddo, I.T.   *(Not Including Freedmen)*   FIELD NO. 3664

Dawes' Roll No.	NAME	Relationship to Person	AGE	SEX	BLOOD	TRIBAL ENROLLMENT		
						Year	County	No.
10359	1 Bouton, William I ²⁷	First Named	24	M	1/4	1896	Blue	1556
	2							
	3							
	4							
	5							
	6							
	7							
	8							
	9							
	10							
	11							
	12							
	13							
	14							
	15							
	16							
	17							

ENROLLMENT
OF NOS. 1   HEREON
APPROVED BY THE SECRETARY
OF INTERIOR   FEB 4 1903

TRIBAL ENROLLMENT OF PARENTS

	Name of Father	Year	County	Name of Mother	Year	County
1	Madison Bouton	Dead	Non Citz	Christina A. Bates		Blue
2						
3						
4						
5						
6						
7		On 1896 roll as W. J. Bouton				
8						
9						
10						
11						
12						
13						
14						Date of Application for Enrollment.
15						Aug 22/99
16						
17						

Choctaw By Blood Enrollment Cards 1898-1914

RESIDENCE: Blue   COUNTY. **Choctaw Nation**   **Choctaw Roll**   CARD NO.
POST OFFICE: Caddo, I.T.   *(Not Including Freedmen)*   FIELD NO. 3665

Dawes' Roll No.	NAME	Relationship to Person Named	AGE	SEX	BLOOD	TRIBAL ENROLLMENT		
						Year	County	No.
10360	1 Sutherland, Lena D ⁴⁶	First Named	43	F	1/8	1896	Blue	11589
15026	2 " Valeria E ¹⁷	Dau	18	F	1/16	1896	"	11590
I.W. 688	3 " Henry ⁵³	Hus	52	M	IW	1896	Atoka	15066
	4	No2 restored to roll by Departmental authority of January 10 1909 (File 5-51)						
	5	No2 transferred from Choctaw card R 291, August 15, 1903. See decision						
	6	of July 30, 1903.						
	7	ENROLLMENT						
	8	OF NOS. 1 HEREON APPROVED BY THE SECRETARY						
	9	OF INTERIOR FEB 4 1903						
	10							
	11	ENROLLMENT						
	12	OF NOS. 2 HEREON APPROVED BY THE SECRETARY						
	13	OF INTERIOR OCT 15 1903						
	14							
	15	ENROLLMENT OF NOS. 3 HEREON						
	16	APPROVED BY THE SECRETARY OF INTERIOR MAR 26 1904						
	17							

TRIBAL ENROLLMENT OF PARENTS

	Name of Father	Year	County	Name of Mother	Year	County
1	William Bilbo	Dead	Non Citz	Henrietta Bilbo	Dead	in Mississippi
2	Henry Sutherland		noncitizen	No1		
3	Danl Sutherland		noncitizen	Elizabeth Sutherland		noncitizen
4						
5						
6						
7						
8						
9	On 1896 roll as Lena Southerland					
10	Enrollment of No.3 cancelled by order of Department March 1, 1909					
11	No1 is the mother of Valeria E Sutherland on Choctaw rejected card #R291; also wife of Henry Sutherland on Choctaw					
12	doubtful card #D483					
13	No3 on 1896 Choctaw roll as Henry Southerland					
14	No3 transferred from Choctaw card D483 January 25, 1904				Date of Application for Enrollment	
15	See decision of January 7, 1904					
	No3 denied by Commission in 1896 Choctaw case No 138. No appeal.				Aug 22/99	
16						
17						

65

Choctaw By Blood Enrollment Cards 1898-1914

RESIDENCE: Blue   COUNTY. **Choctaw Nation**   Choctaw Roll   CARD No.
POST OFFICE: Caddo, I.T.   (Not Including Freedmen)   FIELD No. 3666

Dawes' Roll No.	NAME	Relationship to Person First Named	AGE	SEX	BLOOD	TRIBAL ENROLLMENT Year	County	No.
DEAD	1 Travis, Ozie DEAD 39	First Named	36	F	1/8	1896	Blue	12403
I.W. 340	2 Travis, Robert A 49	husband	49	M	I.W.			
15635	3 " Robbie 16	Dau	16	F	1/16	1896	Blue	12404
15636	4 " William 14	Son	14	M	1/16	1896	"	12405
15637	5 " Marie 12	Dau	12	F	1/16	1896	"	12406
	6	No 1 admitted by act of Choctaw Council of April 8, 1891						
	7	No. 1 HEREON DISMISSED UNDER						
	8	ORDER OF THE COMMISSION TO THE FIVE CIVILIZED TRIBES OF MARCH 31, 1905.						
	9	ENROLLMENT						
	10	OF NOS. 2 HEREON						
	11	APPROVED BY THE SECRETARY OF INTERIOR SEP 12 1903						
	12							
	13	#1 DISMISSED						
	14	SEP 9 1904						
	15	ENROLLMENT						
		#5 – Suite 411 Colcard Bldg. Okla City, Okla	OF NOS. 3,4 and 5 HEREON APPROVED BY THE SECRETARY OF INTERIOR OCT 21 1904						

TRIBAL ENROLLMENT OF PARENTS

	Name of Father	Year	County	Name of Mother	Year	County
1	William Bilbo	Dead	Non Citz	Henrietta Bilbo	Dead	in Mississippi
2	Wm Travis		non-citizen	Martha Travis		non-citizen
3	Nº2			Nº1		
4	Nº2			Nº1		
5	Nº2			Nº1		
6						
7						
8	No 1 is mother of Nos 1,2 and 3 on Choctaw rejected card R #306					
9	No 2 restored to roll by Departmental authority of January 19, 1909 (File 5-51)					
10	Enrollment of No.2 cancelled by order of Department March 4 1904					
11	No 1 died Dec 31, 1900; proof of death filed Nov 26 1902					
12	Nº2 transferred from Choctaw card #D484. See decision of April 22, 1903					
13	Nos 3-4&5 transferred from Choctaw card #R306. See decision of Sept 9, 1904			Sept 24 1904[sic]
14	For child of No3 see NB (Apr 26-06) Card #721			Date of Application for Enrollment
15	No.2 denied by Commission in 1896 Choctaw Case #438			Aug 22/99
16	No appeal. All papers on case of Robert A Travis forwarded to			
17	Court of Indian Affairs Oct 3/08. See telegram from Couser Chief Clerk of Oct 3/08			

See 7-R-306.

66

Choctaw By Blood Enrollment Cards 1898-1914

RESIDENCE:	Blue	COUNTY:								
POST OFFICE:	Caddo, I.T.		**Choctaw Nation**				**Choctaw Roll** *(Not Including Freedmen)*		CARD No.	
									FIELD No.	3667

Dawes' Roll No.	NAME	Relationship to Person	AGE	SEX	BLOOD	TRIBAL ENROLLMENT		
						Year	County	No.
10361	1 Pearce, John M ¹⁵	First Named	12	M	1/16	1896	Blue	10510
10362	2 " Helen M ¹²	Sister	9	F	1/16	1896	"	10511
10363	3 " Lillian ¹⁰	"	7	"	1/16	1896	"	10512
I.W 975	4 " Thornton D ⁴⁷	Father	47	M	I W	1896	"	14941
	5							
	6	ENROLLMENT OF NOS. 1,2 and 3 HEREON APPROVED BY THE SECRETARY OF INTERIOR FEB 4 1903						
	7							
	8							
	9							
	10	ENROLLMENT OF NOS. ~ 4 ~ HEREON APPROVED BY THE SECRETARY OF INTERIOR sep 22 1904						
	11							
	12							
	13							
	14							
	15							
	16							
	17							

TRIBAL ENROLLMENT OF PARENTS

	Name of Father	Year	County	Name of Mother	Year	County
1	Thornton D Pearce		Intermarried	Permelia A Pearce	Dead	Blue
2	" " "		"	" " "	"	"
3	" " "		"	" " "	"	"
4	F. M. Pearce	Dead	noncitizen	Eliz. Pearce	"	noncitizen
5						
6						
7						
8						
9			No1 on 1896 roll as John Pierce			
10			No2 " 1896 " " Myrtle "			
11			No3 " 1896 " " Lillian "			
			~~Father of these children on Choctaw Card D.344~~			
12						
13			No4 transferred from Choctaw card D#344, June 6, 1904			
14			~~Decision of Commission of March 9, 1904 enrolling No.4 affirmed~~			Date of Application for Enrollment.
15			by Department May 21, 1904 (I.T.D. 4060-1904)			Aug 22/99
16			For children of No4 see NB (Apr 26 '06) #1131			
17						

67

Choctaw By Blood Enrollment Cards 1898-1914

RESIDENCE: Jackson   COUNTY. **Choctaw Nation**   **Choctaw Roll**   CARD NO.
POST OFFICE: Jackson, I.T.   (Not Including Freedmen)   FIELD NO. 3668

Dawes' Roll No.	NAME		Relationship to Person First Named	AGE	SEX	BLOOD	TRIBAL ENROLLMENT		
							Year	County	No.
10364	1 Scott, Aaron	30	First Named	27	M	Full	1896	Jackson	11558
10365	2 " Sila	43	Wife	40	F	"	1896	"	11559
	3								
	4								
	5								
	6								
	7								
	8								
	9								
	10								
	11								
	12								
	13								
	14								
	15								
	16								
	17								

ENROLLMENT
OF NOS. 1 and 2   HEREON
APPROVED BY THE SECRETARY
OF INTERIOR FEB 4 1903

TRIBAL ENROLLMENT OF PARENTS

Name of Father	Year	County	Name of Mother	Year	County
1 Abner Scott	Dead	Jackson	Sealy Scott		Jackson
2 Ise-hok-shok	"	Red River	Sah-ko	Dead	Jacks Fork
3					
4					
5					
6					
7		No2 on 1896 roll as Matahama Scott			
8					
9					
10					
11					
12					
13					
14				Date of Application for Enrollment.	
15				Aug 22/99	
16					
17					

Choctaw By Blood Enrollment Cards 1898-1914

RESIDENCE: Jackson   COUNTY.   **Choctaw Nation**   Choctaw Roll   CARD NO.
POST OFFICE: Jackson, I.T.   *(Not Including Freedmen)*   FIELD NO. 3669

Dawes' Roll No.	NAME	Relationship to Person First Named	AGE	SEX	BLOOD	TRIBAL ENROLLMENT Year	County	No.
10366 1	Belvin, Craven N ⁵⁶	First Named	53	M	Full	1896	Jackson	1514
10367 2	" Eliza ⁵³	Wife	50	F	"	1896	"	1515
10368 3	" Thomas ²⁷	Son	24	M	"	1896	"	1517
10369 4	" Abel ²⁵	"	22	"	"	1896	"	1518
10370 5	" Ella ²¹	Dau	18	F	"	1896	"	1520
10371 6	Williams, Incy ¹⁷	Niece	14	"	"	1896	"	13811
7								
8								
9								
10								
11								
12								
13								
14								
15								
16								
17								

ENROLLMENT
OF NOS. 1,2,3,4,5 and 6 HEREON
APPROVED BY THE SECRETARY
OF INTERIOR FEB 4 1903

TRIBAL ENROLLMENT OF PARENTS

	Name of Father	Year	County	Name of Mother	Year	County
1	Tom Belvin	Dead	Red River	Ho-ka-te-ma	Dead	Red River
2	Ma-kin-ta	"	Jackson	Char-ka-sey	"	Jackson
3	No 1			Bessie Belvin	"	"
4	No 1			" "	"	"
5	No 1			" "	"	"
6	A-sho-mo-ta	Dead	Jacks Fork	Selina	"	Jacks Fork
7						
8						
9						
10			No 1 on 1896 roll as G. N. Belvin			
11						
12			For child of No3 see NB (Apr 26-06) Card #377			
13						
14						
15				Date of Application for Enrollment Aug 22/99		
16				Date of Application for Enrollment.		
17						

69

Choctaw By Blood Enrollment Cards 1898-1914

RESIDENCE: Jackson COUNTY. **Choctaw Nation** Choctaw Roll CARD NO.
POST OFFICE: Jackson, I.T. (Not Including Freedmen) FIELD NO. 3670

Dawes' Roll No.	NAME		Relationship to Person	AGE	SEX	BLOOD	TRIBAL ENROLLMENT		
							Year	County	No.
10372	1 Belvin, Lamos	23	First Named	20	M	Full	1896	Jackson	1519
10373	2 " Sis	23	Wife	20	F	Full	1896	"	5941
	3								
	4								
	5	ENROLLMENT OF NOS. 1 and 2 HEREON							
	6	APPROVED BY THE SECRETARY							
	7	OF INTERIOR FEB 4 1903							
	8								
	9								
	10								
	11								
	12								
	13								
	14								
	15								
	16								
	17								

TRIBAL ENROLLMENT OF PARENTS

	Name of Father	Year	County	Name of Mother	Year	County
1	Craven Belvin		Jackson	Bessie Belvin	Dead	Jackson
2	Jas. Harrison		"	Liza A Harrison	"	"
3						
4						
5						
6						
7						
8			No2 on 1896 roll as Sis Harrison			
9						
10			For child of Nos 1&2 see NB (Apr 26-06) Card #378			
11						
12						
13						
14						Date of Application for Enrollment:
15						Aug 22/99
16						
17						

Choctaw By Blood Enrollment Cards 1898-1914

RESIDENCE: Jackson   COUNTY. **Choctaw Nation**   Choctaw Roll   CARD No.
POST OFFICE: Jackson, I.T.   *(Not Including Freedmen)*   FIELD NO. 3671

Dawes' Roll No.	NAME		Relationship to Person Named	AGE	SEX	BLOOD	TRIBAL ENROLLMENT		
							Year	County	No.
10374	1 Wilson, Allington	33	First Named	31	M	Full	1896	Jackson	13837
10375	2 " Becky	28	Wife	25	F	"	1896	"	13838
10376	3 " Henry	10	Son	7	M	"	1896	"	13839
	4								
	5								
	6								
	7	ENROLLMENT							
	8	OF NOS. 1, 2 and 3 HEREON APPROVED BY THE SECRETARY							
	9	OF INTERIOR FEB 4 1903							
	10								
	11								
	12								
	13								
	14								
	15								
	16								
	17								

TRIBAL ENROLLMENT OF PARENTS

	Name of Father	Year	County	Name of Mother	Year	County
1	On-tan-tubbee	Dead	Jackson	To-nah	Dead	Red River
2	Wilson Davis	"	"	Susan Davis	"	Jackson
3	No1			No2		
4						
5						
6						
7	No.2 "Died prior to September 25, 1902; not entitled to land or money."					
8	(See Indian Office letter of June 20, 1910. D.C. #848-1910)					
9						
10						
11						
12						
13						
14				Date of Application for Enrollment.		Aug 22/99
15						
16						
17						

Choctaw By Blood Enrollment Cards 1898-1914

RESIDENCE: Blue   COUNTY. **Choctaw Nation**   Choctaw Roll   CARD NO.
POST OFFICE: Caddo, I.T.   *(Not Including Freedmen)*   FIELD NO. 3672

Dawes' Roll No.		NAME		Relationship to Person	AGE	SEX	BLOOD	TRIBAL ENROLLMENT		
								Year	County	No.
I.W. 925	1	Baxter, Elisha	(48)	First Named	44	M	I.W	1896	Blue	14322
15465	2	" Caroline	45	Wife	42	F	1/8	1896	"	1647
15466	3	" Granville	23	Son	20	M	1/16	1896	"	1648
15467	4	" Walter W.	20	"	17	"	1/16	1896	"	1649
15468	5	" Daisy	14	Dau	11	F	1/16	1896	"	1650
15469	6	" Gaynell	12	"	9	"	1/16	1896	"	1651
15470	7	" Charles E	3	Son	1mo	M	1/16			
I.W. 1217	8	" Alta	20	Wife of No.4	20	F	I.W.			
	9	ENROLLMENT								
	10	OF NOS. 1 HEREON								
	11	APPROVED BY THE SECRETARY OF INTERIOR AUG 3 1904								
	12									
	13	ENROLLMENT								
	14	OF NOS. -2-3-4-5-6-7 HEREON								
	15	APPROVED BY THE SECRETARY OF INTERIOR MAY 9 1904								
	16									
	17									

TRIBAL ENROLLMENT OF PARENTS

	Name of Father	Year	County	Name of Mother	Year	County
1	William Baxter	Dead	Non Citz	Adaline Baxter	Dead	Non Citz
2	Geo Staurt[sic]	"	" "	Cyntha Stuart	"	Kiamitia
3	No1			No2		
4	No1			No2		
5	No1	ENROLLMENT OF NOS. ~8~ HEREON		No2		
6	No1	APPROVED BY THE SECRETARY OF INTERIOR DEC 13 1904		No2		
7	No1			No2		
8	Ewing Pierce		non citizen	Mary J. Pierce		non citizen
9						
10						
11	No1 Admitted by Dawes Com. Case No 196.					
12	No1 on 1896 roll as Elijah Bexter					
13	No.4 is now the husband of Alta Baxter on Choctaw card #D.741 July 14, 1902					
14	No.8 and No.4 were married June 29, 1902. See testimony of July 14, 1902					
15	No8 originally listed for enrollment on Choctaw card #D-741 July 14, 1902: transferred to this card Nov. 26, 1904. See decision of Nov. 8, 1904			Date of Application for Enrollment	Aug 22/99	
16	For child of No.5 see N.B. (Apr 26, 1906) Card No. 42. " " " " 4 " " " " " " " 123.			No7 enrolled Nov 2/99		
17	" " " " 4 " " Mar. 3 '05) #256					

72

Choctaw By Blood Enrollment Cards 1898-1914

RESIDENCE: Jackson COUNTY.								
POST OFFICE: Jackson, I.T.		**Choctaw Nation**				**Choctaw Roll** *(Not Including Freedmen)*	CARD NO. FIELD NO. 3673	

Dawes' Roll No.	NAME	Relationship to Person	AGE	SEX	BLOOD	TRIBAL ENROLLMENT		
						Year	County	No.
10377	1 Belvin, Moses ³³	First Named	30	M	Full	1896	Jackson	1490
10378	2 " Phoebe ⁴⁴	Wife	41	F	"	1896	"	1491
10379	3 Ramsey, Ellis ¹⁵	Ward	12	M	"	1896	"	10880
	4							
	5							
	6							
	7							
	8							
	9							
	10							
	11							
	12							
	13							
	14							
	15							
	16							
	17							

ENROLLMENT
OF NOS. 1 2 and 3 HEREON
APPROVED BY THE SECRETARY
OF INTERIOR FEB 4 1903

TRIBAL ENROLLMENT OF PARENTS

Name of Father	Year	County	Name of Mother	Year	County
1 Impson Belvin	Dead	Jackson	Lucy Belvin	Dead	Jackson
2 E-lam-bey	"	Kiamitia	Ah-chi-ya-ho-na	"	Kiamitia
3 Elias Ramsey	"	Jackson	Piley Ramsey	"	Jackson
4					
5					
6					
7					
8					
9					
10					
11					
12					
13					
14				Date of Application for Enrollment.	
15				Aug 22/99	
16					
17					

Choctaw By Blood Enrollment Cards 1898-1914

RESIDENCE: Jackson COUNTY. **Choctaw Nation** **Choctaw Roll** CARD No.
POST OFFICE: Bennington, I.T. *(Not Including Freedmen)* FIELD No. 3674

Dawes' Roll No.	NAME		Relationship to Person First Named	AGE	SEX	BLOOD	TRIBAL ENROLLMENT		
							Year	County	No.
10380	1 Jones, Zack	48	First Named	45	M	1/2	1896	Jackson	7152
I.W. 570	2 " Malinda	46	Wife	43	F	I.W	1896	"	14699
10381	3 " Ellis	22	Son	19	M	1/4	1896	"	7153
10382	4 " Amelia	13	Dau	10	F	1/4	1896	"	7155
10383	5 " John	8	Son	5	M	1/4	1896	"	7156
10384	6 " Missie	6	Dau	3	F	1/4	1896	"	7157
	7								
	8								
	9	ENROLLMENT							
	10	OF NOS. 1,3,4,5 and 6 HEREON APPROVED BY THE SECRETARY							
	11	OF INTERIOR FEB 4 1903							
	12								
	13	ENROLLMENT OF NOS. 2 HEREON							
	14	APPROVED BY THE SECRETARY							
	15	OF INTERIOR FEB -8 1904							
	16								
	17								

TRIBAL ENROLLMENT OF PARENTS

	Name of Father	Year	County	Name of Mother	Year	County
1	Rayson Jones	Dead	Jackson	Rhoda Jones	Dead	Jackson
2	John Morrison	"	Non Citz	Eliz. Morrison	"	Non Citz
3	No1			No2		
4	No1			No2		
5	No1			No2		
6	No1			No2		
7						
8						
9						
10						
11	No2 As to marriage, see testimony					
12	of No1 and Phoebe LeFlore					
13	No4 on 1896 roll as Annelia Jones No6 " 1896 " " Messie "					
14	For child of No.3 see NB (March 3 1905) #839					Date of Application for Enrollment.
15	" " " " " " (April 26,1906) #281					Aug 22/99
16	Date of application for enrollment					
17						

74

Choctaw By Blood Enrollment Cards 1898-1914

RESIDENCE: Jackson   COUNTY.   **Choctaw Nation**   Choctaw Roll   CARD No.
POST OFFICE: Bennington, I.T.   *(Not Including Freedmen)*   FIELD No. 3675

Dawes' Roll No.	NAME	Relationship to Person First Named	AGE	SEX	BLOOD	TRIBAL ENROLLMENT Year	County	No.
10385	1 Butler Lizzie 19	Named	16	F	1/4	1896	Jackson	7154
10386	2 Davis George 4	Son	6mo	M	1/8			
10387	3 Butler Abbie 1	Dau	10mo	F	1/8			
	4							
	5							
	6							
	7	ENROLLMENT						
	8	OF NOS. 1 2 and 3 HEREON APPROVED BY THE SECRETARY						
	9	OF INTERIOR FEB 4 1903						
	10							
	11							
	12							
	13							
	14							
	15							
	16							
	17							

TRIBAL ENROLLMENT OF PARENTS

	Name of Father	Year	County	Name of Mother	Year	County
1	Zack Jones		Jackson	Malinda Jones		Intermarried
2	Dud Davis		Non Citz	No1		
3	J. F. Butler		" "	N⁰1		
4						
5						
6						
7						

8   For child of No.1 see NB (March 3, 1905) #1188
9   No1 on 1896 roll as Lizzie Jones – As to
10   marriage of parents, see testimony of
     Zack Jones and Phoebe LeFlore in the
11   matter of the enrollment of Zack Jones, Card
12   No 3674
13   No2 Affidavit of birth to be
     supplied:-   Recd Oct 7/99
14   N⁰1 is now the wife of J.F. Butler, a non-citizen   Evidence
15   of marriage filed July 25, 1902.
16   N⁰3 Born Sept/ 26, 1901: enrolled July 25, 1902.
17

#1&2
Date of Application for Enrollment.   Aug 22/99

75

Choctaw By Blood Enrollment Cards 1898-1914

RESIDENCE: Jackson COUNTY. **Choctaw Nation** Choctaw Roll CARD NO.
POST OFFICE: Bennington, I.T. *(Not Including Freedmen)* FIELD NO. 36__

Dawes' Roll No.	NAME		Relationship to Person First Named	AGE	SEX	BLOOD	TRIBAL ENROLLMENT		
							Year	County	No.
10388	1 Jones, Phoebe	39	First Named	36	F	3/4	1896	Jackson	8142
10389	2 Battiest, Frank	19	Son	16	M	3/4	1896	"	1506
10390	3 " Mary	17	Dau	14	F	3/4	1896	"	1507
10391	4 LeFlore, Clemon	6	Son	3	M	5/8	1896	"	8146
10392	5 " Mollie	17	S.Dau	14	F	3/4	1896	"	8145
	6								
	7	ENROLLMENT OF NOS. 1,2,3,4 and 5 HEREON APPROVED BY THE SECRETARY OF INTERIOR FEB 4 1903							
	8								
	9								
	10								
	11								
	12								
	13								
	14								
	15								
	16								
	17								

TRIBAL ENROLLMENT OF PARENTS

	Name of Father	Year	County	Name of Mother	Year	County
1	Francis Battiest	Dead	Kiamitia	Mary Battiest	Dead	Kiamitia
2	Nelson Battiest	"	Jacks Fork	No1		
3	" "	"	" "	No1		
4	Colbert LeFlore	"	Jackson	No1		
5	" "	"	"	Siney	Dead	Jackson
6						
7						
8	No1 is wife of Willis Jones on Choctaw card #5611 – a Choctaw delinquent					
9	who appeared before the Commission at Atoka 11/20'02					
10	For child of No3 see NB (March 3, 1905) #1036					
11						
12						
13						
14						
15					Date of Application for Enrollment	Aug 22/99
16						
17						

Choctaw By Blood Enrollment Cards 1898-1914

RESIDENCE:	Blue	COUNTY.					Choctaw Roll	CARD NO.	
POST OFFICE:	Bok Chito, I.T.		**Choctaw Nation**				*(Not Including Freedmen)*	FIELD NO. 3677	

Dawes' Roll No.	NAME	Relationship to Person Named	AGE	SEX	BLOOD	TRIBAL ENROLLMENT		
						Year	County	No.
10393	1 Impson, Middleton M. 51	First Named	48	M	1/4	1896	Blue	6314
I.W. 157	2 " Angeline 48	Wife	45	F	I.W	1896	"	14680
10394	3 " Hiram W. C. 10	Son	7	M	1/8	1896	"	6316
10395	4 " Robert E. L 8	"	5	"	1/8	1896	"	6317
10396	5 " John A. M 26	"	23	"	1/8	1896	"	6315
	6							
	7							
	8	ENROLLMENT						
	9	OF NOS. 1,3,4 and 5 HEREON APPROVED BY THE SECRETARY						
	10	OF INTERIOR FEB 4 1903						
	11							
	12	ENROLLMENT						
	13	OF NOS. 2 HEREON APPROVED BY THE SECRETARY						
	14	OF INTERIOR JUN 13 1903						
	15							
	16							
	17							

TRIBAL ENROLLMENT OF PARENTS

	Name of Father	Year	County	Name of Mother	Year	County
1	John Impson	Dead	Blue	Louisa Impson	Dead	Blue
2	John Boydston		Non Citz	Poline Boydston	"	Non Citz
3	No1			No2		
4	No1			No2		
5	No1			Mary Impson	Dead	Non Citz
6						
7	No2 Evidence of marriage to be					
8	supplied: Recd Oct 7/99					
9	No3 on 1896 roll as Hiran W Impson					
	No4 " 1896 " " Robt E. L. "					
10	No5 " 1896 " " Jno. A. "					
11	No5 Evidence of marriage of parents					
12	to be supplied:- Recd Oct 7/99					
13						
14					Date of Application for Enrollment.	
15					Aug 22/99	
16						
17						

Choctaw By Blood Enrollment Cards 1898-1914

	NAME	Relationship to Person First Named	AGE	SEX	BLOOD	TRIBAL ENROLLMENT Year	County	No.
1	Lawrence, Sarah J 60	First Named	57	F	I W	1896	Blue	14773
2	" Frank T 29	Son	26	M	1/4	1896	"	8191
3	" Joseph R 27	"	24	"	1/4	1896	"	8192
4	Nicholson Mannie E 24	Dau	21	F	1/4	1896	"	8193
5	Manning Nannie H 20	"	17	"	1/4	1896	"	8194
6	Lawrence Thelma Anna	G.Dau	1mo	F	1/8	ENROLLMENT		
7	Manning Annie E 1	Grand dau	1wk	F	1/4	OF NOS. 8 and 9 HEREON APPROVED BY THE SECRETARY		
8	Lawrence Ida V 21	Wife of No2	21	F	I W	OF INTERIOR MAR 26 1904		
9	" Sudie 20	Wife of No3	20	F	I W			
10						No.5 is now the wife of Arthur		
11						F. Manning on Choctaw roll card		
12						#3923 Dec 24, 1901		
13								
14								
15						ENROLLMENT		
16						OF NOS. 1 HEREON APPROVED BY THE SECRETARY		
17						OF INTERIOR SEP 12 1903		

ENROLLMENT OF NOS. 2,3,4,5,6 and 7 HEREON APPROVED BY THE SECRETARY OF INTERIOR FEB 4 1903

For child of No5 see NB (March 3,1905) #783

Nº4 is the wife of Omer R Nicholson on Choctaw card #7-5903 Sept 19, 1902

No.2 is husband of Ida V Lawrence on Choc D.643

TRIBAL ENROLLMENT OF PARENTS

	Name of Father	Year	County	Name of Mother	Year	County
1	Jas. Thurmond	Dead	Non Citz	Mary Thurmond	Dead	Non Citz
2	Jos. R. Lawrence	"	Towson	No1		
3	" " "	"	"	No1		
4	" " "	"	"	No1		
5	" " "	"	"	No1		
6	No.3			Sudie Lawrence		
7	Arthur F. Manning	1896	Blue	No.5		
8	Columbus Washington		noncitizen	Nancy Washington		noncitizen
9	Thomas Sanford		noncitizen	Fannie Sanford		noncitizen
10						
11	No2 on 1896 roll as Frank Laurence			No.7 born Dec.18,1901; Enrolled Dec 24, 1901		
12	No3 " 1896 " " J. R. "			No8 transferred from Choctaw card D.643		
13	No4 " 1896 " " Mannie "			Jan 23,1904. See decision of Jan 6 1904		
14	No5 " 1896 " " Nannie "					
15	No1 Admitted by Dawes Commission, Case No. 857			Date of Application for Enrollment. Aug 22/99		
16	No.3 is now the husband of Sudie Lawrence on Choctaw card #D.617; Feby 23d, 1901			No8 transferred from Choctaw		
17	No 6 Enrolled Oct 10, 1901			Jan 23,1904. See decision of Ja		

For child of No4 see NB (Mar 3-1905) Card #540
" " " " 2 " " " " " " #258

Choctaw By Blood Enrollment Cards 1898-1914

RESIDENCE:	Atoka	COUNTY.							
POST OFFICE:	Owl, I.T.	**Choctaw Nation**				**Choctaw Roll** (Not Including Freedmen)		CARD NO. FIELD NO. 3679	

Dawes' Roll No.	NAME		Relationship to Person	AGE	SEX	BLOOD	TRIBAL ENROLLMENT		
							Year	County	No.
10403	1 Harkins, George W	43	First Named	40	M	1/2	1896	Atoka	5978
I.W. 342	2 " Hattie	37	Wife	33	F	I W	1896	"	14654
10404	3 " Pike	17	Son	14	M	1/4	1896	"	5979
10405	4 " Elizabeth	15	Dau	12	F	1/4	1896	"	6033
10406	5 " Willy	12	Son	9	M	1/4	1896	"	5980
10407	6 " Memory	10	"	7	"	1/4	1896	"	5981
10408	7 " Lorena	4	Dau	9mo	F	1/4			
10409	8 " Organ Carnelias	2	Son	1mo	M	1/4			
	9								
	10								
	11	ENROLLMENT							
	12	OF NOS. 1,3,4,5,6,7 and 8 HEREON APPROVED BY THE SECRETARY							
	13	OF INTERIOR FEB 4 1903							
	14	ENROLLMENT							
	15	OF NOS. 2 HEREON APPROVED BY THE SECRETARY							
	16	OF INTERIOR SEP 12 1903							
	17								

TRIBAL ENROLLMENT OF PARENTS

	Name of Father	Year	County	Name of Mother	Year	County
1	Dave Harkins	Dead	Atoka	Isabelle Harkins	Dead	Atoka
2	George Beard		Non Citz	Martha M Beard	"	Non Citz
3	No1			No2		
4	No1			No2		
5	No1			No2		
6	No1			No2		
7	No1			No2		
8	No 1			No 2		
9						
10						
11	No1 on 1896 roll as G. W. Harkins					
12	No2 " 1896 " " Hallie "			#1 to 7
13	No7 Affidavit of birth to be					
14	supplied:- Recd Dec. 18/99. Irregular			Date of Application for Enrollment.
15	and returned for correction Dec 19/99			Aug 22/99
16	Recd & filed Jany 17, 1900					
17	No8 Enrolled March 21, 1901.					
	For child of No3 see NB (Apr 26-06) #1253					
	" " " " 1 " " " Mar 3'05) #258					

79

Choctaw By Blood Enrollment Cards 1898-1914

RESIDENCE: Jackson COUNTY.
POST OFFICE: Bennington I.T.

Choctaw Nation

Choctaw Roll (Not Including Freedmen)
CARD NO.
FIELD NO. 3680

Dawes' Roll No.	NAME	Relationship to Person First Named	AGE	SEX	BLOOD	TRIBAL ENROLLMENT Year	County	No.
DP 7/7/06	1 Risener, Jack		65	M	I W	1896	Jackson	14982
10410	2 " Tryfenia 46	Wife	43	F	1/2	1896	"	10867
	3							
	4							
	5							
	6							
	7							
	8							
	9							
	10							
No1	11							
	12							
	13							
	14							
No1	15							
	16							
	17							

ENROLLMENT OF NOS. ~~~2~~~ HEREON APPROVED BY THE SECRETARY OF INTERIOR Feb 4 – 1903

ACTION APPROVED BY SECRETARY OF INTERIOR. MAR 4 1907

NOTICE OF DEPARTMENTAL ACTION MAILED PARTIES HEREIN. APR 22 1907

TRIBAL ENROLLMENT OF PARENTS

	Name of Father	Year	County	Name of Mother	Year	County
1	George Risener	Dead	Non Citz	Rebecca Risener	Dead	Non Citz
2	Wm Smallwood		Kiamitia	Levina Smallwood	"	Jackson
3						
4						
5						
6						
7	No1 was denied by Dawes Commission Case No 643					
8	No1 on list – see case on file in office of Dawes Com at Muskogee I.T.					
9	No1 on 1896 roll as Jackson Risener					
10	No2 " 1896 " " Tryphina "					
11	No1 See Dawes Commission Record 1896 – Case 643 Jack Risener					
12	denied and no record of an appeal					
13	Evidence of marriage between Nos 1 and 2 filed Jany 5-1903					
14						
15						
16						
17						

No1 - REFUSED JUL 28 1906

RECORD FORWARDED DEPARTMENT.

Date of Application for Enrollment. Aug 22-99

80

Choctaw By Blood Enrollment Cards 1898-1914

RESIDENCE: Jackson COUNTY.
POST OFFICE: Bennington, I.T. **Choctaw**

FIELD NO. 5081

Dawes' Roll No.	NAME	Relationship to Person First Named	AGE	SEX	BLOOD	TRIBAL ENROLLMENT		
						Year	County	No.
DEAD.	1 Risener John	Named	31	M	I.W.	1896	Blue	14985
10411	2 Pace Harriet 26	Wife	23	F	1/2	1896	"	10911
10412	3 Risener Adelaide 11	Dau	8	"	1/4	1896	"	10912
10413	4 " Benjamin 9	Son	6	M	1/4	1896	"	10913
10414	5 " Rufus 6	"	3	"	1/4			
10415	6 " Vivian 4	Dau	9mo	F	1/4			
DEAD	7 Pace Tennessee READ. 2	Dau	3mo	F	1/4			
	8							
	9 No7 Died Feby 17,1902: Proof of death filed Dec 30 1902							
	10							
	11 No. 1 and 7 HEREON DISMISSED UNDER							
	12 ORDER OF THE COMMISSION TO THE FIVE							
	13 CIVILIZED TRIBES OF MARCH 31, 1905.							
	14 Proof of death of No1 filed June 26, 1901							
	15 ENROLLMENT							
	16 OF NOS. HEREON APPROVED BY THE SECRETARY							
	17 OF INTERIOR							

Name of Fathe

1 Jack Risener		Intermarriage	Eliz. Risener	Dead	[Illegible]
2 Benj. Battiest	Dead	Jackson	Kizzie Battiest		Jackson
3 No1			No2		
4 No1			No2		
5 No1			No2		
6 No1			No2		
7 Robert L. Pace		noncitizen	No2		
8					
9					
10					

11 No1 was admitted by Dawes Commission
12 Case No 647.
No1 as to marriage of parents, see #1 to 6 inc
13 testimony of Jack Risener Date of Application for Enrollment.
14 Nos 5-6 Affidavits of birth to be
15 supplied:- Recd Oct 7/99 Aug 22/99
16 No.1 is dead. Evidence of death requested May 9 1901 See letter of R.L. Pace filed 5/9/01
No2 is now the wife of Robert L Pace, a noncitizen Marriage license and
17 certificate filed herein May 9. 1901
No.7 Enrolled May 9, 1901

Choctaw By Blood Enrollment Cards 1898-1914

RESIDENCE: Jackson   COUNTY. **Choctaw Nation**   Choctaw Roll   CARD No.
POST OFFICE: Jackson,   *(Not Including Freedmen)*   FIELD No. 3682

Dawes' Roll No.		NAME		Relationship to Person First Named	AGE	SEX	BLOOD	TRIBAL ENROLLMENT		
								Year	County	No.
10416	1	Sharkey, Impson	42	Named	39	M	Full	1896	Jackson	11570
10417	2	" Elsie	45	Wife	42	F	"	1896	"	11571
10418	3	" Emma	15	Dau	12	"	"	1896	"	11575
10419	4	Washington, Albert	19	Ward	16	M	"	1896	"	11572
10420	5	" Edward	18	"	15	"	"	1896	"	11573
10421	6	" Asie	12	"	9	"	"	1896	"	11574
	7									
	8									
	9	ENROLLMENT								
	10	OF NOS. 1,2,3,4,5 and 6 HEREON APPROVED BY THE SECRETARY								
	11	OF INTERIOR FEB 4 1903								
	12									
	13									
	14									
	15	For children of No1 see NB (Apr 26-06) Card #379								
	16									
	17									

	TRIBAL ENROLLMENT OF PARENTS					
	Name of Father		County	Name of Mother	Year	County
1	Sharkey		Jackson	Lottie Sharkey	Dead	Jackson
2	Payson		Jacks Fork	Siney	"	Jacks Fork
3	No1			Kizzie Sharkey	"	Jackson
4	George Washington		Jackson	Siss Washington	"	"
5	" "		"	" "	"	"
6	" "		"	" "	"	"
7						
8						
9						
10						
11	Surnames of Nos 4-5-6 appear on 1896 roll as Sharkey					
12						
13						
14	No4 lives with Silas Bacon at Hugo, I.T.					Date of Application for Enrollment.
15	Nos 5 and 6 live with Robert Belvin, Choc. #3685					Aug 22/99
16	Died prior to Sept 25,1902; not entitled to land or money (See I.O. letter of July 24 1911 No. 1206-1911					
17						

Choctaw By Blood Enrollment Cards 1898-1914

RESIDENCE: Jackson   COUNTY. **Choctaw Nation**   **Choctaw Roll**   CARD No.
POST OFFICE: Jackson, I.T.   *(Not Including Freedmen)*   FIELD No. 3683

NAME	Relationship to Person Named	AGE	SEX	BLOOD	TRIBAL ENROLLMENT Year	County	No.
1 Frazier, Sallie A 28	First Named	25	F	Full	1893	Jackson	643
2 " Frances 6	Dau	3	"	"	1896	"	4303
3 Belvin Silwe 2	Dau	27mo	F	"			
4							
5							
6							
7	ENROLLMENT						
8	OF NOS. 1 and 2 HEREON APPROVED BY THE SECRETARY						
9	OF INTERIOR FEB 4 1903						
10							
11	ENROLLMENT						
12	OF NOS. 3 HEREON APPROVED BY THE SECRETARY						
13	OF INTERIOR MAY 21 1903						
14							
15							
16							
17							

TRIBAL ENROLLMENT OF PARENTS

Name of Father	Year	County	Name of Mother	Year	County
1 Osborne Frazier		Jackson	Elsie Impson		Jackson
2 Bob Belvin	1896	"	No1		
3 Robert Belvin	1896	"	Nº1		
4					
5					
6					
7	No1 on 1893 Pay Roll, Page 74, No 643,				
8	Jackson Co., a Sallian Wilson				
9					
10	Nº3 Born Sept 1, 1900, application made Dec 23, 1902, Proof of birth filed Feb. 12, 1903				
11	For child of No.1 see N.B. (Apr 26, 1906) Card No. 34				
12					
13					
14				#1&2	
15			Date of Application for Enrollment.	Aug 22/99	
16					
17					

Choctaw By Blood Enrollment Cards 1898-1914

RESIDENCE: **Blue** COUNTY. **Choctaw Nation** **Choctaw Roll** (Not Including Freedmen) Card No.
POST OFFICE: **Bok Chito, I.T.** Field No. 3684

Dawes' Roll No.	NAME	Relationship to Person First Named	AGE	SEX	BLOOD	TRIBAL ENROLLMENT		
						Year	County	No.
10424	1 Beams, Calvin S ²¹	First Named	18	M	Full	1896	Blue	1600
	2							
	3							
	4							
	5	ENROLLMENT						
	6	OF NOS. 1 HEREON APPROVED BY THE SECRETARY						
	7	OF INTERIOR FEB 4 1903						
	8							
	9							
	10							
	11							
	12							
	13							
	14							
	15							
	16							
	17							

TRIBAL ENROLLMENT OF PARENTS

	Name of Father	Year	County	Name of Mother	Year	County
1	Calvin Beams	Dead	Blue	Eliza Beams		Blue
2						
3						
4						
5						
6	No. 1 also on 1896 Choctaw roll, page 42, No. 1726					
7	as Limon Beams					
8						
9						
10						
11						
12						
13						
14						
15				Date of Application for Enrollment.	Aug 22/99	
16						
17						

Choctaw By Blood Enrollment Cards 1898-1914

RESIDENCE: Jackson
POST OFFICE: Jackson, I.T.

COUNTY. **Choctaw Nation**

Choctaw Roll *(Not Including Freedmen)*

CARD NO.
FIELD NO. 3685

Dawes' Roll No.	NAME	Relationship to Person	AGE	SEX	BLOOD	TRIBAL ENROLLMENT		
						Year	County	No.
10425	1 Belvin, Robert ²⁸	First Named	25	M	Full	1896	Jackson	1484
DEAD	2 " Mollie ²⁵	Wife	22	F	"	1896	"	1480
	3							
	4							
	5							
	6							

ENROLLMENT OF NOS. 1 HEREON APPROVED BY THE SECRETARY OF INTERIOR FEB 4 1903

No. 2 HEREON DISMISSED UNDER ORDER OF THE COMMISSION TO THE FIVE CIVILIZED TRIBES OF MARCH 31, 1905.

TRIBAL ENROLLMENT OF PARENTS

	Name of Father	Year	County	Name of Mother	Year	County
1	James Belvin	Dead	Jackson	Eliza Belvin		Jackson
2	Chas Farlis	"	"	Tennessee Farlis	Dead	"

No2 on 1896 roll a Mary Belvin

No2 died April 15, 1901; proof of death Dec 6, 1902
For child of No.1 see NB (Apr. 26, 1906) Card No.34

Date of Application for Enrollment. Aug 22/99

85

Choctaw By Blood Enrollment Cards 1898-1914

RESIDENCE: Jackson COUNTY. **Choctaw Nation** **Choctaw Roll** (Not Including Freedmen) CARD NO.
POST OFFICE: Jackson, I.T. FIELD NO. 3686

Dawes' Roll No.	NAME		Relationship to Person	AGE	SEX	BLOOD	TRIBAL ENROLLMENT		
							Year	County	No.
10426	1 Frazier, David	40	First Named	37	M	Full	1896	Jackson	4277
10427	2 " Josephine	34	Wife	31	F	"	1896	"	4278
10428	3 " Elizabeth	12	Dau	9	"	"	1896	"	4280
10429	4 " Robert	4	Son	10mo	M	"			
	5								
	6								
	7								
	8								
	9								
	10								
	11								
	12								
	13								
	14								
	15								
	16								
	17								

ENROLLMENT
OF NOS. 1,2,3 and 4 HEREON
APPROVED BY THE SECRETARY
OF INTERIOR FEB 4 1903

TRIBAL ENROLLMENT OF PARENTS

	Name of Father	Year	County	Name of Mother	Year	County
1	Eden Frazier	Dead	Jackson	Betsy Frazier	Dead	Jackson
2	George James	"	Kiamitia	Manda James	"	Kiamitia
3	No1			No2		
4	No1			No2		
5						
6						
7	No1 on 1896 roll as Davis Frazier					
8	No4 Affidavit of birth to be					
9	supplied:- Filed Nov 2/99					
10						
11						
12						
13						
14						
15				Date of Application for Enrollment.	Aug 22/99	
16						
17						

RESIDENCE: Jackson   COUNTY. **Choctaw Nation**   **Choctaw Roll**   CARD No.
POST OFFICE: Bennington, I.T.   *(Not Including Freedmen)*   FIELD No. **3687**

Dawes' Roll No.	NAME		Relationship to Person	AGE	SEX	BLOOD	TRIBAL ENROLLMENT		
							Year	County	No.
10430	1 Jones, Henry	27	First Named	24	M	Full	1896	Jackson	7120
10431	2 " Susan	26	Wife	23	F	"	1896	"	7121
10432	3 " Reason	7	Son	4	M	"	1896	"	7122
10433	4 " Robert Henderson	2	Son	8mo	M	"			
	5								
	6								
	7	ENROLLMENT							
	8	OF NOS. 1,2,3 and 4 HEREON APPROVED BY THE SECRETARY							
	9	OF INTERIOR Feb 4 1903							
	10								
	11								
	12								
	13								
	14								
	15								
	16								
	17								

TRIBAL ENROLLMENT OF PARENTS

	Name of Father	Year	County	Name of Mother	Year	County
1	Wallace Jones		Jackson	Liza Jones		Jackson
2	Morris Mosley	Dead	Blue	Mary Mosley	Dead	Blue
3	No1			No2		
4	No1			No2		
5						
6						
7						
8			No4 Enrolled Oct 1 1901			
9						
10						
11						
12						
13					#1 to 3	
14					Date of Application for Enrollment	
15					Aug 22/99	
16						
17						

Choctaw By Blood Enrollment Cards 1898-1914

RESIDENCE:	Blue		COUNTY.						
POST OFFICE:	Bennington, I.T.								

Choctaw Nation

Choctaw Roll *(Not Including Freedmen)*

CARD N█
FIELD N█

Dawes' Roll No.	NAME	Relationship to Person First Named	AGE	SEX	BLOOD	TRIBAL ENROLLMENT		
						Year	County	No.
I.W. 1534	1 McClard, William C 24		21	M	I W			
DEAD	2 " Louisa DEAD	Wife	18	F	3/4	1896	Blue	9420
10434	3 " Myrtle 3	Dau	2yr	F	3/8			
	4							
	5							
	6	ENROLLMENT						
	7	OF NOS. 3 HEREON						
		APPROVED BY THE SECRETARY						
	8	OF INTERIOR FEB 4 1903						
	9							
	10	NO. 2 HEREON DISMISSED UNDER						
	11	ORDER OF THE COMMISSION TO THE FIVE						
	12	CIVILIZED TRIBES OF MARCH 31, 1905.						
	13	ENROLLMENT						
	14	OF NOS. ~~~~1~~~~ HEREON						
		APPROVED BY THE SECRETARY						
	15	OF INTERIOR MAR 14 1906						
	16							
	17							

TRIBAL ENROLLMENT OF PARENTS

	Name of Father	Year	County	Name of Mother	Year	County
1	Caleb McClard		Non Citz	Tabitha McClard	Dead	Non Citz
2	Edmond McCurtain	Dead	Sans Bois	Lucy Risener		Blue
3	No1			No2		
4						
5						
6				GRANTED		NOV 11 1905
7	No2 on 1896 roll as Louisa McCurtain					
8	No.2 Died June 15, 1900 Evidence					
9	of death filed October 10, 1901.					
10						
11	No3 Enrolled Sept 28, 1901.					
12						
13						
14				#1&2		
15				Date of Application for Enrollment.		Aug 22/99
16						
17	Hot Springs, Ark 5/21/05					

Choctaw By Blood Enrollment Cards 1898-1914

RESIDENCE:	Blue	COUNTY.								
POST OFFICE:	Bennington, I.T.									

Choctaw Nation

Choctaw Roll *(Not Including Freedmen)*

CARD NO.
FIELD NO. 3689

Dawes' Roll No.	NAME	Relationship to Person First Named	AGE	SEX	BLOOD	Year	County	No.
10435	₁ Smith, Morris S ²⁸	First Named	25	M	1/4	1896	Jackson	11552
10436	₂ " Caroline ²⁵	Wife	22	F	1/4	1896	"	11553
10437	₃ " Ruth ⁵	Dau	2	"	1/4			
10438	₄ " George G. ³	Son	4mo	M	1/4			
10439	₅ " Geo. Homer Colbert ¹	Son	8mo	M	1/4			
	6							
	7							
	8	ENROLLMENT						
	9	OF NOS. 1,2,3,4 and 5 HEREON APPROVED BY THE SECRETARY						
	10	OF INTERIOR FEB 4 1903						
	11							
	12							
	13							
	14							
	15							
	16							
	17							

TRIBAL ENROLLMENT OF PARENTS

	Name of Father	Year	County	Name of Mother	Year	County
₁	George Smith	Dead	Non Citz	Tryfenia Risener		Jackson
₂	George Risener		" "	Sealey Risener		"
₃	No1			No2		
₄	No1			No2		
₅	"			"		
6						
7						
8		No1 on 1896 roll as M. S. Smith				
9		No2 " 1896 " " Carrie "				
10		Nos 3-4 Affidavits of birth to be supplied:- Reed.				
11						
12		No5 born March 28, 1902; enrolled Nov 28, 1902				
13						
14					Date of Application for Enrollment.	
15					Aug 22/99	
16						
17						

89

Choctaw By Blood Enrollment Cards 1898-1914

RESIDENCE:	Jackson	COUNTY.			

RESIDENCE: Jackson COUNTY. **Choctaw Nation** Choctaw Roll CARD NO.
POST OFFICE: Bennington, I.T. (Not Including Freedmen) FIELD NO. 3690

Dawes' Roll No.	NAME	Relationship to Person	AGE	SEX	BLOOD	TRIBAL ENROLLMENT		
						Year	County	No.
10440	1 Rishor, Cealy	First Named	50	F	Full	1896	Jackson	10888
	2							
	3							
	4							
	5							
	6							
	7							
	8							
	9							
	10							
	11							
	12							
	13							
	14							
	15							
	16							
	17							

DIED PRIOR TO SEPTEMBER 25 1902

ENROLLMENT
OF NOS. 1 HEREON
APPROVED BY THE SECRETARY
OF INTERIOR FEB 4 1903

TRIBAL ENROLLMENT OF PARENTS

	Name of Father	Year	County	Name of Mother	Year	County
1	Ta-nap-ya-ho-ma	Dead	Blue	E-mi-na	Dead	Blue
2						
3						
4						
5						
6						
7	No1 died Feb. 14, 1902: Enrollment cancelled by Department Sept. 16, 1904					
8						
9						
10						
11						
12						
13						
14						Date of Application for Enrollment.
15						Aug 22/99
16						
17						

RESIDENCE:	Blue	COUNTY.							
POST OFFICE:	Ego, I.T.								

Choctaw Nation

Choctaw Roll *(Not Including Freedmen)*

CARD No. FIELD No. **3691**

Dawes' Roll No.	NAME	Relationship to Person	AGE	SEX	BLOOD	TRIBAL ENROLLMENT		
						Year	County	No.
10441 ₁	Moran, Daniel S ⁴²	First Named	39	M	1/16	1896	Blue	8761
I.W.343 ₂	" Willie Agnes ²⁹	Wife	25	F	I.W	1896	"	14831
10442 ₃	" Marmaduke L¹⁰	Son	7	M	1/32	1896	"	8762
10443 ₄	" Imet B ⁴	"	8mo	"	1/32			
DEAD ₅	" ~~Curtis~~ DEAD	"	2mo	"	1/32			
10444 ₆	" Ora S ¹	Son	3mo	M	1/32			
₇								
₈	No. 5 HEREON DISMISSED UNDER ORDER OF THE COMMISSION TO THE FIVE CIVILIZED TRIBES OF MARCH 31, 1905.							
₉								
₁₀								
₁₁	No5 died Aug, 1901; proof of death filed Nov 26 1902							
₁₂	ENROLLMENT							
₁₃	OF NOS. 1,3,4,and 6 HEREON APPROVED BY THE SECRETARY							
₁₄	OF INTERIOR FEB 4 1903							
₁₅	ENROLLMENT							
₁₆	OF NOS. 2 HEREON APPROVED BY THE SECRETARY							
₁₇	OF INTERIOR SEP 12 1903							

TRIBAL ENROLLMENT OF PARENTS

	Name of Father	Year	County	Name of Mother	Year	County
₁	C. H. Moran	Dead	Non Citz	Eliz. Moran		Blue
₂	Frank Melton	"	"	Candis Melton		Non Citz
₃	No1			No2		
₄	No1			No2		
₅	No1			No 2		
₆	Nº1			Nº2		
₇						
₈						
₉	No1 admitted by Act of Choctaw Council of Nov. 3 1879					
₁₀	No2 on 1896 toll as Willis M. Moran					
₁₁						
₁₂	No4 Affidavit of birth to be					
₁₃	supplied:- Recd Oct 7/99					#1 to 4
₁₄	No.2 admitted as an intermarried citizen by Dawes Commission in 1896, Choctaw Case #481. No appeal.					Date of Application for Enrollment.
₁₅				No5 Enrolled 6/4/1900		Aug 22/99
₁₆	Nº6 Born Oct 12, 1901; enrolled Jan. 11, 1902.					
₁₇						

Choctaw By Blood Enrollment Cards 1898-1914

RESIDENCE: Blue   COUNTY.   **Choctaw Nation**   **Choctaw Roll**   CARD No.
POST OFFICE: Ego, I.T.   *(Not Including Freedmen)*   FIELD No. 3692

Dawes' Roll No.	NAME	Relationship to Person First Named	AGE	SEX	BLOOD	TRIBAL ENROLLMENT		
						Year	County	No.
10445	1 Moran, Elizabeth 82	First Named	79	F	1/8	1896	Blue	8759
10446	2 " Charles H 51	Son	48	M	1/16	1896	"	8760
	3							
	4							
	5	ENROLLMENT						
	6	OF NOS. 1 and 2 HEREON APPROVED BY THE SECRETARY						
	7	OF INTERIOR FEB 4 1903						
	8							
	9							
	10							
	11							
	12							
	13							
	14							
	15							
	16							
	17							

TRIBAL ENROLLMENT OF PARENTS

	Name of Father	Year	County	Name of Mother	Year	County
1	Buckholtz	Dead	Non Citz	Betsey Buckholtz	Dead	in Alabama
2	C H Moran	"	" "	No 1		
3						
4						
5						
6						
7	Nos 1 and 2 admitted by act of Choctaw Council of Nov 3, 1879					
8						
9						
10						
11						
12						
13						
14					Date of Application for Enrollment.	
15					Aug 22/99	
16						
17						

Choctaw By Blood Enrollment Cards 1898-1914

RESIDENCE: Blue   COUNTY. **Choctaw Nation**   **Choctaw Roll**   CARD NO.
POST OFFICE: Ego, I.T.   (Not Including Freedmen)   FIELD NO. 3693

Dawes' Roll No.	NAME	Relationship to Person First Named	AGE	SEX	BLOOD	TRIBAL ENROLLMENT Year	County	No.
10447	1 Moran, John B 49	First Named	46	M	1/16	1896	Blue	8756
I.W. 1416	2 " Mary 40	Wife	37	F	I.W.	1896	"	14835
10448	3 Overstreet, Addie 16	Dau	13	"	1/32	1896	"	8757
10449	4 Moran Charles 11	Son	8	M	1/32	1896	"	8758
10450	5 " Robert R 6	"	3	"	1/32			
10451	6 Overstreet, Nora May 1	Dau of No 3	4mo	F	1/64			
	7 Enrollment of No.2 cancelled by order of Department March 4 1907							
	8 No1 was admitted by act of Choctaw Council of Nov. 3, 1879							
	9 ENROLLMENT							
	10 OF NOS. 1,3,4,5 and 6 HEREON APPROVED BY THE SECRETARY							
	11 OF INTERIOR FEB 4 1903							
	12 No3 is now married to N.W. Overstreet					ENROLLMENT OF NOS. 2 HEREON		
	13 a noncitizen: evidence of marriage					APPROVED BY THE SECRETARY		
	14 filed Dec 5, 1902 Her correct name					OF INTERIOR JUN 12 1905		
	15 is Addie A Overstreet: see copy of							
	16 letter from No.1 filed herein dated							
	Dec. 3, 1902							
	17 For child of No3 see NB (Mar 3"05) #1182							

TRIBAL ENROLLMENT OF PARENTS

	Name of Father	Year	County	Name of Mother	Year	County
1	C H Moran	Dead	Non Citz	Elizabeth Moran		Blue
2	Nathaniel Ross	" "		Susanna Ross	Dead	Non Citz
3	No1			No2		
4	No1			No2		
5	No1			No2		
6	N.W. Overstreet (?)			No 3		
7						
8						
9	No1 on 1896 roll as John Moran					
10	No5 Affidavit of birth to be					
11	supplied:- Recd Oct 7/99					
12	See if she was denied by Dawes Commission in 1896: Case No 750					
13	Dec. 6/99 See if she was denied					
14	by Dawes Commission in 1896, Case No 750			No2 restored to roll by Departmental		
15	For child of No.3 see NB (Apr 26-06) No 806			authority of January 19, 1909 (File 5-51)		
16	No2 was denied by Dawes Commission in 1896					
17	in Choctaw case #350: No appeal.			Date of Application for Enrollment.	Aug 22/99	
	No6 born July 3, 1902: enrolled Nov 26, 1902					
	No3 PO Kemp IT 6/5 03					

93

Choctaw By Blood Enrollment Cards 1898-1914

RESIDENCE: Jackson   COUNTY, **Choctaw Nation**   Choctaw Roll   CARD NO.
FICE: Jackson, I.T.   *(Not Including Freedmen)*   FIELD NO. 3694

NAME	Relationship to Person	AGE	SEX	BLOOD	TRIBAL ENROLLMENT		
					Year	County	No.
1 Follis, Silway ²⁴	First Named	21	F	Full	1896	Jackson	4274
2 " Sila ²¹	Sister	18	"	"	1896	"	4275
3 " Stephen ¹⁴	Bro	11	M	"	1896	"	4276
4 Belvin Wilson ²	Son of Nº2	2 1/3	"	"			
5 " Lizzy ¹	Dau of Nº2	9mo	F	"			
6	ENROLLMENT						
7	OF NOS. 1,2 and 3 HEREON APPROVED BY THE SECRETARY						
8	OF INTERIOR FEB 4 1903						
9							
10	ENROLLMENT						
11	OF NOS. 5 HEREON APPROVED BY THE SECRETARY						
12	OF INTERIOR MAY 20 1903						
13							
14	ENROLLMENT						
15	OF NOS. ～～4～～ HEREON APPROVED BY THE SECRETARY						
16	OF INTERIOR FEB 16 1904						
17							

TRIBAL ENROLLMENT OF PARENTS

Name of Father	Year	County	Name of Mother	Year	County
1 Charles Follis	Dead	Jackson	Tennessee Follis	Dead	Jackson
2 " "	"	"	" "	"	"
3 " "	"	"	" "	"	"
4 Solomon Belvin	1896	"	Nº2		
5 " "	1896	"	Nº2		
6					
7					
8	No1 on 1896 roll as Silway Follies				
9	No2 " 1896 " " Sallie "				
10	No3 " 1896 " " Stephen "				
11					
12	Nº4 Born Sept 18, 1900: enrolled Dec. 24, 1902.				
13	Nº5 Born March 4, 1902: enrolled Dec. 24, 1902.			#1 to 3 inc	
14				Date of Application for Enrollment.	
15				Aug 22/99	
16					
17					

94

Choctaw By Blood Enrollment Cards 1898-1914

| RESIDENCE: | Jackson | COUNTY. | **Choctaw Nation** | Choctaw Roll | CARD No. |
| POST OFFICE: | Mayhew, I.T. | | | (Not Including Freedmen) | FIELD No. 3695 |

Dawes' Roll No.	NAME	Relationship to Person	AGE	SEX	BLOOD	TRIBAL ENROLLMENT		
						Year	County	No.
10455	1 James, Laura A 27	First Named	24	F	1/2	1896	Jackson	7145
10456	2 " Juanita 7	Dau	4	"	1/4	1896	"	
DEAD.	3 " Addie DEAD 4	"	7mo	"	1/4			
10457	4 " Columbus 1	Son	4mo	M	1/4			
	5							
	6							
	7	ENROLLMENT						
	8	OF NOS. 1, 2 and 4 HEREON						
		APPROVED BY THE SECRETARY						
	9	OF INTERIOR FEB 4 1903						
	10	No. 3 HEREON DISMISSED UNDER						
	11	ORDER OF THE COMMISSION TO THE FIVE						
	12	CIVILIZED TRIBES OF MARCH 31, 1905.						
	13							
	14							
	15							
	16							
	17							

TRIBAL ENROLLMENT OF PARENTS

	Name of Father	Year	County	Name of Mother	Year	County
1	Nelson Harris		Colored man	Jincey Harris		Jackson
2	John James		" "	No1		
3	" "		" "	No1		
4	" "		" "	No1		
5						
6						
7			No1 on 1896 roll as Laura James			
8			No2 " 1896 " " Warnetta "			
9			No3 Affidavit of birth to be			
10			supplied:- Recd Oct 7/99			
			No.4 Enrolled Sept 7, 1901			
11						
12			No3 died Sept 3, 1902; proof of death filed Nov 28 1902			
13			For child of No.1 see NB (March 3 1905) #823			
14					Date of Application for Enrollment.	
15					Aug 22/99	
16						
17						

Choctaw By Blood Enrollment Cards 1898-1914

RESIDENCE: Jackson COUNTY. **Choctaw Nation** Choctaw Roll CARD No.
POST OFFICE: Jackson, I.T. (Not Including Freedmen) FIELD No. 3696

Dawes' Roll No.	NAME		Relationship to Person	AGE	SEX	BLOOD	TRIBAL ENROLLMENT		
							Year	County	No.
19458	1 Scott, John	38	First Named	35	M	Full	1896	Jackson	11560
10459	2 " Sibby	43	Wife	40	F	"	1896	"	11561
	3								
	4								
	5	ENROLLMENT							
	6	OF NOS. 1 and 2 HEREON APPROVED BY THE SECRETARY							
	7	OF INTERIOR FEB 4 1903							
	8								
	9								
	10								
	11								
	12								
	13								
	14								
	15								
	16								
	17								

TRIBAL ENROLLMENT OF PARENTS

	Name of Father	Year	County	Name of Mother	Year	County
1	Abner Scott	Dead	Jackson	Sealy Scott		Jackson
2	Silas Cota	"	"	Nancy Cota	Dead	"
3						
4						
5						
6						
7						
8						
9						
10						
11						
12						
13						
14						
15				Date of Application for Enrollment.		Aug 22/99
16						
17						

Choctaw By Blood Enrollment Cards 1898-1914

RESIDENCE: Jackson COUNTY. **Choctaw Nation** **Choctaw Roll** CARD No.
POST OFFICE: Jackson, I.T. *(Not Including Freedmen)* FIELD No. 3697

Dawes' Roll No.	NAME		Relationship to Person	AGE	SEX	BLOOD	TRIBAL ENROLLMENT		
							Year	County	No.
10460	1 Follis, Jincy	23	First Named	20	F	Full	1896	Jackson	4263
10461	2 " Lymsia[sic]	5	Dau	2	"	"			
10462	3 " Jacob	3	Son	3mo	M	"			
10463	4 Battiest, Eunice		Dau	1	F	"			
	5								
	6								
	7	ENROLLMENT OF NOS. 1, 2 and 3 HEREON APPROVED BY THE SECRETARY OF INTERIOR FEB 4 1903							
	8								
	9								
	10	ENROLLMENT OF NOS. 4 HEREON APPROVED BY THE SECRETARY OF INTERIOR NOV 24 1905							
	11								
	12								
	13								
	14								
	15								
	16								
	17								

TRIBAL ENROLLMENT OF PARENTS

	Name of Father	Year	County	Name of Mother	Year	County
1	George Allen	Dead	Jackson	Sibbey Scott		Jackson
2	Aaron Follis	"	"	No1		
3	" "	"	"	No1		
4	Ratio Battiest		Choctaw	No1		
5						
6						
7	Notify L. D Horton Boswell IT of approval of No4					
8	" V Brough Boswell IT of approval of No 4 10/25/05					
9						
10	No1 on 1896 roll as Jincy Follies					
11	Nos 2-3 Affidavits of birth to be					
12	supplied:- Filed Nov 2/99					
13	N°4 Proof of birth to be supplied 12/5/02 Originally listed hereon as Unice Battiest					#1 to 3 inc
14	No 4 was born Oct. 23, 1902:					Date of Application for Enrollment.
15						Aug 22/99
16						
17	P.O. Mayhew I.T.					

Choctaw By Blood Enrollment Cards 1898-1914

RESIDENCE: Blue
POST OFFICE: Caddo, I.T.

COUNTY.

Choctaw Nation

Choctaw Roll *(Not Including Freedmen)*

CARD NO.
FIELD NO. **3698**

Dawes' Roll No.	NAME	Relationship to Person	AGE	SEX	BLOOD	TRIBAL ENROLLMENT		
						Year	County	No.
10463	1 Boydstun John F 21	First Named	18	M	1/4	1896	Blue	1615
10464	2 " Alfred E 19	Bro	16	"	1/4	1896	"	1616
See 5351	3 " Lucetta	Sister	16	F	1/4	1896	"	1617
10465	4 " Ellis M 16	Bro	13	M	1/4	1896	"	1618
10466	5 " Robert 14	"	11	"	1/4	1896	"	1619
10467	6 " Ada 12	Dau	9	F	1/4	1896	"	1620
10468	7 " Ethel 10	"	7	"	1/4	1896	"	1621
10469	8 Gardner Raymon R 6	Cousin	3	M	1/4	1896	"	4929
I.W. 1125	9 Boydstun, George A 48	Father	48	M	IW	1896	"	14334
15841	10 " John Francis	Son	1	M	1/8			
	11	No 1 on 1896 roll as Jno B. Boydston						
	12	No 2 " 1896 " " Alfred E						
	13	No 3 " 1896 " " Lucy E						
	14	No 4 " 1896 " " Ellis						
	15	No 5 " 1896 " " Robert						
	16	No 6 " 1896 " " Ada						
		No 7 " 1896 " " Ethel						
	17	No 8 " 1896 " " Raymon Gardner						

(left margin: Wife of No on Choctaw card #6060)

TRIBAL ENROLLMENT OF PARENTS

	Name of Father	Year	County	Name of Mother	Year	County
1	Geo. A Boydstun		Intermarried	Mary Boydstun	Dead	Blue
2	" " "		"	" "	"	"
3	" " "		"	" "	"	"
4	" " "		ENROLLMENT	"	ENROLLMENT"
5	" " "		OF NOS. ~~ 10 ~~ HEREON APPROVED BY THE SECRETARY OF INTERIOR Jun 12 1905	"	OF NOS. ~~ 9 ~~ HEREON APPROVED BY THE SECRETARY OF INTERIOR Nov 16 1904
6	" " "			"	
7	" " "		"	" "	"	"
8	Daniel Gardner		Blue	Mary J Gardner now Boydstun		Intermarried
9	John Boydstun		non-citizen	Annie J Boydstun	dead	non citizen
10	No. 1			Hattie Boydstun	ENROLLMENT OF NOS. 1,2,4,5,6,7 and 8 HEREON APPROVED BY THE SECRETARY OF INTERIOR Feb 4 1903
11					
12	Father of first seven is on Card No D 345				#1 to 8 inc
13	Mother of No 8 " " " " 345 as to her marriage to Daniel Gardner see evidence				Date of Application for Enrollment.
14	attached to card No D345				Aug 22/99
15	No 9 transferred from Choctaw card #D-345 Oct 31,1904: See decision of Oct 15,1904				
16	No 3 transferred to Choctaw card #5351 with her husband Dec 6th, 1900				
17	No. 9 on 1896 Choc census roll as Geo. A. Boydston				

No 10 Born Dec 4 1901: Application received April 18,1905   For child of No 9 see NB(Apr 26-06) #1089

98

Choctaw By Blood Enrollment Cards 1898-1914

RESIDENCE: Blue   COUNTY. **Choctaw Nation**   **Choctaw Roll** CARD NO.
POST OFFICE: Caddo, I.T.   *(Not Including Freedmen)*   FIELD NO. **3699**

Dawes' Roll No.	NAME		Relationship to Person	AGE	SEX	BLOOD	TRIBAL ENROLLMENT		
							Year	County	No.
10470	1 Folsom, Finis E	50	First Named	47	M	1/4	1896	Blue	4333
10471	2 " Mollie	41	Wife	38	F	1/4	1896	"	4334
10472	3 " Ewing	21	Son	18	M	1/4	1896	"	4336
10473	4 " Columbus	19	"	16	"	1/4	1896	"	4337
10474	5 " Carril	16	"	13	"	1/4	1896	"	4338
10475	6 " Irmer	8	Dau	5	F	1/4	1896	"	4339
10476	7 " Jewell L	4	"	9mo	F	1/4			
10477	8 " Push-ma-ta-ha	2	Son	2mo	M	1/4			
	9								
	10								
	11	ENROLLMENT							
	12	OF NOS. 1,2,3,4,5,6,7 and 8 HEREON APPROVED BY THE SECRETARY							
	13	OF INTERIOR Feb 4 1903							
	14								
	15								
	16								
	17								

TRIBAL ENROLLMENT OF PARENTS

	Name of Father	Year	County	Name of Mother	Year	County
1	Israel Folsom	Dead	Blue	Louvicey Folsom	Dead	Blue
2	Push Pitchlynn	"	Eagle	Mary Williams		Non Citz
3	No 1			No 2		
4	No 1			No 2		
5	No 1			No 2		
6	No 1			No 2		
7	No 1			No 2		
8	No 1			No 2		
9						
10			No 1 on 1896 roll as F. E. Folsom			
11			No 5 " 1896 " " Carrol "			
12			No 2 As to marriage of parents see enrollment of Minnie Semple			
13			No 8 Enrolled Oct 1st 1900	#1 to 7		
14				Date of Application for Enrollment.		
15				Aug 22/99		
16						
17						

Choctaw By Blood Enrollment Cards 1898-1914

RESIDENCE: **Blue**
POST OFFICE: **Caddo, I.T.**

COUNTY. **Choctaw Nation**

Choctaw Roll *(Not Including Freedmen)*

CARD No.
FIELD No. **3700**

Dawes' Roll No.	NAME		Relationship to Person	AGE	SEX	BLOOD	TRIBAL ENROLLMENT		
							Year	County	No.
10478	1 Brewer Minnie	23	First Named	20	F	1/4	1896	Blue	4335
I.W. 195	2 " Lake		husband	28	M	I.W.			
	3								
	4								
	5	ENROLLMENT OF NOS. 1 HEREON APPROVED BY THE SECRETARY OF INTERIOR Feb 4 1903							
	6								
	7								
	8								
	9								
	10								
	11	ENROLLMENT OF NOS. ~ 2 ~ HEREON APPROVED BY THE SECRETARY OF INTERIOR Jun 13 1903							
	12								
	13								
	14								
	15								
	16								
	17								

TRIBAL ENROLLMENT OF PARENTS

	Name of Father	Year	County	Name of Mother	Year	County
1	Finis E. Folsom		Blue	Mollie Folsom		Blue
2	Ben Brewer		non-citz	Tennie Brewer		non-citz
3						
4						
5						
6			On roll 1896 Minnie Folsom			
7						
8			Nº2 transferred from Choctaw card #D.351. See decision of May 5, 1903			
9						
10						
11						
12						
13						
14						Date of Application for Enrollment.
15						Aug 22/99
16						
17						

100

Choctaw By Blood Enrollment Cards 1898-1914

RESIDENCE:	Blue	COUNTY.	**Choctaw Nation**		**Choctaw Roll**		CARD No.	
POST OFFICE:	Caney, I.T.				*(Not Including Freedmen)*		FIELD No. **3701**	

Dawes' Roll No.	NAME		Relationship to Person First Named	AGE	SEX	BLOOD	TRIBAL ENROLLMENT		
							Year	County	No.
I.W. 344	1 Perkins, Lena E	27	First Named	24	F	I.W.	1896	Blue	14943
10479	2 " Simon H	11	Son	8	M	3/8	1896	"	10485
10480	3 " William H	9	"	6	"	3/8	1896	"	10486
10481	4 " David A	8	"	5	"	3/8	1896	"	10487
10482	5 " Lavina H	6	Dau	2	F	3/8			
10483	6 " Cornelius E	3	Son	5mo	M	3/8			
	7								
	8	ENROLLMENT							
	9	OF NOS. 2,3,4,5 and 6 HEREON APPROVED BY THE SECRETARY							
	10	OF INTERIOR Feb 4 1903							
	11								
	12	ENROLLMENT							
	13	OF NOS. 1 HEREON APPROVED BY THE SECRETARY							
	14	OF INTERIOR Sep 12 1903							
	15								
	16								
	17								

TRIBAL ENROLLMENT OF PARENTS

	Name of Father	Year	County	Name of Mother	Year	County
1	A. G. Brown		Non Citz	Serilda Brown	Dead	Non Citz
2	Henry Perkins	Dead	Blue	No 1		
3	" "	"	"	No 1		
4	" "	"	"	No 1		
5	" "	"	"	No 1		
6	" "	"	"	No 1		
7						
8			No1 on 1896 roll as Lena A. Perkins – was			
9			also admitted by Dawes Com Case No 569, as			
10			Mrs. Henry H Perkins.			
11			No3 on 1896 roll as Wᵐ H Perkins			
12			No4 " 1896 " " Davis A "			
13			Nos 5-6 Affidavits of birth to be			
14			supplied:- Rec'd Oct 7/99			Date of Application for Enrollment.
15						Aug 22/99
16						
17	11/21/02 P.O. Boggy Depot I.T.					

Choctaw By Blood Enrollment Cards 1898-1914

RESIDENCE: Gaines   COUNTY: **Choctaw Nation**   **Choctaw Roll** *(Not Including Freedmen)*   CARD No.

POST OFFICE: Featherston, I.T.   FIELD No. **3702**

Dawes' Roll No.		NAME	Relationship to Person First Named	AGE	SEX	BLOOD	TRIBAL ENROLLMENT		
							Year	County	No.
I.W. 1218	1	McBride, William P ³⁴	First Named	31	M	I.W	1896	Tobucksy	14866
15471	2	" Philip P ?	Son	4	"	1/16	1896	"	9219
	3								
	4								
	5								
	6								
	7								
	8								
	9	ENROLLMENT							
	10	OF NOS. ~ 2 ~~~ HEREON APPROVED BY THE SECRETARY							
	11	OF INTERIOR May 9 1904							
	12								
	13	ENROLLMENT							
	14	OF NOS. ~ 1 ~~~ HEREON APPROVED BY THE SECRETARY							
	15	OF INTERIOR Dec 13 1904							
	16								
	17								

TRIBAL ENROLLMENT OF PARENTS

	Name of Father	Year	County	Name of Mother	Year	County
1	P. T. McBride		Non Citz	Mary E McBride	Dead	Non Citz
2	No 1			Minnie I McBride	"	Tobucksy
3						
4						
5						
6						
7						
8	Nos 1 and 2 were admitted by Dawes Com.					
9	Case No 1291. No appeal					
10	No 1 on 1896 roll as Wᵐ P. McBride No 2 " 1896 " " Pleas P "					
11	See testimony of Nº 1 taken October 16, 1902					
12	No.1 formerly husband of Minnie I. McBride					
13	a recognized Choctaw by blood, who died on June 28, 1896 For child of No 1 see NB (Apr 26 '06) #1124					
14						
15				Date of Application for Enrollment.	Aug 22/99	
16						
17	P.O. Womack, I.T.					

Choctaw By Blood Enrollment Cards 1898-1914

RESIDENCE: Jackson COUNTY. **Choctaw Nation** Choctaw Roll CARD No.
POST OFFICE: Mayhew, I.T. (Not Including Freedmen) FIELD No. 3703

Dawes' Roll No.	NAME	Relationship to Person First Named	AGE	SEX	BLOOD	TRIBAL ENROLLMENT		
						Year	County	No.
10484	1 James, Mary	24	21	F	1/4	1893	Jackson	325
DEAD	2 " Minnie	Dau	1½	"	1/8			
10485	3 " Edward	3 Son	2m	M	1/8			
10486	4 " Jasper	2 Son	6m	M	1/8			
	5							
	6							
	7	ENROLLMENT OF NOS. 1, 3 and 4 HEREON APPROVED BY THE SECRETARY OF INTERIOR FEB 4 1903						
	8							
	9							
	10	NO. 2 HEREON DISMISSED UNDER ORDER OF THE COMMISSION TO THE FIVE CIVILIZED TRIBES OF MARCH 31, 1905.						
	11							
	12							
	13							
	14							
	15							
	16							
	17							

TRIBAL ENROLLMENT OF PARENTS

	Name of Father	Year	County	Name of Mother	Year	County
1	Nelson Harris		Colored man	Jincey Harris		Jackson
2	Tom James		" "	No 1		
3	" "		" "	No 1		
4	" "		" "	No 1		
5						
6						
7						
8			No 1 on 1893 Pay Roll, Page 37, No 325,			
9			Jackson Co., as Mary Harris			
10			No.4 enrolled Sept 5, 1901.			
11			No2 died December, 1900: proof of death filed Nov 26 1902			
12						
13			For two (2) children of No1 see NB (Apr 26-06) Card #695			
14						Date of Application for Enrollment.
15			Date of application for enrollment			Aug 22/99
16						No3 enrolled Nov 2/99
17						

103

Choctaw By Blood Enrollment Cards 1898-1914

| RESIDENCE: Blue | COUNTY. | **Choctaw Nation** | Choctaw Roll | CARD No. |
| POST OFFICE: Caddo, I.T. | | | (Not Including Freedmen) | FIELD No. 3704 |

Dawes' Roll No.	NAME	Relationship to Person First Named	AGE	SEX	BLOOD	TRIBAL ENROLLMENT Year	County	No.
10487	1 Hawkins, Milton 39		36	M	Full	1896	Skullyville	5194
I.W.926	2 " Margaret (14)	Wife	14	F	I.W.			
	3							
	4	ENROLLMENT OF NOS. 1 HEREON APPROVED BY THE SECRETARY OF INTERIOR FEB 4 1903						
	5							
	6							
	7							
	8							
	9	ENROLLMENT OF NOS. 2 HEREON APPROVED BY THE SECRETARY OF INTERIOR AUG 3 1904						.
	10							
	11							
	12							
	13							
	14							
	15							
	16							
	17							

TRIBAL ENROLLMENT OF PARENTS

	Name of Father	Year	County	Name of Mother	Year	County
1	Wᵐ Harkins	Dead	Blue	Elzira Harkins	Dead	Blue
2	John W Pasley	"	non citizen	Nancy Coppedge		non citizen
3						
4						
5						
6	No.2 transferred from Choctaw card #D.708 July 7-04. See decision of June 21 –'04					
7	No.1 is now the husband of Margaret Harkins on Choctaw Card #D708. Mch 10 1902					
8	No1 now spells his surname "Hawkins" ~~See his statement and that of A Telle relative thereto~~					
9	Nᵒ1 was formerly husband of Mary Benton on Choctaw card #3803. See					
10	affidavit of Henry Byington as to divorce between the parties filed with					
11	Choctaw #D805 Sept. 30, 1902 ~~For child of No.1 see NB (Apr 26, 1906) No.546~~					
12						
13						
14					Date of Application for Enrollment.	
15					Aug 22/99	
16						
17						

RESIDENCE: Blue
POST OFFICE: Caddo, I.T.
COUNTY.

Choctaw Nation

Choctaw Roll
(Not Including Freedmen)

CARD No.
FIELD No. 3705

Dawes' Roll No.	NAME	Relationship to Person	AGE	SEX	BLOOD	TRIBAL ENROLLMENT		
						Year	County	No.
10488	₁ Johnson, Bankston ⁴¹	First Named	38	M	Full	1896	Blue	7198
I.W. 1500	₂ " Roselia	Wife	17	F	I.W.			
	₃							
	₄	ENROLLMENT						
	₅	OF NOS. 1 HEREON APPROVED BY THE SECRETARY						
	₆	OF INTERIOR FEB 4 1903						
	₇	ENROLLMENT						
	₈	OF NOS. 2 HEREON APPROVED BY THE SECRETARY						
	₉	OF INTERIOR NOV 27 1905						
	₁₀							
	₁₁							
	₁₂							
	₁₃							
	₁₄							
	₁₅							
	₁₆							
	₁₇							

TRIBAL ENROLLMENT OF PARENTS

	Name of Father	Year	County	Name of Mother	Year	County
₁	Jas Johnson	Dead	in Louisiana	Sophie Johnson	Dead	in Louisiana
₂	Joe Batise	dead	--	Lou Batise		
₃						
₄						
₅						
₆						
₇						
₈	On 1896 roll as Banks Johnson					
₉						
₁₀	Also on 1896 roll, Page 178, No 7231					
₁₁	No.1 is now the husband of Roselia Johnson on Choctaw card #D.738					
₁₂				June 30, 1901		
₁₃	No2 transferred from Choctaw card D738 October 20, 1905				#1	
₁₄	See decision of October 4, 1905				Date of Application for Enrollment.	
₁₅	No2 was also applicant for identification as Mississippi Choctaw Application was refused March 15, 1904 and action approved				Aug 22/99	
₁₆	by Secretary of Interior August 6, 1904					
₁₇						

Choctaw By Blood Enrollment Cards 1898-1914

RESIDENCE: **Blue** COUNTY. **Choctaw Nation** Choctaw Roll CARD No.
POST OFFICE: **Caddo, I.T.** (Not Including Freedmen) FIELD No. **3706**

Dawes' Roll No.	NAME	Relationship to Person First Named	AGE	SEX	BLOOD	TRIBAL ENROLLMENT Year	County	No.
10489	1 Paddock, William A 27	First Named	24	M	1/16	1896	Blue	10473
I.W. 345	2 " Mollie 27	Wife	24	F	I.W.	1896	Blue	14945
10490	3 " Lydia 6	Dau	3	"	1/32	18906	Blue	10474
10491	4 " Florence 5	"	2	"	1/32			
	5							
	6							
	7	ENROLLMENT						
	8	OF NOS. 1,3 and 4 HEREON APPROVED BY THE SECRETARY						
	9	OF INTERIOR FEB 4 1903						
	10	ENROLLMENT						
	11	OF NOS. 2 HEREON APPROVED BY THE SECRETARY						
	12	OF INTERIOR SEP 12 1903						
	13							
	14							
	15							
	16							
	17							

TRIBAL ENROLLMENT OF PARENTS

	Name of Father	Year	County	Name of Mother	Year	County
1	Reuben Paddock		Non Citz	Eliza Paddock	Dead	Blue
	Jno Templeton		" "	Lydia Templeton		Non Citz
3	No1			No2		
4	No1			No2		
5						
6						
7	No1 on 1896 roll as Wm A Paddock					
8	No3 " 1896 " " Lidda "					
9	7/23/02 No1 was admitted by Act of Council approved Nov. 5, 1888 See Choc. D-20					
	No2 On 1896 roll as Mollie Pedock					
10						
11						
12						
13						
14					Date of Application for Enrollment.	
15					Aug 22/99	
16						
17	PO Sugden IT 8/1/0?					

Choctaw By Blood Enrollment Cards 1898-1914

Dawes' Roll No.	NAME		Relationship to Person	AGE	SEX	BLOOD	TRIBAL ENROLLMENT		
							Year	County	No.
10492	1 Fry, Billy	58	First Named	55	M	Full	1896	Blue	4394
10493	2 " Vicey	43	Wife	40	F	"	1896	"	4395
10494	3 " Lena	19	Dau	16	"	"	1896	"	4397
10495	4 " Robert	17	Son	14	M	"	1896	"	4398
10496	5 " Allington	15	"	12	"	"	1896	"	4399
10497	6 " Emma	11	Dau	8	F	"	1896	"	4401
10498	7 " Natt	9	"	6	"	"	1896	"	4402
10499	8 " James	20	Ward	17	M	"	1896	"	4403
10500	9 " Edmond	24	"	21	"	"	1896	"	4400
	10								
	11								
	12	ENROLLMENT							
	13	OF NOS. 1,2,3,4,5,6,7,8 and 9 HEREON APPROVED BY THE SECRETARY							
	14	OF INTERIOR FEB 4 1903							
	15								
	16								
	17								

TRIBAL ENROLLMENT OF PARENTS

	Name of Father	Year	County	Name of Mother	Year	County
1	Ita Fry	Dead	Bok Tuklo	Ca-non-te-ma	Dead	Blue
2	Che-co-pa	"	Blue		"	"
3	No1			No2		
4	No1			No2		
5	No1			No2		
6	No1			No2		
7	No1			No2		
8	Pusley Fry	Dead	Blue	Bessie Fry	Dead	Blue
9	" "	"	"	" "	"	"
10						
11			No8 on 1896 roll as Jim Fry.			
12						
13					Date of Application for Enrollment.	
14			For child of No3 see NB (Apr 26-06) Card #377			
15					Aug 22/99	
16						
17						

Choctaw By Blood Enrollment Cards 1898-1914

RESIDENCE: Jackson   COUNTY. **Choctaw Nation**   **Choctaw Roll**   CARD No.
POST OFFICE: Jackson, I.T.   *(Not Including Freedmen)*   FIELD No. 3708

Dawes' Roll No.	NAME	Relationship to Person	AGE	SEX	BLOOD	TRIBAL ENROLLMENT		
						Year	County	No.
I.W. 1332	1 Sutton, Rachel A 40	First Named	35	F	IW	1896	Jackson	14533
10501	2 Freeny, John W 16	Son	13	M	1/4	1896	"	4283
	3							
	4							
	5	ENROLLMENT						
	6	OF NOS. 2 HEREON						
	7	APPROVED BY THE SECRETARY OF INTERIOR FEB 4 1903						
	8							
	9	ENROLLMENT OF NOS. 1 HEREON						
	10	APPROVED BY THE SECRETARY OF INTERIOR MAR 14 1905						
	11							
	12							
	13							
	14							
	15							
	16							
	17							

TRIBAL ENROLLMENT OF PARENTS

	Name of Father	Year	County	Name of Mother	Year	County
1	Henry Hate	Dead	Non Citz	Lizzie Hate		Non Citz
2	Henry Freeny	"	Kiamitia	No 1		
3						
4						
5						
6						
7						
8						
9	No 1 on 1896 roll as R. A. Freeny					
10	No 2 " 1896 " " Jno. W. "					
11	No 1 as to marriage and separation, see testimony of No 1					
12	No.2 formerly wife of Henry Freeny, 1885 Kiamitia, No 173, who died					
13	about 1888. No.1 also formerly wife of Daniel Smallwood, Choctaw roll No 10860, approved Feb. 4, 1903. Now wife of William M. Sutton,					
14	a white man.					Date of Application for Enrollment.
15	No.1 originally listed on this card as Rachel A Smallwood.					Aug 22/99
16						
17						

108

RESIDENCE: Blue COUNTY. **Choctaw Nation** **Choctaw Roll** CARD NO.
POST OFFICE: Caddo, I.T. *(Not Including Freedmen)* FIELD NO. 3709

Dawes' Roll No.	NAME	Relationship to Person Named	AGE	SEX	BLOOD	TRIBAL ENROLLMENT		
						Year	County	No.
I.W. 746	1 Lane, Bartholomew (76)	First Named	74	M	IW	1896	Blue	14775
10502	2 " Frances 48	Wife	45	F	3/4	1896	"	8196
10503	3 " Edward 24	Son	21	M	3/8	1896	"	8197
10504	4 " Bartholomew Jr 22	"	19	"	3/8	1896	"	8198
10505	5 " Rosa 10	Dau	7	F	3/8	1896	"	8200
10506	6 " Daisy 8	"	5	"	3/8	1896	"	8201
	7							
	8 DECISION PREPARED #1	Oct. 29, '03						
	9 ENROLLMENT							
	10 OF NOS. 2 3 4 5 and 6 HEREON APPROVED BY THE SECRETARY							
	11 OF INTERIOR FEB 4 1903							
	12							
	13 ENROLLMENT							
	14 OF NOS. ~~~ 1 ~~~ HEREON APPROVED BY THE SECRETARY							
	15 OF INTERIOR MAY -7 1904							
	16							
	17							

TRIBAL ENROLLMENT OF PARENTS

	Name of Father	Year	County	Name of Mother	Year	County
1	Daniel Lane	Dead	Non Citz	Mary Lane	Dead	Non Citz
2	Simpson Jones	"	Blue	Jincey Jones		Blue
3	No1			No2		
4	No1			No2		
5	No1			No2		
6	No1			No2		
7						
8	No1 See Decision of March 2 '04					
9	No1 was admitted by Dawes Com., Case					
10	No 1252. No appeal					
11	No1 on 1896 roll as Batt Lane					
	No4 " 1896 " " Bart Lane					
12						
13						
14				Date of Application for Enrollment		
15				Aug 22/99		
16						
17						

Choctaw By Blood Enrollment Cards 1898-1914

RESIDENCE:	Blue	COUNTY.						CARD No.	
POST OFFICE:	Caddo, I.T.	Choctaw Nation		Choctaw Roll (Not Including Freedmen)				FIELD No. 3710	

Dawes' Roll No.	NAME		Relationship to Person	AGE	SEX	BLOOD	TRIBAL ENROLLMENT		
							Year	County	No.
10507	1 Smith, Louvina	36	First Named	36	F	1/2	1896	Blue	11591
10508	2 " Ella L	15	Dau	12	"	1/4	1896	"	11592
10509	3 " Claude	11	Son	8	M	1/4	1896	"	11593
	4								
	5								
	6	ENROLLMENT							
	7	OF NOS. 1, 2 and 3 HEREON							
	8	APPROVED BY THE SECRETARY OF INTERIOR FEB 4 1903							
	9								
	10								
	11								
	12								
	13								
	14								
	15								
	16								
	17								

TRIBAL ENROLLMENT OF PARENTS

	Name of Father	Year	County	Name of Mother	Year	County
1	Edmond Bohanan	Dead	Jackson	Louvina Smith	Dead	Jackson
2	W.T. Smith		white man	No1		
3	" " "		" "	No1		
4						
5						
6			No2 on 1896 roll as Ella Lee Smith			
7			No1 is wife of William T. Smith on Choctaw card #5653			
8						
9						
10						
11						
12						
13						
14					Date of Application for Enrollment.	
15					Aug 22/99	
16						
17						

Choctaw By Blood Enrollment Cards 1898-1914

RESIDENCE: Blue   COUNTY. **Choctaw Nation**   **Choctaw Roll**   CARD No.
POST OFFICE: Bok Chito, I.T.   *(Not Including Freedmen)*   FIELD No. 3711

Dawes' Roll No.	NAME	Relationship to Person	AGE	SEX	BLOOD	TRIBAL ENROLLMENT		
						Year	County	No.
10510	1 Clark Edward 26	First Named	23	M	Full	1896	Blue	2898
	2							
	3							
	4	ENROLLMENT						
	5	OF NOS. 1 HEREON APPROVED BY THE SECRETARY						
	6	OF INTERIOR FEB 4 1903						
	7							
	8							
	9							
	10							
	11							
	12							
	13							
	14							
	15							
	16							
	17							

TRIBAL ENROLLMENT OF PARENTS

Name of Father	Year	County	Name of Mother	Year	County
1 Adam Clark	Dead	Atoka	Jincy Clark	Dead	Blue
2					
3					
4					
5					
6					
7					
8					
9					
10					
11					
12					
13					
14				Date of Application for Enrollment.		
15				Aug 22/99		
16						
17 P.O. Hugo, I.T. 12/1/02						

Choctaw By Blood Enrollment Cards 1898-1914

Dawes' Roll No.	NAME		Relationship to Person First Named	AGE	SEX	BLOOD	TRIBAL ENROLLMENT		
							Year	County	No.
10511	1 Folsom, Joseph	28	First Named	25	M	Full	1896	Jackson	4284
10512	2 " Sissie	23	Wife	20	F	"	1896	"	4285
10513	3 " Wilson	5	Son	2	M	"			
10514	4 " Louie	3	"	3mo	"	"			
10515	5 " Saul	1	Son	4mo	M	"			
	6								
	7								
	8	ENROLLMENT							
	9	OF NOS. 1,2,3,4 and 5 HEREON APPROVED BY THE SECRETARY							
	10	OF INTERIOR FEB 4 1903							
	11								
	12								
	13								
	14								
	15								
	16								
	17								

TRIBAL ENROLLMENT OF PARENTS

	Name of Father	Year	County	Name of Mother	Year	County
1	Stewart Folsom	Dead	Jackson	Kizzie Folsom	Dead	Jackson
2	Rayson Anderson	"	"	Bicey Anderson	"	Atoka
3	No1			No2		
4	No1			No2		
5	No.1			No.2		
6						
7	No1 on 1896 roll as Joe Folsom					
8	Nos 3-4 Affidavits of birth to					
9	be supplied:- Recd Oct 7/99					
10	No.5 Born Dec 2, 1901: enrolled March 31, 1902. For child of Nos 1&2 see NB (Mar. 3, 1905) card #586					
11					#1 to 4	
12						
13				DATE OF APPLICATION FOR ENROLLMENT		
14				Aug 22/99		
15						
16	P.O. Matoy I.T. 3/29/05					
17						

Choctaw By Blood Enrollment Cards 1898-1914

RESIDENCE: Jackson   COUNTY. **Choctaw Nation**   **Choctaw Roll**   CARD NO.
POST OFFICE: Bennington, I.T.   *(Not Including Freedmen)*   FIELD NO. 3713

Dawes' Roll No.	NAME		Relationship to Person	AGE	SEX	BLOOD	TRIBAL ENROLLMENT		
							Year	County	No.
10516	1 Folsom, Alfred	26	First Named	23	M	Full	1896	Jackson	4289
	2								
	3								
	4	ENROLLMENT							
	5	OF NOS. 1 HEREON APPROVED BY THE SECRETARY							
	6	OF INTERIOR FEB 4 1903							
	7								
	8								
	9								
	10								
	11								
	12								
	13								
	14								
	15								
	16								
	17								

TRIBAL ENROLLMENT OF PARENTS

	Name of Father	Year	County	Name of Mother	Year	County
1	Stewart Folsom	Dead	Jackson	Kizzie Folsom	Dead	Jackson
2						
3						
4						
5						
6						
7			On 1896 roll as Alfred Folsom, Jr.			
8						
9						
10						
11						
12						
13						
14						
15				Date of Application for Enrollment.	Aug 22/99	
16						
17						

Choctaw By Blood Enrollment Cards 1898-1914

RESIDENCE: Blue   COUNTY. **Choctaw Nation**   **Choctaw Roll**   CARD No.
POST OFFICE: Bennington, I.T.   *(Not Including Freedmen)*   FIELD No. 3714

Dawes' Roll No.	NAME	Relationship to Person First Named	AGE	SEX	BLOOD	TRIBAL ENROLLMENT		
						Year	County	No.
10517	1 Anderson, Gibbie ²¹	First Named	18	M	Full	1896	Blue	418
	2							
	3							
	4							
	5	ENROLLMENT OF NOS. 1 HEREON APPROVED BY THE SECRETARY						
	6	OF INTERIOR FEB 4 1903						
	7							
	8							
	9							
	10							
	11							
	12							
	13							
	14							
	15							
	16							
	17							

TRIBAL ENROLLMENT OF PARENTS

	Name of Father	Year	County	Name of Mother	Year	County
1	Rayson Anderson	Dead	Atoka	Bicey Anderson	Dead	Atoka
2						
3						
4						
5						
6						
7						
8						
9						
10						
11						
12						
13						
14						Date of Application for Enrollment.
15						Aug 22/99
16						
17						

Choctaw By Blood Enrollment Cards 1898-1914

RESIDENCE: Jackson   COUNTY.   **Choctaw Nation**   **Choctaw Roll**   CARD NO.
POST OFFICE: Mayhew, I.T.   *(Not Including Freedmen)*   FIELD NO. **3715**

Dawes' Roll No.	NAME	Relationship to Person	AGE	SEX	BLOOD	TRIBAL ENROLLMENT		
						Year	County	No.
10518	1 Wade, Kennedy ²⁹	First Named	26	M	Full	1896	Jackson	13836
	2							
	3							
	4							
	5	ENROLLMENT OF NOS. 1 HEREON						
	6	APPROVED BY THE SECRETARY						
	7	OF INTERIOR Feb 4 1903						
	8							
	9							
	10							
	11							
	12							
	13							
	14							
	15							
	16							
	17							

TRIBAL ENROLLMENT OF PARENTS

	Name of Father	Year	County	Name of Mother	Year	County
1	Eastman Wade	Dead	Kiamitia	Siley Frazier	Dead	Jackson
2						
3						
4						
5						
6						
7			On 1896 roll as Cunningham Wade			
8						
9						
10						
11			No.1 in Jail at Atoka 11/21 '02			
12						
13						
14					Date of Application for Enrollment.	
15					Aug 22/99	
16			Bro. on 7-1846			
17						

115

Choctaw By Blood Enrollment Cards 1898-1914

RESIDENCE:	Blue	COUNTY.								
POST OFFICE:	Caddo, I.T.		**Choctaw Nation**				**Choctaw Roll** *(Not Including Freedmen)*		CARD No. FIELD NO. **3716**	

Dawes' Roll No.	NAME		Relationship to Person First Named	AGE	SEX	BLOOD	TRIBAL ENROLLMENT		
							Year	County	No.
Void Chickasaw	1 Frazier, William		Named	30	M	Full	1896	Blue	4408
10519	2 " Louisa	31	Wife	28	F	"	1896	"	4409
10520	3 " Sarah	13	Dau	10	"	3/4	1896	"	4410
	4								
	5								
	6								
	7	ENROLLMENT OF NOS. 2 and 3 HEREON							
	8	APPROVED BY THE SECRETARY							
	9	OF INTERIOR Feb 4 1903							
	10								
	11								
	12								
	13								
	14								
	15								
	16								
	17								

TRIBAL ENROLLMENT OF PARENTS

	Name of Father	Year	County	Name of Mother	Year	County
1	Daniel Frazier	Dead	Blue	Ho-te-a-ho-ke	Dead	Blue
2	Adam Nicholas	"	"	Mulsey Nicholas	"	"
3	No1			No2		
4						
5						
6		Husband, William Frazier on				
7		Chickasaw Card No 1530				
8		For child of No.3 see NB (Apr. 26, 1906) Card No. 142.				
9						
10						
11						
12						
13						
14					Date of Application for Enrollment.	
15					Aug 22/99	
16						
17						

RESIDENCE: Blue
POST OFFICE: Caddo, I.T.

COUNTY. **Choctaw Nation**

Choctaw Roll
(Not Including Freedmen)

CARD NO.
FIELD NO. 3717

Dawes' Roll No.	NAME		Relationship to Person	AGE	SEX	BLOOD	TRIBAL ENROLLMENT		
							Year	County	No.
10521	1 Wade, Abel	44	First Named	41	M	Full	1896	Blue	13879
10522	2 " Agnes	41	Wife	38	F	"	1896	"	13880
10523	3 " Elsie	20	Dau	17	"	"	1896	"	13881
10524	4 " Jefferson	18	Son	15	M	"	1896	"	13882
10525	5 " Sarah	15	Dau	12	F	"	1896	"	13883
10526	6 " Lena	13	"	10	"	"	1896	"	13884
10527	7 " Sam	11	Son	8	M	"	1896	"	13885
10528	8 " Thomas	9	"	6	"	"	1896	"	13886
10529	9 " Dora	4	Dau	1	F	"			
16116	10 Wade, Albert	1	Son of No. 3	1	M	"			
	11								
	12								
	13								
	14								
	15								
	16								
	17								

ENROLLMENT
OF NOS. 1,2,3,4,5,6,7,8,9 and 10 HEREON
APPROVED BY THE SECRETARY
OF INTERIOR FEB 4 1903

ENROLLMENT
OF NOS. ____10____ HEREON
APPROVED BY THE SECRETARY
OF INTERIOR FEB 21 1907

TRIBAL ENROLLMENT OF PARENTS

	Name of Father	Year	County	Name of Mother	Year	County
1	Henry Wade	Dead	Red River	Ish-ta-la-ma	Dead	Red River
2	Judson Frazier	"	Blue	Tennessee Frazier	"	Blue
3	No1			No2		
4	No1			No2		
5	No1			No2		
6	No1			No2		
7	No1			No2		
8	No1			No2		
9	No1			No2		
10	Reed Bond		Choctaw	No3		
11						
12	No3 on 1896 roll as Elcie Wade					
13	No9 Affidavit of birth to be				#1 to 9 inc	
14	supplied:- Recd Oct 7/99				Date of Application for Enrollment.	
15	No10 was born June 3, 1902. application received and No10				Aug 22/99	
16	placed on this card April 4, 1905, under Act of Congress					
17	approved March 3, 1905.					

No10 GRANTED JAN 16 1907

117

Choctaw By Blood Enrollment Cards 1898-1914

RESIDENCE: Jackson   COUNTY. **Choctaw Nation**   **Choctaw Roll**   CARD NO.
POST OFFICE: Jackson, I.T.   *(Not Including Freedmen)*   FIELD NO. 3718

Dawes' Roll No.	NAME	Relationship to Person First Named	AGE	SEX	BLOOD	TRIBAL ENROLLMENT Year	County	No.
10530	1 Pruden, Tecumseh ²⁴	First Named	21	M	Full	1896	Jackson	10463
	2							
	3							
	4							
	5							
	6							
	7							
	8							
	9							
	10							
	11							
	12							
	13							
	14							
	15							
	16							
	17							

ENROLLMENT
OF NOS. 1 HEREON
APPROVED BY THE SECRETARY
OF INTERIOR FEB 4 1903

TRIBAL ENROLLMENT OF PARENTS

	Name of Father	Year	County	Name of Mother	Year	County
1	Henry Pruden	Dead	Red River	Siney Pruden	Dead	Red River
2						
3						
4						
5						
6						
7						
8						
9						
10						
11						
12						
13						
14					Date of Application for Enrollment.	
15					Aug 22/99	
16						
17						

Choctaw By Blood Enrollment Cards 1898-1914

RESIDENCE: Blue
POST OFFICE: Caney, I.T.

COUNTY. **Choctaw Nation**

Choctaw Roll
(Not Including Freedmen)

CARD No.
FIELD No. 3719

Dawes' Roll No.		NAME	Relationship to Person	AGE	SEX	BLOOD	TRIBAL ENROLLMENT		
							Year	County	No.
10531	1	Washington, Marcus 24	First Named	21	M	Full	1896	Blue	13903
	2								
	3								
	4								
	5								
	6	ENROLLMENT							
	7	OF NOS. 1 HEREON APPROVED BY THE SECRETARY							
	8	OF INTERIOR Feb 4 1903							
	9								
	10								
	11								
	12								
	13								
	14								
	15								
	16								
	17								

TRIBAL ENROLLMENT OF PARENTS

	Name of Father	Year	County	Name of Mother	Year	County
1	Ben Washington	Dead	Blue	Seliney Washington	Dead	Blue
2						
3						
4						
5						
6	No.1 is now the husband of Ellen Frazier on Choctaw card #4228 Nov 5, 1902					
7						
8	For child of No1 see NB (Apr 26-06) Card #604					
9						
10						
11						
12						
13						
14						
15				Date of Application for Enrollment. Aug 22/99		
16						
17						

Choctaw By Blood Enrollment Cards 1898-1914

RESIDENCE: Blue
POST OFFICE: Caddo, I.T.

COUNTY. **Choctaw Nation**

Choctaw Roll
(Not Including Freedmen)

CARD No.
FIELD No. **3720**

Dawes' Roll No.	NAME		Relationship to Person First Named	AGE	SEX	BLOOD	TRIBAL ENROLLMENT		
							Year	County	No.
10532	1 McDaniel, Nicholas	68	First Named	65	M	Full	1896	Blue	9416
I.W. 1655	2 " Mollie	✓	Wife	28	F	I.W.			
I.W. 1126	3 " Ida	38	Wife	38	F	I.W.			
	4								
	5								
	6								
	7 ENROLLMENT OF NOS. 1 HEREON								
	8 APPROVED BY THE SECRETARY								
	9 OF INTERIOR Feb 4 1903								
	10								
	11 ENROLLMENT								
	12 OF NOS. ~ 3 ~ HEREON APPROVED BY THE SECRETARY								
	13 OF INTERIOR Nov 16 1904								
	14								
	15 ENROLLMENT OF NOS. ~ 2 ~ HEREON								
	16 APPROVED BY THE SECRETARY OF INTERIOR Mar 2– 1907								
	17								

TRIBAL ENROLLMENT OF PARENTS

	Name of Father	Year	County	Name of Mother	Year	County
1	Caldwell McDaniel	Dead	Red River	Te-ho-na	Dead	Eagle
2	James Burke		non citizen	Sarah Burke	"	non citizen
3	Henry Campbell	dead	" "	Mary Campbell	"	" " "
4						
5						

6   No.2 maiden name was Mary Burke   No2 is dead. See letter of

7   J M Burke her father of

8   No2 Enrolled June 7, 1900.   Jan 10 1906

No.1 was divorced from No.2 Aug. 15th 1900.

9   See bill of divorce filed Sept. 14th, 1900

10   No1 is now married to Ida McDaniel on

Choctaw Card #D602, December 11, 1900

11   Jan 11/1901: Enrollment of No2 will be refused on presentation of evidence of

12   notice of contest by Choctaw attorneys as by agreement of Dec. 11 1900.

13   No.3 transferred from Choctaw card #D-602 Oct 31, 1904: see decision of Oct 15,1904

		Date of Application for Enrollment.
14		
15		Aug 22/99
16		
17	No.3 P.O. Durant I.T	Granted Jan 10. 1907

120

Choctaw By Blood Enrollment Cards 1898-1914

RESIDENCE: Blue	COUNTY.		
POST OFFICE: Caddo, I.T.	**Choctaw Nation**	**Choctaw Roll** (Not Including Freedmen)	CARD NO. FIELD NO. 3721

Dawes' Roll No.	NAME	Relationship to Person	AGE	SEX	BLOOD	TRIBAL ENROLLMENT		
						Year	County	No.
10533	₁ Manning, Forbis ³¹	First Named	28	M	1/4	1896	Blue	8750
I.W. 346	₂ " Laura ²⁷	Wife	25	F	I W	1896	"	14832
10534	₃ " Lizzie ¹²	Dau	9	"	1/8	1896	"	8751
10535	₄ " Edgar ¹¹	Son	8	M	1/8	1896	"	8752
10536	₅ " Eula ⁶	Dau	3	F	1/8	1896	"	8753
	6							
	7							
	8	ENROLLMENT OF NOS. 1,3,4 and 5 HEREON						
	9	APPROVED BY THE SECRETARY OF INTERIOR FEB 4 1903						
	10							
	11	ENROLLMENT OF NOS. 2 HEREON						
	12	APPROVED BY THE SECRETARY						
	13	OF INTERIOR SEP 12 1903						
	14							
	15							
	16							
	17							

TRIBAL ENROLLMENT OF PARENTS

	Name of Father	Year	County	Name of Mother	Year	County
1	T. J. Manning	Dead	Non Citz	Matilda Manning	Dead	Blue
2	Griffith	"	" "	Manda Griffith		Non Citz
3	No1			Judie Manning	Dead	" "
4	No1			" "	"	" "
5	No1			No2		
6						
7						
8	No2 was admitted by Dawes Com Case					
9	No 395 as Mrs. Laura Manning					
10	For child of No⁵ 1&2 see (NB Apr. 26, 1906) Card #60					
11	No⁵ 3-4 as to marriage of parents, see testimony of No1 and Peter Maytubby					
12	For child of No1 see NB (Act Mar 3-05) #259					
13						
14					Date of Application for Enrollment.	
15					Aug 22/99	
16						
17						

121

Choctaw By Blood Enrollment Cards 1898-1914

| RESIDENCE: Jackson | COUNTY. | Choctaw Nation | Choctaw Roll | CARD NO. |
| POST OFFICE: Jackson, I.T. | | | (Not Including Freedmen) | FIELD NO. 3722 |

Dawes' Roll No.	NAME	Relationship to Person First Named	AGE	SEX	BLOOD	TRIBAL ENROLLMENT		
						Year	County	No.
DEAD dead	1 Frazier, Susan DEAD.	First Named	35	F	Full	1896	Jackson	4288
VOID	2 " Bessie	Dau	2	"	"			
	3							
	4							
	5							
	6	No. 1 HEREON DISMISSED UNDER						
	7	ORDER OF THE COMMISSION TO THE FIVE						
	8	CIVILIZED TRIBES OF MARCH 31, 1905.						
	9							
	10							
	11							
	12							
	13							
	14							
	15							
	16							
	17							

TRIBAL ENROLLMENT OF PARENTS

	Name of Father	Year	County	Name of Mother	Year	County
1	Nicholas McDaniel		Jackson	Bicey McDaniel	Dead	Jackson
2	Fisher Frazier		"	No1		
3						
4						
5						
6						
7						
8		No2 Affidavit of birth to be supplied:-				
9		No2 is duplicate enrollment of No.3 on Choctaw Card No 1667				
10						
11		No.1 died October, 1901; proof of death filed Nov 26 1902				
12						
13						
14					Date of Application for Enrollment.	
15					Aug 22/99	
16						
17						

CANCELLED

No1 died prior to ratification of Choctaw-Chickasaw agreement Sept 25, 1902

No2 is same as No.3 on Choctaw card #1667

Choctaw By Blood Enrollment Cards 1898-1914

RESIDENCE: Jackson COUNTY. **Choctaw Nation** **Choctaw Roll** CARD NO.
POST OFFICE: Jackson, I.T. *(Not Including Freedmen)* FIELD NO. 3723

Dawes' Roll No.	NAME	Relationship to Person	AGE	SEX	BLOOD	TRIBAL ENROLLMENT		
						Year	County	No.
10537	1 Scott, Salina 63	First Named	60	F	Full	1896	Jackson	11557
10538*	2 Belvin, Johnson 24	Son	21	M	"	1896	"	1475
10539	3 " Elisha 21	"	18	"	"	1896	"	1476
	4							
	5							
	6	ENROLLMENT						
	7	OF NOS. 1, 2 and 3 HEREON						
	8	APPROVED BY THE SECRETARY OF INTERIOR FEB 4 1903						
	9							
	10							
	11							
	12							
	13							
	14							
	15							
	16							
	17							

TRIBAL ENROLLMENT OF PARENTS

	Name of Father	Year	County	Name of Mother	Year	County
1	Ma-kin-ta	Dead	Jackson		Dead	Jackson
2	Jesse Belvin	"	"	No1		
3	" "	"	"	No1		
4						
5						
6						
7	* "Died prior to Sept. 25, 1902; not entitled to land or money." See DC09 - Sec 11, 1914					
8						
9						
10						
11						
12						
13					Date of Application for Enrollment.	
14						
15					Aug 22/99	
16						
17						

123

Choctaw By Blood Enrollment Cards 1898-1914

RESIDENCE: **Blue**   COUNTY.   **Choctaw Nation**   **Choctaw Roll**   CARD NO.
POST OFFICE: **Jackson I.T.**   (Not Including Freedmen)   FIELD NO. **3724**

Dawes' Roll No.	NAME		Relationship to Person First Named	AGE	SEX	BLOOD	TRIBAL ENROLLMENT		
							Year	County	No.
10540	1 Julius, Solomon	47	First Named	44	M	Full	1896	Blue	7219
10541	2 " Serena	47	Wife	44	F	"	1896	"	7220
10542	3 " Eli	21	Son	18	M	"	1896	"	7221
10543	4 " Jane	18	Dau	15	F	"	1896	"	7222
10544	5 " Sallie	14	"	11	"	"	1896	"	7223
10545	6 " Rosa	10	"	7	"	"	1896	"	7224
10546	7 " Gilbert	7	Son	4	M	"	1896	"	7225
10547	8 " Adam	5	"	2	"	"			
	9								
	10								
	11								
	12								
	13								
	14								
	15								
	16								
	17								

ENROLLMENT
OF NOS. 1,2,3,4,5,6,7 and 8 HEREON
APPROVED BY THE SECRETARY
OF INTERIOR Feb 4 1903

TRIBAL ENROLLMENT OF PARENTS

	Name of Father	Year	County	Name of Mother	Year	County
1	Julius Boys	Dead	Blue	Pe-sa-hu-na	Dead	Blue
2	Solomon Byington	"	Chick Dist	Sally A Byington	"	Chick Dist
3	No1			No2		
4	No1			No2		
5	No1			No2		
6	No1			No2		
7	No1			No2		
8	No1			No2		

9 For child of No1 see NB (Act of April 26, 1906) Card No.245
10 No1 on 1896 roll as Solomon Julious
11 No2 " 1896 " " Zorena "   For child of No3 see NB (Mar 3-05) #863
    No3 " 1896 " " Eli "   " " " " " " (Apr 26'06) #245
12 No6 " 1896 " " Russey "
13 No7 " 1896 " " Colbert "
14 No8 Affidavit of birth to   Date of Application for Enrollment.
   be supplied:- Filed Nov 2/99
15 For child of Nos 1 and 2 see NB (Mar 3 '05) #498   Aug 22/99
16
17 P.O. Bennington 1/6/03

Choctaw By Blood Enrollment Cards 1898-1914

RESIDENCE: Jackson COUNTY. **Choctaw Nation** **Choctaw Roll** CARD No.
POST OFFICE: Jackson, I.T. *(Not Including Freedmen)* FIELD No. **3725**

Dawes' Roll No.	NAME	Relationship to Person Named	AGE	SEX	BLOOD	TRIBAL ENROLLMENT		
						Year	County	No.
10548	1 Hayes Ellis 54	First Named	51	M	Full	1896	Jackson	5824
10549	2 ~~Lizzie~~ DIED PRIOR TO SEPTEMBER 25,1902	Dau	12	F	"	1896	"	5825
	3							
	4							
	5							
	6	ENROLLMENT						
	7	OF NOS. 1 and 2 HEREON APPROVED BY THE SECRETARY						
	8	OF INTERIOR Feb 4 1903						
	9							
	10							
	11							
	12							
	13							
	14							
	15							
	16							
	17							

TRIBAL ENROLLMENT OF PARENTS

	Name of Father	Year	County	Name of Mother	Year	County
1	Billy Hayes		Jackson		dead	Jackson
2	~~No1~~			~~Susan Hayes~~	"	"
3						
4						
5						
6						
7	No2 died June 28, 1900: Enrollment cancelled by Department July 8, 1904					
8						
9						
10						
11						
12						
13						
14					Date of Application for Enrollment.	
15					Aug 22/99	
16						
17						

Choctaw By Blood Enrollment Cards 1898-1914

RESIDENCE: Armstrong Academy COUNTY.
POST OFFICE: Academy, I.T.

Choctaw Nation

Choctaw Roll
(Not Including Freedmen)

CARD NO.
FIELD NO. 3726

Dawes' Roll No.	NAME	Relationship to Person First Named	AGE	SEX	BLOOD	TRIBAL ENROLLMENT		
						Year	County	No.
10550	1 Fulsom, Robert	19 First Named	16	M	1/2	1896	Tobucksy	4008
	2							
	3							
	4							
	5	ENROLLMENT OF NOS. 1			Duplicate enrollment of No. 12674: not entitled			
	6	APPROVED BY THE SECRETARY HEREON			to land or money under this number.			
	7	OF INTERIOR Feb 4 1903			[See Indian Office letter Aug. 5-1910. D.C. #1112-1910			
	8							
	9							
	10							
	11							
	12							
	13							
	14							
	15							
	16							
	17							

TRIBAL ENROLLMENT OF PARENTS

	Name of Father	Year	County	Name of Mother	Year	County
1						
2						
3						
4						
5						
6			On 1896 roll as Robt. Fulsom			
7						
8			Information respecting parents waived			
9			by Commissioners			
10						
11						
12						
13						
14					Date of Application for Enrollment.	
15					Aug 22/99	
16						
17						

Choctaw By Blood Enrollment Cards 1898-1914

RESIDENCE: Armstrong Academy COUNTY.   **Choctaw Nation**   **Choctaw Roll**   CARD NO.

POST OFFICE: Academy I.T.   *(Not Including Freedmen)*   FIELD NO. **3727**

Dawes' Roll No.	NAME	Relationship to Person	AGE	SEX	BLOOD	TRIBAL ENROLLMENT Year	County	No.
10551	1 Bell, Robert E 22	First Named	19	M	1/4	1896	Tobucksy	914
	2							
	3							
	4							
	5							
	6	ENROLLMENT OF NOS. 1 HEREON						
	7	APPROVED BY THE SECRETARY OF INTERIOR Feb 4 1903						
	8							
	9							
	10							
	11							
	12							
	13							
	14							
	15							
	16							
	17							

TRIBAL ENROLLMENT OF PARENTS

	Name of Father	Year	County	Name of Mother	Year	County
1						
2						
3						
4						
5						
6						
7						
8						
9						
10						
11						
12						
13						
14					Date of Application for Enrollment.	
15					Aug 22/99	
16						
17						

Choctaw By Blood Enrollment Cards 1898-1914

RESIDENCE: Armstrong Academy COUNTY. **Choctaw Nation** Choctaw Roll (*Not Including Freedmen*) CARD NO.
POST OFFICE: Academy, I.T. FIELD NO. **3728**

Dawes' Roll No.	NAME	Relationship to Person First Named	AGE	SEX	BLOOD	TRIBAL ENROLLMENT Year	County	No.
10552	1 Tracey, John H 14	First Named	11	M	1/8	1896	Sans Bois	11876
	2							
	3							
	4							
	5	ENROLLMENT						
	6	OF NOS. 1 HEREON APPROVED BY THE SECRETARY						
	7	OF INTERIOR Feb 4 1903						
	8							
	9							
	10							
	11							
	12							
	13							
	14							
	15							
	16							
	17							

TRIBAL ENROLLMENT OF PARENTS

Name of Father	Year	County	Name of Mother	Year	County
1 John Tracey	Dead	Non Citz	Ruthy Mosby		Sans Bois
2					
3					
4					
5					
6		On 1896 roll as Jno. H Tracy.			
7		Guardian of No.1 James H. Boatwright on Choc. 4505. Letters			
8		of guardianship filed Oct. 28, 1902			
9					
10					
11					
12					
13					
14					
15			Date of Application for Enrollment.		Aug 22/99
16					
17					

Choctaw By Blood Enrollment Cards 1898-1914

RESIDENCE: Armstrong Academy COUNTY. **Choctaw Nation**   **Choctaw Roll**   CARD No.
POST OFFICE: Academy, I.T.   *(Not Including Freedmen)*   FIELD No. 3729

Dawes' Roll No.	NAME	Relationship to Person	AGE	SEX	BLOOD	TRIBAL ENROLLMENT		
						Year	County	No.
10553	1 Lucas, Adam 22	First Named	19	M	3/4	1896	Tobucksy	7861
	2							
	3							
	4							
	5	ENROLLMENT OF NOS. 1 HEREON						
	6	APPROVED BY THE SECRETARY OF INTERIOR FEB 4 1903						
	7							
	8							
	9							
	10							
	11							
	12							
	13							
	14							
	15							
	16							
	17							

TRIBAL ENROLLMENT OF PARENTS

	Name of Father	Year	County	Name of Mother	Year	County
1						
2						
3						
4						
5						
6						
7						
8						
9						
10						
11						
12						
13						
14						Date of Application for Enrollment.
15						Aug 22/99
16						
17						

Choctaw By Blood Enrollment Cards 1898-1914

RESIDENCE: Armstrong Academy COUNTY. **Choctaw Nation** **Choctaw Roll** CARD No.
POST OFFICE: Academy, I.T. *(Not Including Freedmen)* FIELD No. 3730

Dawes' Roll No.	NAME	Relationship to Person First Named	AGE	SEX	BLOOD	TRIBAL ENROLLMENT		
						Year	County	No.
10554	1 Bascom, Charles 26	First Named	23	M	Full	1896	Sans Bois	681
	2							
	3							
	4							
	5	ENROLLMENT						
	6	OF NOS. 1 HEREON APPROVED BY THE SECRETARY						
	7	OF INTERIOR FEB 4 1903						
	8							
	9							
	10							
	11							
	12							
	13							
	14							
	15							
	16							
	17							

TRIBAL ENROLLMENT OF PARENTS

	Name of Father	Year	County	Name of Mother	Year	County
1	Cornelius Bascomb[sic]	Dead	Skullyville	Mary Bascomb	Dead	Skullyville
2						
3						
4						
5						
6	No.1 is now the husband of Jincy Carney on Chickasaw card #1561. Feby 4, 1901					
7						
8	P.O. address of No.1 Featherstone, I.T. – Feby 14, 1901					
9	As to parents of No1 see letter filed this date Feby 28, 1901					
10	For child of No1 see NB (March 3,1905) #1353 " " " " ' " (April 26,1906) #341					
11						
12						
13						
14					Date of Application for Enrollment.	
15					Aug 22/99	
16						
17	PO Quinton 7/1/03					

Choctaw By Blood Enrollment Cards 1898-1914

RESIDENCE: Armstrong Academy COUNTY.   **Choctaw Nation**   **Choctaw Roll** CARD No.
POST OFFICE: Academy, I.T.   *(Not Including Freedmen)*   FIELD No. 3731

Dawes' Roll No.	NAME	Relationship to Person First Named	AGE	SEX	BLOOD	TRIBAL ENROLLMENT		
						Year	County	No.
1	Morris, Sampson ~~16~~	First Named	13	M	3/4	1896	Blue	8807
2								
3								
4								
5								
6								
7								
8								
9								
10								
11								
12								
13								
14								
15								
16								
17								

TRIBAL ENROLLMENT OF PARENTS

	Name of Father	Year	County	Name of Mother	Year	County
1						
2						
3						
4						
5						
6						
7						
8						
9						
10						
11						
12						
13						
14						
15						
16						
17						

Nº1 is duplicate of Nº3 on Choctaw card #2477. See letter of Thompson Barnett in Gen Office files #23301-1903.

Date of Application for Enrollment.
Aug 22/99

CANCELLED

Duplicate of Nº3 on Choctaw #2477

131

Choctaw By Blood Enrollment Cards 1898-1914

RESIDENCE: Armstrong Academy COUNTY. **Choctaw Nation** Choctaw Roll CARD No.
POST OFFICE: Academy, I.T. *(Not Including Freedmen)* FIELD No. 3732

Dawes' Roll No.	NAME	Relationship to Person First Named	AGE	SEX	BLOOD	TRIBAL ENROLLMENT		
						Year	County	No.
1	Gardner, Wilson 20		17	M	Full	1896	Blue	4939
2								
3								
4								
5								
6								
7								
8								
9								
10								
11								
12								
13								
14								
15								
16								
17								

Duplicate of #4 on 7-1354
Authority W.O.B. 9/8/05.

CANCELLED

TRIBAL ENROLLMENT OF PARENTS

	Name of Father	Year	County	Name of Mother	Year	County
1						
2						
3						
4						
5						
6						
7	Not No1 duplicate enrollment of No4 on 7-1354?					
8	He undoubtedly [illegible....] have been received from inquiries					
9						
10						
11						
12						
13						Date of Application for Enrollment.
14						
15						Aug 22/99
16						
17						

132

Choctaw By Blood Enrollment Cards 1898-1914

RESIDENCE: Armstrong Academy COUNTY. **Choctaw Nation** **Choctaw Roll** CARD No.
POST OFFICE: Academy, I.T. *(Not Including Freedmen)* FIELD No. 3733

Dawes' Roll No.	NAME	Relationship to Person	AGE	SEX	BLOOD	TRIBAL ENROLLMENT		
						Year	County	No.
10555	1 Colbert, Gaines ^16	First Named	13	M	Full	1896	Blue	2906
	2							
	3							
	4							
	5							
	6							
	7							
	8							
	9							
	10							
	11							
	12							
	13							
	14							
	15							
	16							
	17							

ENROLLMENT OF NOS. 1 HEREON APPROVED BY THE SECRETARY OF INTERIOR FEB 4 1903

TRIBAL ENROLLMENT OF PARENTS

	Name of Father	Year	County	Name of Mother	Year	County
1						
2						
3						
4						
5						
6						
7						
8						
9						
10						
11						
12						
13						
14						
15						
16						
17						

Duplicate enrollment of No. 934, not entitled to land or money under this number.
(See Indian Office letter Aug 5-1910 (D.C. #1108-1910))

Date of Application for Enrollment.
Aug 22/99

Choctaw By Blood Enrollment Cards 1898-1914

RESIDENCE: Armstrong Academy COUNTY.
POST OFFICE: Academy, I.T.

Choctaw Nation

Choctaw Roll
(Not Including Freedmen)

CARD NO.
FIELD NO. 3734

Dawes' Roll No.	NAME	Relationship to Person	AGE	SEX	BLOOD	TRIBAL ENROLLMENT		
						Year	County	No.
10556	1 Clay, Solomon 21	First Named	18	M	Full	1896	Blue	2905
	2							
	3							
	4							
	5							
	6							
	7							
	8							
	9							
	10							
	11							
	12							
	13							
	14							
	15							
	16							
	17							

ENROLLMENT
OF NOS. 1
APPROVED BY THE SECRETARY HEREON
OF INTERIOR FEB 4 1903

TRIBAL ENROLLMENT OF PARENTS

Name of Father	Year	County	Name of Mother	Year	County
1 James Clay	dd	Towson	Patsey Clay	Dd	
2					
3					
4					
5					
6					
7 No.1 also on 1896 Choctaw census roll: page 63; No. 2654					
8					
9					
10					
11					
12					
13					
14					Date of Application for Enrollment.
15					Aug 22/99
16					
17					

Choctaw By Blood Enrollment Cards 1898-1914

RESIDENCE: Armstrong Academy COUNTY. **Choctaw Nation** **Choctaw Roll** CARD NO.
POST OFFICE: Academy, I.T. *(Not Including Freedmen)* FIELD NO. 3735

Dawes' Roll No.	NAME	Relationship to Person First Named	AGE	SEX	BLOOD	TRIBAL ENROLLMENT Year	County	No.
10557	1 Williams, Daniel 21		18	M	3/4	1896	Blue	13916
	2							
	3							
	4							
	5							
	6							
	7							
	8							
	9							
	10							
	11							
	12							
	13							
	14							
	15							
	16							
	17							

ENROLLMENT
OF NOS. 1
APPROVED BY THE SECRETARY HEREON
OF INTERIOR FEB 4 1903

TRIBAL ENROLLMENT OF PARENTS

	Name of Father	Year	County	Name of Mother	Year	County
1	Ellis Williams	Dd	Choctaw	Sallie Williams	Dd	Choctaw
2						
3						
4						
5						
6						
7						
8						
9						
10						
11						
12						
13						
14						
15				Date of Application for Enrollment.		Aug 22/99
16						
17						

135

Choctaw By Blood Enrollment Cards 1898-1914

RESIDENCE: Armstrong Academy COUNTY. **Choctaw Nation** Choctaw Roll CARD NO.
POST OFFICE: Academy, I.T. (Not Including Freedmen) FIELD NO. 3736

Dawes' Roll No.	NAME	Relationship to Person First Named	AGE	SEX	BLOOD	TRIBAL ENROLLMENT		
						Year	County	No.
10558	1 Battice, Marcus 22		19	M	1/2	1896	Towson	1110
	2							
	3							
	4	ENROLLMENT						
	5	OF NOS. 1 HEREON APPROVED BY THE SECRETARY						
	6	OF INTERIOR FEB 4 1903						
	7							
	8							
	9							
	10							
	11							
	12							
	13							
	14							
	15							
	16 No1 Died Dec 19, 1905							
	17							

TRIBAL ENROLLMENT OF PARENTS

	Name of Father	Year	County	Name of Mother	Year	County
1						
2						
3						
4						
5						
6						
7						
8						
9						
10						
11						
12						
13						
14						
15				Date of Application for Enrollment.	Aug 22/99	
16						
17 P.O. Miah IT 5/12/03						

Choctaw By Blood Enrollment Cards 1898-1914

RESIDENCE: Armstrong Academy COUNTY.
POST OFFICE: Academy, I.T.

Choctaw Nation

Choctaw Roll
(Not Including Freedmen)

CARD NO.
FIELD NO. 3737

Dawes' Roll No.	NAME	Relationship to Person First Named	AGE	SEX	BLOOD	TRIBAL ENROLLMENT		
						Year	County	No.
10559	1 Pisahabe, Harrison 21	First Named	18	M	Full	1893	Jackson	537
	2							
	3							
	4	ENROLLMENT						
	5	OF NOS. 1 HEREON APPROVED BY THE SECRETARY						
	6	OF INTERIOR FEB 4 1903						
	7							
	8							
	9							
	10							
	11							
	12							
	13							
	14							
	15							
	16							
	17							

TRIBAL ENROLLMENT OF PARENTS

	Name of Father	Year	County	Name of Mother	Year	County
1						
2						
3						
4						
5						
6		On 1893 Pay Roll, Page 62, No. 537				
7		Jackson Co., as Harrison Pisachabbie				
8						
9						
10						
11						
12						
13	"Duplicate enrollment of No. 4466; not entitled to land or money				Date of Application for Enrollment.	
14	under this number." (See Indian Office letter of Sept 2 1910 No 1449-1910)					
15					Aug 22/99	
16						
17						

Choctaw By Blood Enrollment Cards 1898-1914

RESIDENCE: Armstrong Academy COUNTY.
POST OFFICE: Academy, I.T. **Choctaw Nation**
Choctaw Roll
(Not Including Freedmen)
CARD No.
FIELD No. 3738

Dawes' Roll No.	NAME	Relationship to Person First Named	AGE	SEX	BLOOD	TRIBAL ENROLLMENT Year	County	No.
10560	1 Jackson, Sampson 18	First Named	15	M	Full	1896	Jackson	7091
	2							
	3							
	4							
	5							
	6							
	7	ENROLLMENT						
	8	OF NOS. 1 HEREON APPROVED BY THE SECRETARY						
	9	OF INTERIOR FEB 4 1903						
	10							
	11							
	12							
	13							
	14							
	15							
	16							
	17 No.1 also on 1896 Roll No. 7242							

TRIBAL ENROLLMENT OF PARENTS

	Name of Father	Year	County	Name of Mother	Year	County
1	Davis Jackson	Dead	Jackson	Mary Jackson	Dead	Jackson
2						
3						
4						
5						
6						
7						
8						
9						
10						
11						
12						
13						
14						
15				Date of Application for Enrollment.	Aug 22/99	
16						
17						

Choctaw By Blood Enrollment Cards 1898-1914

RESIDENCE: Armstrong Academy ~~COUNTY.~~ **Choctaw Nation**   **Choctaw Roll**   CARD NO.

POST OFFICE: Academy, I.T.   *(Not Including Freedmen)*   FIELD NO. 3739

Dawes' Roll No.	NAME	Relationship to Person First Named	AGE	SEX	BLOOD	TRIBAL ENROLLMENT Year	County	No.
10561	1 Armstrong, Moses ¹⁶	First Named	13	M	1/2	1896	Atoka	416
	2							
	3							
	4							
	5							
	6							
	7							
	8							
	9							
	10							
	11							
	12							
	13							
	14							
	15							
	16							
	17							

ENROLLMENT
OF NOS. 1   HEREON
APPROVED BY THE SECRETARY
OF INTERIOR   FEB 4 1903

TRIBAL ENROLLMENT OF PARENTS

Name of Father	Year	County	Name of Mother	Year	County
1 B Armstrong	Dd				
2					
3					
4					
5					
6					
7					
8					
9					
10					
11					
12					
13					
14				Date of Application for Enrollment.	
15				Aug 22/99	
16					
17					

139

Choctaw By Blood Enrollment Cards 1898-1914

RESIDENCE: Armstrong Academy COUNTY. **Choctaw Nation** **Choctaw Roll** CARD NO.
POST OFFICE: Academy, I.T. *(Not Including Freedmen)* FIELD NO. 3740

Dawes' Roll No.	NAME	Relationship to Person First Named	AGE	SEX	BLOOD	TRIBAL ENROLLMENT		
						Year	County	No.
10562	1 Moore, Willis 20	First Named	17	M	Full	1896	Atoka	8831
	2							
	3							
	4	ENROLLMENT						
	5	OF NOS. 1 HEREON						
		APPROVED BY THE SECRETARY						
	6	OF INTERIOR FEB 4 1903						
	7							
	8							
	9							
	10							
	11							
	12							
	13							
	14							
	15							
	16							
	17							

TRIBAL ENROLLMENT OF PARENTS

Name of Father	Year	County	Name of Mother	Year	County
1 Thomas Moore	Dead			Dead	
2					
3					
4					
5					
6					
7 No.1 is a duplicate of No.1 on Choctaw card #4348.					
8 No.1 is the husband of Fannie Moore on Choctaw card #4206.					
9 For child of No.1 see NB (March 3,1905) #1347					
10					
11					
12					
13					
14				Date of Application for Enrollment	
15				Aug 22/99	
16					
17 P.O. Calloway, I.T. Dec 3 1904					

140

Choctaw By Blood Enrollment Cards 1898-1914

RESIDENCE: Armstrong Academy COUNTY. **Choctaw Nation** **Choctaw Roll** CARD No.
POST OFFICE: Academy, I.T. (Not Including Freedmen) FIELD No. 3741

Dawes' Roll No.	NAME	Relationship to Person	AGE	SEX	BLOOD	TRIBAL ENROLLMENT		
						Year	County	No.
10563	1 Nicholas, Ephraim	First Named	16	M	Full	1896	Blue	9827
	2							
	3							
	4							
	5							
	6							
	7							
	8							
	9							
	10							
	11							
	12							
	13							
	14							
	15							
	16							
	17							

ENROLLMENT HEREON
OF NOS. 1
APPROVED BY THE SECRETARY
OF INTERIOR FEB 4 1903

TRIBAL ENROLLMENT OF PARENTS

	Name of Father	Year	County	Name of Mother	Year	County
1						
2						
3						
4						
5						
6						
7						
8						
9						
10						
11						
12						
13						
14						Date of Application for Enrollment.
15						Aug 22/99
16						
17						

141

Choctaw By Blood Enrollment Cards 1898-1914

RESIDENCE: **Blue**   COUNTY.

POST OFFICE: Bok Chito, I.T.   **Choctaw Nation**

Choctaw Roll *(Not Including Freedmen)*

CARD NO.

FIELD NO. 3742

Dawes' Roll No.	NAME		Relationship to Person	AGE	SEX	BLOOD	TRIBAL ENROLLMENT		
							Year	County	No.
10564	1 Senter, Lavinia S	55	First Named	52	F	1/8	1896	Blue	11606
10565	2 Lewis, Florence E	32	Dau	29	"	1/16	1896	"	11607
10566	3 " Rush C	28	Son	25	M	1/16	1896	Blue	8211
10567	4 " Dora L	25	Dau	22	F	1/16	1896	"	8212
10568	5 " James W	16	Son	13	M	1/16	1896	"	8213
	6								
	7								
	8								
	9	ENROLLMENT							
	10	OF NOS. 1,2,3,4 and 5 HEREON APPROVED BY THE SECRETARY							
	11	OF INTERIOR FEB 4 1903							
	12								
	13								
	14								
	15								
	16								
	17								

TRIBAL ENROLLMENT OF PARENTS

	Name of Father	Year	County	Name of Mother	Year	County
1	Chas. F. Stewart	Dead	Non Citz	Triphena Stewart	Dead	Jackson
2	Charles Lewis		" "	No1		
3	" "		" "	No1		
4	" "		" "	No1		
5	" "		" "	No1		
6						
7	No1 on 1896 roll as Lavina S Senter					
8	All were admitted by Act of Choctaw Council, No 13. Approved October 29, 1887.					
9	No1 was admitted as Lavinia S. Lewis					
10	No2 " " " James F Lewis					
11	As to residence of above parties, see testimony of No1					
12	No.2 also on 1896 roll, page 300, #11607 as Florence E. Stewart					
13						
14					Date of Application for Enrollment.	
15					Aug 22/99	
16						
17	P.O. Antlers, I.T. 12/6 '02					

Choctaw By Blood Enrollment Cards 1898-1914

RESIDENCE: Blue		COUNTY. **Choctaw Nation**		**Choctaw Roll** (Not Including Freedmen)	CARD NO.	
POST OFFICE: Caddo, I.T.					FIELD NO. 3743	

Dawes' Roll No.	NAME	Relationship to Person First Named	AGE	SEX	BLOOD	Year	TRIBAL ENROLLMENT County	No.
1	Smith, Thomas H. P.	Named	36	M	1/8		D	
2	" Martha J	Wife	27	F	I.W.		D	
3	" Mary M	Dau	9	"	1/16		D	
4	" Annie	"	7	"	1/16		D	
5	" Laura V	"	22mo	"	1/16		Dis	
6	" Addie	"	3mo	"	1/16		Dis	
7	" Thomas H.P. Jr	Son	2mo	M	1/16		Dis	
8								
9								
10	#5-6-7 DISMISSED							
11	NOV 12 1904							

DENIED CITIZENSHIP BY THE CHOCTAW AND
Nos 3&4 CHICKASAW CITIZENSHIP COURT

TRIBAL ENROLLMENT OF PARENTS

	Name of Father	Year	County	Name of Mother	Year	County
1	W.H.P. Smith	Dead	Non Citz	Mary A. Loving		Choctaw
2	H.W. Anderson		" "	Mary Anderson	Dead	Non Citz
3	No1			No2		
4	No1			No2		
5	No1			No2		
6	No.1			No.2		
7	Nº1			Nº2		

9 Nos 1,2,3,4 denied in 96 Case #546 (2,3 & 4 ?)
10 All but No5 were admitted by U.S. Court Central Dist., Sept 11/97, Case No 71. As
11 to residence and birth of No5 Oct. 19/97,
12 see testimony of No1
13 Judgment of U.S. Ct admitting Nos 1 to 4 inc vacated and set aside by Decree of Choctaw Chickasaw Cit Court Decr 17'02
14 No.6 Enrolled, June 7, 1900
15 Nº7 Born July 25, 1902: enrolled Sept 24, 1902.
Nos 1 to 7 inc now in C.C.C.C. Case #107
17 P.O. Matoy I.T. 9/24/02

Date of Application for Enrollment.
Aug 22/99

Nos 5,6&7 dismissed by C.C.C.C. for want of [illegible]

143

Choctaw By Blood Enrollment Cards 1898-1914

RESIDENCE: **Blue**   COUNTY. **Choctaw Nation**   **Choctaw Roll**   CARD NO.
POST OFFICE: Caddo, I.T.   *(Not Including Freedmen)*   FIELD NO. **3744**

Dawes' Roll No.	NAME		Relationship to Person First Named	AGE	SEX	BLOOD	TRIBAL ENROLLMENT		
							Year	County	No.
10569	1 Folsom, Alice	36	First Named	33	F	Full	1896	Blue	4346
10570	2 " Tandy	16	Son	13	M	"	1896	"	4347
10571	3 " Annie	9	Dau	6	F	"	1896	"	4348
10572	4 " Oscar	8	Son	5	M	"	1896	"	4349
10573	5 " Junior	4	Dau	1	F	"			
	6								
	7								
	8								
	9								
	10								
	11								
	12								
	13								
	14								
	15								
	16								
	17								

ENROLLMENT
OF NOS. 1,2,3,4 and 5 HEREON
APPROVED BY THE SECRETARY
OF INTERIOR FEB 4 1903

TRIBAL ENROLLMENT OF PARENTS

	Name of Father	Year	County	Name of Mother	Year	County
1	Impson Jones	Dead	Blue	Jincey Jones		Blue
2	John Folsom		"	No1		
3	" "		"	No1		
4	" "		"	No1		
5	" "		"	No1		
6						
7						
8			No5 Affidavit of birth to be			
9			supplied:- Recd Oct 7/99			
10			No.3 on 1896 Roll as Fannie Folsom.			
11						
12						
13						
14					Date of Application for Enrollment.	
15					Aug 22/99	
16						
17						

Choctaw By Blood Enrollment Cards 1898-1914

RESIDENCE: Blue
POST OFFICE: Caddo, I.T.

COUNTY. **Choctaw Nation**

Choctaw Roll CARD NO.
(Not Including Freedmen) FIELD NO. 3745

Dawes' Roll No.	NAME	Relationship to Person First Named	AGE	SEX	BLOOD	TRIBAL ENROLLMENT Year	County	No.
10574	1 Fletcher, Melvina 43	First Named	40	F	1/2	1896	Blue	4323
10575	2 Lewis, Joslin 23	Son	20	M	3/4	1893	"	756
10576	3 " Peter 20	"	17	"	3/4	1896	"	8240
10577	4 Fletcher, Sophia 14	Dau	11	F	3/4	1896	"	4324
	5							
	6	ENROLLMENT						
	7	OF NOS. 1,2,3 and 4 HEREON						
	8	APPROVED BY THE SECRETARY OF INTERIOR FEB 4 1903						
	9							
	10							
	11							
	12							
	13							
	14							
	15							
	16							
	17							

TRIBAL ENROLLMENT OF PARENTS

Name of Father	Year	County	Name of Mother	Year	County
1 Jas. Loving	Dead	Chickasaw	Martha Washington	Dead	Blue
2 Abel Lewis	"	Blue	No1		
3 " "	"	"	No1		
4 Jackson Fletcher	"	"	No1		
5					
6					
7					
8	No2 on 1893 Pay roll, Page 72, No 756, Blue Co				
9	No.2 also on 1896 Choctaw roll as Julious Lewis, page 205, #8239				
10					
11					
12					
13					
14					
15			Date of Application for Enrollment	Aug 22/99	
16					
17					

145

Choctaw By Blood Enrollment Cards 1898-1914

RESIDENCE: **Blue**   COUNTY. **Choctaw Nation**   **Choctaw Roll** CARD NO.

POST OFFICE: **Caddo, I.T.**   *(Not Including Freedmen)* FIELD NO. **3746**

Dawes' Roll No.	NAME	Relationship to Person	AGE	SEX	BLOOD	TRIBAL ENROLLMENT		
						Year	County	No.
10578	1 Johnson, Agnes 24	First Named	21	F	Full	1893	Blue	770
	2							
	3							
	4							
	5	ENROLLMENT						
	6	OF NOS. 1 HEREON APPROVED BY THE SECRETARY						
	7	OF INTERIOR FEB 4 1903						
	8							
	9							
	10							
	11							
	12							
	13							
	14							
	15							
	16							
	17							

TRIBAL ENROLLMENT OF PARENTS

Name of Father	Year	County	Name of Mother	Year	County
1 Eastman Brewer	Dead	Blue	Minerva Brewer	Dead	Blue
2					
3					
4					
5					
6	On 1893 Pay roll, Page 73, No 770, Blue Co.,				
7	as Agnes Brewer				
8	For child of No1 see NB (Act Mar 3 '05) Card #263				
9					
10					
11					
12					
13					
14					
15				Date of Application for Enrollment.	Aug 22/99
16					
17					

RESIDENCE:	Blue	COUNTY.	**Choctaw Nation**		**Choctaw Roll** *(Not Including Freedmen)*	CARD No.
POST OFFICE:	Caddo, I.T.					FIELD No. 3747

Dawes' Roll No.	NAME		Relationship to Person	AGE	SEX	BLOOD	TRIBAL ENROLLMENT		
							Year	County	No.
I.W. 347	1 Halpin, Michael	44	First Named	41	M	IW	1896	Blue	14646
10579	2 " Margaret	26	Wife	23	F	1/2	1896	Blue	5853
10580	3 " Oscar	6	Son	3	M	1/4	1896	"	5854
	4								
	5								
	6	ENROLLMENT OF NOS. 2 and 3 HEREON							
	7	APPROVED BY THE SECRETARY							
	8	OF INTERIOR FEB 4 1903							
	9	ENROLLMENT OF NOS. 1 HEREON							
	10	APPROVED BY THE SECRETARY							
	11	OF INTERIOR SEP 12 1903							
	12								
	13								
	14								
	15								
	16								
	17								

TRIBAL ENROLLMENT OF PARENTS

	Name of Father	Year	County	Name of Mother	Year	County
1	John Halpin		Non Citz	Mary Halpin		Non Citz
2	Bartholomew Lane		Intermarried	Frances Lane		Blue
3	No 1			No 2		
4						
5						
6						
7	No 1 was admitted by Dawes Com. Case No 406					
8	No 1 on 1896 roll as Michael Helpin					
9	Surname of No's 2 and 3 is Halpine on 1896 Roll.					
10						
11						
12						
13						
14					Date of Application for Enrollment.	
15					Aug 22/99	
16						
17						

Choctaw By Blood Enrollment Cards 1898-1914

RESIDENCE: Jackson   COUNTY. **Choctaw Nation**   **Choctaw Roll**   CARD NO.
POST OFFICE: Crowder, I.T.   *(Not Including Freedmen)*   FIELD NO. **3748**

Dawes' Roll No.	NAME		Relationship to Person First Named	AGE	SEX	BLOOD	TRIBAL ENROLLMENT		
							Year	County	No.
I.W. 976	1 Hunt, John	58	First Named	48	M	I.W.	1896	Jackson	14644
	2								
	3								
	4								
	5								
	6	Take no further action relative to enrollment of No.							
	7	Protest of Attys for Choctaw and Chickasaw Nations							
	8	Jan 25 '04							
	9	Protest overruled March 31, 1904 by Dept.							
	10								
	11								
	12								
	13								
	14	ENROLLMENT							
	15	OF NOS. ~~~ 1 ~~~ HEREON APPROVED BY THE SECRETARY							
	16	OF INTERIOR Sep 22, 1904							
	17								

TRIBAL ENROLLMENT OF PARENTS

	Name of Father	Year	County	Name of Mother	Year	County
1	Andres Hunt	Dead	Non Citz	Polly Hunt	Dead	Non Citz
2						
3						
4						
5						
6	No.1 see decision of July 19 '04					
7						
8	Admitted by Dawes Com, Case No. 192.					
9	On 1896 Roll Jno. Hunt					
10	For child of No1 see NB (Apr 26-06) #1117					
11						
12						
13						
14					Date of Application for Enrollment.	
15					Aug 22/99	
16						
17						

		RESIDENCE:	Jackson						

RESIDENCE: **Jackson** COUNTY. **Choctaw Nation** **Choctaw Roll** CARD No.
POST OFFICE: **Bennington, I.T.** (Not Including Freedmen) FIELD No. **3749**

Dawes' Roll No.	NAME		Relationship to Person	AGE	SEX	BLOOD	TRIBAL ENROLLMENT		
							Year	County	No.
10581	1 Frazier, John	33	First Named	30	M	Full	1896	Jackson	4291
10582	2 " Mary	33	Wife	30	F	"	1896	"	4293
10583	3 " Virgie	11	Dau	8	"	"	1896	"	4294
10584	4 " Ben	9	Son	6	M	"	1896	"	4295
10585	5 " Emma	4	Dau	1	F	"			
DEAD	6 " ~~Phelena~~	2	"	2mo	F	"			
	7								
	8								
	9	ENROLLMENT OF NOS. 1,2,3,4 and 5 HEREON							
	10	APPROVED BY THE SECRETARY OF INTERIOR Feb 4, 1903							
	11	No. 6 hereon dismissed under order of							
	12	~~the Commission to the Five Civilized~~							
	13	~~Tribes of March 31, 1905.~~							
	14								
	15								
	16								
	17								

TRIBAL ENROLLMENT OF PARENTS

	Name of Father	Year	County	Name of Mother	Year	County
1	Ben Frazier	Dead	Blue	Melvina Frazier	Dead	Blue
2	Jackson Stewart	"	"	Siney Stewart	"	"
3	No1			No2		
4	No1			No2		
5	No1			No2		
6	~~No1~~			~~No2~~		
7						
8	No5 Affidavit of birth to be					
9	supplied: filed Nov. 2/99					
10	No6 Enrolled April 1, 1901					
	~~No6 died Aug 20 1902: proof of death filed Dec. 6 1902~~					
11	For child of No.1 see NB (Act Mar. 3095) Card #261					
12						
13						
14					#1 to 5	
15				Date of Application for Enrollment	Aug 22/99	
16						
17	P.O. Mayhew I.T. 12/2 '02					

P.O. Boswell I.T. 3/25/03

Choctaw By Blood Enrollment Cards 1898-1914

RESIDENCE: **Blue** COUNTY. **Choctaw Nation** **Choctaw Roll** CARD NO.
POST OFFICE: **Blue, I.T.** (Not Including Freedmen) FIELD NO. **3750**

Dawes' Roll No.	NAME	Relationship to Person First Named	AGE	SEX	BLOOD	TRIBAL ENROLLMENT Year	County	No.
10586	1 Anderson, Robinson D 43	First Named	40	M	Full	1896	Blue	395
10587	2 " Frank 21	Son	18	"	"	1896	"	397
10588	3 " Gilbert 17	"	14	"	"	1896	"	398
10589	4 " Nancy 7	Dau	4	F	"	1896	"	399
	5							
	6							
	7	ENROLLMENT						
	8	OF NOS. 1,2,3 and 4 HEREON APPROVED BY THE SECRETARY						
	9	OF INTERIOR Feb 4, 1903						
	10							
	11							
	12							
	13							
	14							
	15							
	16							
	17							

TRIBAL ENROLLMENT OF PARENTS

	Name of Father	Year	County	Name of Mother	Year	County
1	Chas. Anderson	Dead	Blue	Sophia Anderson	Dead	Blue
2	No1			Louisa Anderson	"	"
3	No1			" "	"	"
4	No1			Lourena "	"	"
5						
6						
7						
8	No.1 on 1896 roll as R. D. Anderson					
9	No.2 is now the husband of Elsie Baker on Choctaw Card #3832			Aug 4,	1902.	
10						
11	For child of No3 see NB (Apr 26 '06) #1272					
12	" " " 2 " " (Mar 3-05) #255					
13						
14						
15				Date of Application for Enrollment.	Aug 22/99	
16						
17						

Choctaw By Blood Enrollment Cards 1898-1914

RESIDENCE: Jackson   COUNTY.   **Choctaw Nation**   **Choctaw Roll** CARD NO.
POST OFFICE: Jackson, I.T.   *(Not Including Freedmen)*   FIELD NO. **3751**

Dawes' Roll No.	NAME	Relationship to Person Named	AGE	SEX	BLOOD	TRIBAL ENROLLMENT Year	County	No.
10590	₁ Harrison, James D ⁶⁶	First Named	63	M	Full	1896	Atoka	5938
10591	₂ Anderson, Lita ¹⁶	Niece	13	F	"	1893	"	596
15842	₃ LeFlore, Sarah	Dau of No2	1	F	"			
	₄							
	₅							
	₆	ENROLLMENT						
	₇	OF NOS. 1 and 2 HEREON APPROVED BY THE SECRETARY						
	₈	OF INTERIOR Feb 4, 1903						
	₉							
	₁₀	ENROLLMENT						
	₁₁	OF NOS. ~~~ 3 ~~~ HEREON APPROVED BY THE SECRETARY						
	₁₂	OF INTERIOR Jun 12, 1905						
	₁₃							
	₁₄							
	₁₅							
	₁₆							
	₁₇							

TRIBAL ENROLLMENT OF PARENTS

	Name of Father	Year	County	Name of Mother	Year	County
₁	Ton Harrison	Dead	Cedar	E-la-key	Dead	Blue
₂	Henry Anderson	"	Atoka	Edna Anderson	"	Atoka
₃	Joshua LeFlore		Choctaw	No2		
₄						
₅						
₆						
₇						
₈						
₉						
₁₀	No.1 on 1896 roll as J. D. Harrison					
₁₁	No.2 on 1893 Pay Roll Page 57, No 596, Atoka					
₁₂	Co. as Lidda John					
₁₃						
₁₄	No3 was born Aug 3, 1902: Application made and No4 placed on this card March 27, 1905, under Act of Congress approved March 3, 1905.					
₁₅	See 7-4174 for father of No3			Date of Application for Enrollment	Aug 22/99	
₁₆	For child of No 2 see NB (Act March 3 '05) Card #262			➤ 1&2		
₁₇						

No2 P.O. Boswell I.T.   3/25/1901

Choctaw By Blood Enrollment Cards 1898-1914

RESIDENCE: **Blue** COUNTY. **Choctaw Nation** **Choctaw Roll** (Not Including Freedmen) CARD NO.
POST OFFICE: **Bennington, I.T.** FIELD NO. **3752**

Dawes' Roll No.	NAME	Relationship to Person First Named	AGE	SEX	BLOOD	TRIBAL ENROLLMENT		
						Year	County	No.
10592	₁ Hoparkentubbi, David ⁴⁵ ᴰᴵᴱᴰ ᴾᴿᴵᴼᴿ ᵀᴼ ˢᴱᴾᵀᴱᴹᴮᴱᴿ ²⁵ᵗʰ 1902	First Named	42	M	Full	1896	Jackson	5799
14810	₂ " Isabelle ²⁴	Wife	21	F	"	1896	"	5800
10593	₃ " Eastman ¹⁵	Son	12	M	"	1896	"	5805
10594	₄ " Wesley ⁴	"	6mo	"	"			
	₅							
	₆	ENROLLMENT OF NOS. 1, 3 and 4 HEREON APPROVED BY THE SECRETARY OF INTERIOR Feb 4, 1903						
	₇							
	₈							
	₉							
	₁₀							
	₁₁	ENROLLMENT OF NOS. 2 HEREON APPROVED BY THE SECRETARY OF INTERIOR May 20, 1903						
	₁₂							
	₁₃							
	₁₄							
	₁₅							
	₁₆							
	₁₇							

TRIBAL ENROLLMENT OF PARENTS

	Name of Father	Year	County	Name of Mother	Year	County
₁	Simon Hoparkentubbi	Dead	Blue	Siney Hoparkentubbi	Dead	Blue
₂	Eastman M°Gee		Jackson	Sicily Homma		"
₃	No1			Siney Hoparkentubbi	Dead	Jackson
₄	No1			No2		
₅						
₆						
₇						
₈	No4 "Died prior to September 25, 1902, not entitled to land or money." See Indian office letter Feb 29, 1908 (I.T. 3941-1908)					
₉	No4 affidavit of birth to be supplied:- Filed Nov. 2/99					
₁₀						
₁₁	No1 Died May 14, 1902. Proof of death filed Jany 29, 1903					
₁₂	No2 is living. See her letter filed Jany 29, 1903					
₁₃	No1 died May 14, 1902: Enrollment cancelled by Department July 8, 1904 For child of No2 see NB (Apr 26-06) Card #443					
₁₄	" " " " " " " (Mar 3-05) " "263.					
₁₅				Date of Application for Enrollment.	Aug 23/99	
₁₆						
₁₇						

152

Choctaw By Blood Enrollment Cards 1898-1914

RESIDENCE: Blue   COUNTY.   **Choctaw Nation**   **Choctaw Roll**   CARD NO.
POST OFFICE: Bennington, I.T.   *(Not Including Freedmen)*   FIELD NO. 3753

Dawes' Roll No.	NAME	Relationship to Person	AGE	SEX	BLOOD	TRIBAL ENROLLMENT		
						Year	County	No.
10595	1 Houston, Cicily ⁶³	First Named	60	F	Full	1896	Blue	5870
	2							
	3							
	4							
	5	ENROLLMENT OF NOS. 1 HEREON						
	6	APPROVED BY THE SECRETARY						
	7	OF INTERIOR FEB 4 1903						
	8							
	9							
	10							
	11							
	12							
	13							
	14							
	15							
	16							
	17							

TRIBAL ENROLLMENT OF PARENTS

	Name of Father	Year	County	Name of Mother	Year	County
1		Dead	Atoka		Dead	Atoka
2						
3						
4						
5						
6		On 1896 roll as Sisby Huston				
7						
8						
9						
10						
11						
12						
13						
14					Date of Application for Enrollment.	
15					Aug 23/99	
16						
17						

153

Choctaw By Blood Enrollment Cards 1898-1914

RESIDENCE: Jackson   COUNTY. **Choctaw Nation**   **Choctaw Roll** CARD NO.
POST OFFICE: Bennington, I.T.   (Not Including Freedmen)   FIELD NO. 3754

Dawes' Roll No.	NAME		Relationship to Person First Named	AGE	SEX	BLOOD	TRIBAL ENROLLMENT		
							Year	County	No.
10596	1 Durant, Joseph S	41	First Named	38	M	Full	1896	Jackson	3477
10597	2 DIED PRIOR TO SEPTEMBER 25, 2002 Susan		Wife	27	F	"	1896	"	3478
10598	3 " Martha	20	Dau	17	"	"	1896	"	3479
10599	4 " Rena	18	"	15	"	"	1896	"	3480
10600	5 " Hattie	12	"	9	"	"	1896	"	3481
10601	6 " Mollie	10	"	7	"	"	1896	"	3482
10602	7 " Austin	15	Son	12	M	"	1896	"	3483
10603	8 " B.	9	"	6	"	"	1896	"	3484
10604	9 " Mary	3	Dau	2mo	F	"			
	10								
	11	ENROLLMENT							
	12	OF NOS. 1,2,3,4,5,6,7,8,9 HEREON APPROVED BY THE SECRETARY							
	13	OF INTERIOR FEB 4 1903							
	14								
	15								
	16								
	17								

TRIBAL ENROLLMENT OF PARENTS

	Name of Father	Year	County	Name of Mother	Year	County
1	Besand Durant	Dead	Jackson	Liley Durant		Jackson
2	W^m LeFlore		"	Liney LeFlore	Dead	"
3	No1			No2		
4	No1			No2		
5	No1			No2		
6	No1			No2		
7	No1			No2		
8	No1			No2		
9	No1			No2		
10						
11						
12	No1 on 1896 roll as J. S. Durant					
13	No6 " 1896 " " Millie "					
14	No9 Affidavit of birth to be supplied:- Recd Oct 7/99				Date of Application for Enrollment.	
15	No.2 died April 11, 1902; Enrollment cancelled by Department July 8, 1904				Aug 23/99	
16	For child of No4 see NB (Apr 26 '06) Card #254					
17	" " " " 3 " (Mar 3 '05) " #264					

154

RESIDENCE:	Jackson	COUNTY.	**Choctaw Nation**	Choctaw Roll	CARD No.
POST OFFICE:	Bennington, I.T.			*(Not Including Freedmen)*	FIELD No. 3755

Dawes' Roll No.	NAME	Relationship to Person First Named	AGE	SEX	BLOOD	TRIBAL ENROLLMENT		
						Year	County	No.
DEAD: 1	Durant, Lila	Named	60	F	Full	1896	Jackson	3469
DEAD: 2	" Nancy	Dau	35	"	"	1896	"	3471
3								
4	No. 1 and 2 HEREON DISMISSED UNDER							
5	ORDER OF THE COMMISSION TO THE FIVE							
6	CIVILIZED TRIBES OF MARCH 31, 1905.							
7								
8								
9								
10								
11								
12								
13								
14								
15								
16								
17								

TRIBAL ENROLLMENT OF PARENTS

Name of Father	Year	County	Name of Mother	Year	County
1 Benj Battiest	Dead		Susie Battiest	Dead	
2 Besand Durant	"	Jackson	No1		
3					
4					
5					
6					
7		No1 on 1896 roll as Lily Durant			
8					
9		No1 dead May 11, 1902; proof of death filed Nov 28 1902			
10		No2 " Feb. 20, 1902; " " " " " "			
11					
12					
13					
14				Date of Application for Enrollment.	
15				Aug 23/99	
16					
17					

Choctaw By Blood Enrollment Cards 1898-1914

RESIDENCE: Jackson   COUNTY.
POST OFFICE: Bennington, I.T.

Choctaw Nation

Choctaw Roll
(Not Including Freedmen)

CARD No.
FIELD No. 3756

Dawes' Roll No.	NAME	Relationship to Person First Named	AGE	SEX	BLOOD	TRIBAL ENROLLMENT		
						Year	County	No.
10605	1 Durant, Sophia 44		41	F	Full	1896	Jackson	3470
10606	2 Crowder, Rachel DIED PRIOR TO SEPTEMBER 25 1902	Dau	14	"	3/4	1896	"	2839
	3							
	4							
	5							
	6							
	7	ENROLLMENT OF NOS. 1 and 2 HEREON APPROVED BY THE SECRETARY OF INTERIOR FEB 4 1903						
	8							
	9							
	10							
	11							
	12							
	13							
	14							
	15							
	16							
	17							

TRIBAL ENROLLMENT OF PARENTS

	Name of Father	Year	County	Name of Mother	Year	County
1	Besand Durant	Dead	Jackson	Lila Durant		Jackson
2	Josh Crowder	"	"	No 1		
3						
4						
5						
6						
7						
8						
9						
10	No 2 died Feb. 5, 1901; Enrollment cancelled by Department July 8, 1904					
11						
12						
13						
14						Date of Application for Enrollment.
15						Aug 23/99
16						
17						

156

Choctaw By Blood Enrollment Cards 1898-1914

RESIDENCE: **Blue** COUNTY. **Choctaw Nation** CARD NO.
POST OFFICE: **Caddo, I.T.** Choctaw Roll *(Not Including Freedmen)* FIELD NO. **3757**

Dawes' Roll No.	NAME	Relationship to Person First Named	AGE	SEX	BLOOD	TRIBAL ENROLLMENT		
						Year	County	No.
14376	1 Pitchlynn, Edward E ⁴²	First Named	39	M	1/4	1896	Eagle	10402
	2							
	3							
	4	ENROLLMENT OF NOS. 1 HEREON APPROVED BY THE SECRETARY OF INTERIOR APR 11 1903						
	5							
	6							
	7							
	8							
	9							
	10							
	11							
	12							
	13							
	14							
	15							
	16							
	17							

TRIBAL ENROLLMENT OF PARENTS

	Name of Father	Year	County	Name of Mother	Year	County
1	Peter P. Pitchlynn	Dead	Eagle	Carrie Pitchlynn	Dead	Eagle
2						
3						
4						
5						
6	On 1896 roll as Everett Pitchlynn					
7						
8	As to residence see his testimony					
9						
10	No1 admitted as a citizen by blood by Dawes Commission					
11	Choctaw Case #589: No appeal. No.1 is now the husband of Sudie Maytubby on Chickasaw card #1242 July 19, 1901					
12	Evidence of marriage between No1 and Sudie Maytubby filed in Chickasaw Case					
13	#1242 Aug 21, 1901					
14	For child of No1 see NB (Apr 26-06) Chickasaw Card #69				Date of Application for Enrollment.	
15	" " " " " (Mar 3-05) " #190				Aug 23/99	
16						
17						

157

Choctaw By Blood Enrollment Cards 1898-1914

RESIDENCE: **Blue** COUNTY. **Choctaw Nation** Choctaw Roll CARD NO.
POST OFFICE: Bok Chito, I.T. *(Not Including Freedmen)* FIELD NO. 3758

Dawes' Roll No.	NAME	Relationship to Person First Named	AGE	SEX	BLOOD	TRIBAL ENROLLMENT Year	County	No.
DEAD	1 Lauchner, Susan	Named	28	F	1/2	1896	Blue	8195
10607	2 " Fannie M 6	Dau	3	"	1/4			
10608	3 " Fidelia E 4	"	1	"	1/4			
	4							
	5							
	6 ENROLLMENT							
	7 OF NOS. 2 and 3 HEREON APPROVED BY THE SECRETARY							
	8 OF INTERIOR FEB 4 1903							
	9 No. 1 HEREON DISMISSED UNDER							
	10 ORDER OF THE COMMISSION TO THE FIVE							
	11 CIVILIZED TRIBES OF MARCH 31, 1905.							
	12							
	13							
	14							
	15							
	16							
	17							

TRIBAL ENROLLMENT OF PARENTS

Name of Father	Year	County	Name of Mother nee Forman	Year	County
1 Calvin Beams	Dead	Blue	Caroline Beams	Dead	Cherokee
2 Grant Lauchner		Non Citz	No1		
3 " "		" "	No1		
4					
5					
6					
7 No1 on 1893 Pay Roll, Page 10, No 110, Blue Co,					
8 as Susan Beams					
9					
10 No1 See if name of Caroline Foreman, mother, appears on Cherokee Rolls – she died in 1872. No Cherokee rolls back of '80					
11					
12					
13 Nos 2-3 Affidavits of birth to be					
14 supplied:- Recd Oct 7/99					
15 No1 Died May 14, 1901; Proof of death filed Nov 10 1902			Date of Application for Enrollment.	Aug 23/99	
16					
17					

158

Choctaw By Blood Enrollment Cards 1898-1914

RESIDENCE:	Blue	COUNTY.					Choctaw Roll	CARD NO.	
POST OFFICE:	Bok Chito, I.T.	**Choctaw Nation**					(Not Including Freedmen)	FIELD NO. 3759	

Dawes' Roll No.	NAME	Relationship to Person	AGE	SEX	BLOOD	TRIBAL ENROLLMENT		
						Year	County	No.
10609	1 Roberson, Margaret 68	First Named	65	F	1/2	1896	Blue	10927
10610	2 " Ruth 8	Ward	5	"	1/4			
	3							
	4							
	5							
	6							
	7	ENROLLMENT OF NOS. 1 and 2 HEREON						
	8	APPROVED BY THE SECRETARY OF INTERIOR FEB 4 1903						
	9							
	10							
	11							
	12							
	13							
	14							
	15							
	16							
	17							

TRIBAL ENROLLMENT OF PARENTS

	Name of Father	Year	County	Name of Mother	Year	County
1	Lewis Roberson	Dead	Non Citz	Mary Roberson	Dead	Eagle
2	George Quell		" "	Liza Quell	"	Blue
3						
4						
5						
6						
7						
8	No2 As to marriage of parents, see					
9	testimony of No1					
10						
11	Mother of No3 on Blue County Roll 1893 No 224 as Eliza Caldwell					
12						
13						
14					Date of Application for Enrollment.	
15					Aug 23/99	
16						
17						

Choctaw By Blood Enrollment Cards 1898-1914

RESIDENCE: Jackson COUNTY. **Choctaw Nation** Choctaw Roll CARD NO:
POST OFFICE: Bennington, I.T. *(Not Including Freedmen)* FIELD NO. 3760

Dawes' Roll No.	NAME		Relationship to Person First Named	AGE	SEX	BLOOD	TRIBAL ENROLLMENT		
							Year	County	No.
10611	1 Hampton, Joe	49	First Named	46	M	Full	1896	Jackson	5816
10612	2 " Ellen	43	Wife	40	F	"	1896	"	5817
10613	3 " Isaac	24	Son	21	M	"	1896	"	5818
10614	4 " Thomas ~~DIED PRIOR TO SEPTEMBER 25, 1902~~		"	20	"	"	1896	"	5819
10615	5 " Alex	21	"	18	"	"	1896	"	5820
10616	6 " Susan ~~DIED PRIOR TO SEPTEMBER 25, 1902~~		Dau	13	F	"	1896	"	5821
10617	7 " Bennie	10	Son	7	M	"	1896	"	5822
10618	8 " Alice	7	Dau	4	F	"	1896	"	5823
10619	9 " Michael	5	Son	1	M	"			
	10								
	11								
	12	ENROLLMENT OF NOS. 1,2,3,4,5,6,7,8 and 9 HEREON							
	13	APPROVED BY THE SECRETARY							
	14	OF INTERIOR FEB 4 1903							
	15								
	16								
	17								

TRIBAL ENROLLMENT OF PARENTS

	Name of Father	Year	County	Name of Mother	Year	County
1	Isaac Hampton	Dead	Red River	Na-ka-ne-ho-ke	Dead	Bok Tuklo
2	Robin Jones	"	Jackson	Phillis Jones	"	Jackson
3	No1			No2		
4	~~No1~~			~~No2~~		
5	No1			No2		
6	~~No1~~			~~No2~~		
7	No1			No2		
8	No1			No2		
9	No1			No2		
10			No4 on 1896 roll as Tommie Hampton			
11			No9 Affidavit of birth to be supplied:- Filed Nov 2/99			
12			~~No1 died Dec 21, 1901. No2 died Jan 6, 1902. Enrollment cancelled by Department July 8, 1904~~			
13			For child of No3 see NB (Mar 3-05) Card #264			
14					Date of Application for Enrollment.	
15					Aug 23/99	
16						
17						

Choctaw By Blood Enrollment Cards 1898-1914

RESIDENCE:	Blue		
POST OFFICE:	Caddo, I.T.		

COUNTY. **Choctaw Nation**

Choctaw Roll *(Not Including Freedmen)*

CARD NO.

FIELD NO. 376

Dawes' Roll No.	NAME	Relationship to Person	AGE	SEX	BLOOD	TRIBAL ENROLLMENT		
						Year	County	No.
10620	1 Faudree, Dora ⁣ 38	First Named	35	F	1/4	1896	Blue	4344
10621	2 Hampton, Flossie ⁣ 18	Dau	15	"	3/8			5862
10622	3 " Julius C. ⁣ 16	Son	13	M	3/8			5863
10623	4 Faudree, Thomas R ⁣ 1	Son	2mo	M	1/8			
	5							
	6							
	7	ENROLLMENT						
	8	OF NOS. 1,2,3 and 4 HEREON						
	9	APPROVED BY THE SECRETARY OF INTERIOR FEB 6 1903						
	10							
	11							
	12							
	13							
	14							
	15							
	16							
	17							

TRIBAL ENROLLMENT OF PARENTS

Name of Father	Year	County	Name of Mother	Year	County
1 Caleb Impson	Dead	Blue	Melina Freeney		Blue
2 Julius C. Hampton		"	No1		
3 " " "		"	No1		
4 C. J. Faudree		noncitizen	No.1		
5					
6					
7					
8	No.4 Born Feby 24, 1902. Enrolled April 11, 1902				
9					
10					
11					
12					
13				#1 to 3	
14				Date of Application for Enrollment.	
15				Aug 23/99	
16					
17					

161

Choctaw By Blood Enrollment Cards 1898-1914

RESIDENCE: Blue   COUNTY. **Choctaw Nation**   **Choctaw Roll**   CARD NO.
POST OFFICE: Bok Chito, I.T.   *(Not Including Freedmen)*   FIELD NO. **3762**

Dawes' Roll No.	NAME	Relationship to Person	AGE	SEX	BLOOD	TRIBAL ENROLLMENT Year	County	No.
10624	1 Freeny, Malina ⁶⁶	First Named	63	F	1/2	1896	Blue	4326
10625	2 Impson, La Fayette ³²	Son	29	M	1/2	1896	"	6312
10626	3 " Thompson J ²⁶	"	23	"	1/2	1896	"	6313
10627	4 Freeny, Ida M ²³	Dau	20	F	1/2	1896	"	4327
	5							
	6							
	7	ENROLLMENT OF NOS. 1,2,3 and 4 HEREON						
	8	APPROVED BY THE SECRETARY						
	9	OF INTERIOR Feb 4 1903						
	10							
	11							
	12							
	13							
	14							
	15							
	16							
	17							

TRIBAL ENROLLMENT OF PARENTS

Name of Father	Year	County	Name of Mother	Year	County
1 Samuel Folsom	Dead	Blue	Annie Folsom	Dead	Blue
2 Caleb Impson	"	"	No1		
3 " "	"	"	No1		
4 John Freeny	"	"	No1		
5					
6					
7					
8 No1 on 1896 roll as Melina Freeny					
9 No3 " 1896 " " Cap. Inpson					
10 No2 is now the husband of No.1 on 7-4307					
11					
12 For child of No3 see NB (Mar 3-05) Card #1391					
13 " " " " " " " (Apr 26-06) " #437					
14				Date of Application for Enrollment.	
15				Aug 23/99	
16					
17					

Choctaw By Blood Enrollment Cards 1898-1914

RESIDENCE: Blue   COUNTY.   **Choctaw Nation**   **Choctaw Roll**   CARD NO.

POST OFFICE: Caddo, Ind. Ter.   *(Not Including Freedmen)*   FIELD NO. **3763**

Dawes' Roll No.	NAME		Relationship to Person First Named	AGE	SEX	BLOOD	TRIBAL ENROLLMENT		
							Year	County	No.
10628	1 Robinson, Loring	34		31	M	Full	1896	Blue	10899
10629	2 " Betsy	43	Wife	40	F	"	1896	"	10900
10630	3 " Raymond	12	Son	9	M	"	1896	"	10901
10631	4 " Sallie	9	Dau	6	F	"	1896	"	10902
10632	5 Wright, Louisa	12	S.Dau	9	"	"	1896	"	13852
	6								
	7								
	8	ENROLLMENT							
	9	OF NOS. 1,2,3,4 and 5 HEREON APPROVED BY THE SECRETARY							
	10	OF INTERIOR Feb 4, 1903							
	11								
	12								
	13								
	14								
	15								
	16								
	17								

TRIBAL ENROLLMENT OF PARENTS

	Name of Father	Year	County	Name of Mother	Year	County
1	Robinson Makinley	Dead	Jackson	Malind Makinley	Dead	Jackson
2	Edmond Jones	"	Red River	Nohey Jones	"	Red River
3	No1			Minerva Robinson	"	Blue
4	No1			" "	"	"
5	Allen Wright	Dead	Blue	No2		
6						
7						

8   For child of No5 see NB (Apr 26-06) No 694

9   No1 on 1896 Roll as Lowring W Roberson

10   No2 " 1896 " " Betsy "

   No3 " 1896 " " Raymond "

11   No4 " 1896 " " Sallie "

12   It is claimed that mother of Nos 3&4 was a Chickasaw

13   No 3&4 were placed on Chickasaw Card No. 1531

   Nos 3&4 retransferred to this Card Nov 24-1902

14

15

16   Date of Application for Enrollment.

17   Aug 23rd 1899

163

Choctaw By Blood Enrollment Cards 1898-1914

RESIDENCE: Blue			COUNTY.							CARD NO.	
POST OFFICE: Caddo, I.T.			**Choctaw Nation**			**Choctaw Roll** (Not Including Freedmen)				FIELD NO. 3764	

Dawes' Roll No.	NAME	Relationship to Person First Named	AGE	SEX	BLOOD	TRIBAL ENROLLMENT		
						Year	County	No.
10633	1 Jones, Allington 48	First Named	45	M	Full	1896	Blue	7239
10634	2 " Betsy 42	Wife	39	F	"	1896	"	7240
	3							
	4							
	5							
	6	ENROLLMENT						
	7	OF NOS. 1 and 2 HEREON APPROVED BY THE SECRETARY						
	8	OF INTERIOR FEB 4 1903						
	9							
	10							
	11							
	12							
	13							
	14							
	15							
	16							
	17							

TRIBAL ENROLLMENT OF PARENTS

	Name of Father	Year	County	Name of Mother	Year	County
1	Edmond Jones	Dead	Red River	A-no-hey	Dead	Red River
2	Pih-ke-sh-to-be	Dead	Chick Roll	Sha-ta-ho-ye	Dead	Chick Roll
3						
4						
5						
6						
7	N⁰2 on 1896 Chickasaw roll page 75 as Betsey Bell					
8	N⁰2 originally enrolled on Chickasaw card #1527, transferred to					
9	Choctaw card #5478 Oct 20, 1902. Transferred to this card Nov. 19, 1902. for					
10	authority for this action see letter of WO Beall dated Nov. 17, 1902 copy filed herein.					
11						
12						
13						
14					Date of Application for Enrollment	
15					Aug 23/99	
16						
17						

Choctaw By Blood Enrollment Cards 1898-1914

RESIDENCE: Jackson COUNTY.								
POST OFFICE: Bennington, I.T	**Choctaw Nation**			**Choctaw Roll** (Not Including Freedmen)		CARD NO. FIELD NO. 3765		

Dawes' Roll No.	NAME	Relationship to Person First Named	AGE	SEX	BLOOD	TRIBAL ENROLLMENT		
						Year	County	No.
10635	1 LeFlore, Ezekiel ²²	First Named	19	M	Full	1896	Jackson	8143
	2							
	3							
	4	ENROLLMENT						
	5	OF NOS. 1 HEREON APPROVED BY THE SECRETARY						
	6	OF INTERIOR FEB 4 1903						
	7							
	8							
	9							
	10							
	11							
	12							
	13							
	14							
	15							
	16							
	17							

TRIBAL ENROLLMENT OF PARENTS

Name of Father	Year	County	Name of Mother	Year	County
1 Colbert LeFlore	Dead	Jackson	Siney LeFlore	Dead	Jackson
2					
3					
4					
5					
6					
7		On 1896 roll as E. Z. LeFlore			
8					
9					
10					
11					
12					
13					
14					Date of Application for Enrollment.
15					Aug 23/99
16					
17					

Choctaw By Blood Enrollment Cards 1898-1914

Dawes' Roll No.	NAME		Relationship to Person	AGE	SEX	BLOOD	TRIBAL ENROLLMENT		
							Year	County	No.
10636	1	Billy, Willie ⁽³⁷⁾	First Named	34	M	Full	1896	Blue	1652
10637	2	" Esther ⁽⁴⁰⁾	Wife	37	F	"	1896	"	1653
	3								
	4								
	5								
	6								
	7								
	8								
	9								
	10								
	11								
	12								
	13								
	14								
	15								
	16								
	17								

ENROLLMENT
OF NOS. 1 and 2 HEREON
APPROVED BY THE SECRETARY
OF INTERIOR FEB 4 1903

TRIBAL ENROLLMENT OF PARENTS

	Name of Father	Year	County	Name of Mother	Year	County
1	Wallace Billy	Dead	Blue	E-ma-lu-na	Dead	Blue
2	Charles	"	"	Lucy	"	"
3						
4						
5						
6						
7						
8						
9						
10						
11						
12						
13						
14					Date of Application for Enrollment.
15					Aug 23/99
16					
17					

Choctaw By Blood Enrollment Cards 1898-1914

RESIDENCE: Jackson COUNTY.
POST OFFICE: Jackson, I.T.

Choctaw Nation

Choctaw Roll
(Not Including Freedmen)

CARD No.
FIELD No. 3767

Dawes' Roll No.	NAME		Relationship to Person First Named	AGE	SEX	BLOOD	TRIBAL ENROLLMENT		
							Year	County	No.
10638	1 Frazier, Osborne	51	First Named	48	M	Full	1896	Jackson	4317
10639	2 " Sophia	51	Wife	48	F	"	1896	"	4318
10640	3 " Sweeney	18	Son	15	M	"	1896	"	4319
	4								
	5								
	6	ENROLLMENT							
	7	OF NOS. 1, 2 and 3 HEREON							
	8	APPROVED BY THE SECRETARY OF INTERIOR FEB 4 1903							
	9								
	10								
	11								
	12								
	13								
	14								
	15								
	16								
	17								

TRIBAL ENROLLMENT OF PARENTS

	Name of Father	Year	County	Name of Mother	Year	County
1	Tobias Frazier	Dead	Jackson	Che-ma-le-hoke	Dead	Jackson
2	Robinson Wade	"	Blue	Susan Wade	"	Blue
3	No1			Elsie Sharkey		Jackson
4						
5						
6						
7	No1 also on 1896 roll as Aulson Frazier					
8	Page 104, No 4265, Jackson Co					
9						
10	No3 is husband of Minnie Tucker Choctaw card #3852					
11						
12						
13						
14						
15				Date of Application for Enrollment.	Aug 23/99	
16						
17						

Choctaw By Blood Enrollment Cards 1898-1914

RESIDENCE: Jackson   COUNTY. **Choctaw Nation**   **Choctaw Roll** *(Not Including Freedmen)*   CARD No.
POST OFFICE: Jackson, I.T.   FIELD No. **3768**

Dawes' Roll No.	NAME		Relationship to Person	AGE	SEX	BLOOD	TRIBAL ENROLLMENT		
							Year	County	No.
10641	1 Frazier, Sidney	30	First Named	27	M	Full	1896	Jackson	4305
	2								
	3								
	4								
	5	ENROLLMENT							
	6	OF NOS. 1 HEREON							
	7	APPROVED BY THE SECRETARY OF INTERIOR Feb 4-1903							
	8								
	9								
	10								
	11								
	12								
	13								
	14								
	15								
	16								
	17								

TRIBAL ENROLLMENT OF PARENTS

	Name of Father	Year	County	Name of Mother	Year	County
1	Ben Frazier	Dead	Blue	Emily Frazier	Dead	Blue
2						
3						
4						
5						
6						
7						
8						
9						
10						
11						
12						
13						
14						Date of Application for Enrollment.
15						
16						
17						

Choctaw By Blood Enrollment Cards 1898-1914

RESIDENCE:	Blue	COUNTY.			CARD NO.		
POST OFFICE:	Caddo, I.T.	**Choctaw Nation**	**Choctaw Roll** *(Not Including Freedmen)*		FIELD NO. **3769**		

Dawes' Roll No.	NAME	Relationship to Person First Named	AGE	SEX	BLOOD	TRIBAL ENROLLMENT Year	TRIBAL ENROLLMENT County	TRIBAL ENROLLMENT No.
10642	1 Pickens, Austin ⁴⁵	First Named	42	M	Full	1896	Blue	10505
10643	2 " Jefferson ²³	Son	20	"	"	1896	"	10507
	3							
	4							
	5							
	6	ENROLLMENT OF NOS. 1 and 2 HEREON APPROVED BY THE SECRETARY OF INTERIOR Feb 4, 1903						
	7							
	8							
	9							
	10							
	11							
	12							
	13							
	14							
	15							
	16							
	17							

TRIBAL ENROLLMENT OF PARENTS

	Name of Father	Year	County	Name of Mother	Year	County
1	Harris Pickens	Dead	Blue	Bicey Pickens	Dead	Blue
2	No1			Amy Pickens	"	Jackson
3						
4						
5						
6						
7			For child of No.2 see NB (March 3-1905) #1382.			
8						
9						
10						
11						
12						
13						
14					Date of Application for Enrollment.	
15					Aug 23/99	
16						
17						

Choctaw By Blood Enrollment Cards 1898-1914

RESIDENCE: Blue   COUNTY. **Choctaw Nation**   **Choctaw Roll**   CARD NO.
POST OFFICE: Blue, I.T.   *(Not Including Freedmen)*   FIELD NO. 3770

Dawes' Roll No.	NAME	Relationship to Person First Named	AGE	SEX	BLOOD	TRIBAL ENROLLMENT		
						Year	County	No.
10644	1 Moseley, Charles S 26	First Named	23	M	3/4	1896	Blue	8792
	2							
	3							
	4							
	5							
	6							
	7							
	8							
	9							
	10							
	11							
	12							
	13							
	14							
	15							
	16							
	17							

ENROLLMENT
OF NOS. 1   HEREON
APPROVED BY THE SECRETARY
OF INTERIOR   FEB 4 1903

TRIBAL ENROLLMENT OF PARENTS

Name of Father	Year	County	Name of Mother	Year	County
1 Allen Moseley	Dead	Chick Roll	Harriet Moseley	Dead	Blue
2					
3					
4					
5					
6					
7		On 1896 roll as Chas. Moseley			
8					
9					
10					
11					
12					
13					Date of Application for Enrollment.
14					
15					Aug 23/99
16					
17					

Choctaw By Blood Enrollment Cards 1898-1914

Dawes' Roll No.	NAME	Relationship to Person	AGE	SEX	BLOOD	TRIBAL ENROLLMENT		
						Year	County	No.
10645	1 Folsom, John N. ³⁸	First Named	35	M	1/2	1896	Blue	4345
	2							
	3							
	4							
	5							
	6							
	7							
	8							
	9							
	10							
	11							
	12							
	13							
	14							
	15							
	16							
	17							

ENROLLMENT OF NOS. 1 HEREON APPROVED BY THE SECRETARY OF INTERIOR FEB 4 1903

TRIBAL ENROLLMENT OF PARENTS

Name of Father	Year	County	Name of Mother	Year	County
1 Gus Folsom	Dead	Chick Roll	Eliza Folsom	Dead	Blue
2					
3					
4					
5					
6		On 1896 roll as J. N. Folsom			
7		For child of No.1 see NB (March 3, 1905) #1211			
8					
9					
10					
11					
12					
13					Date of Application for Enrollment.
14					
15					Aug 23/99
16					
17					

171

Choctaw By Blood Enrollment Cards 1898-1914

RESIDENCE: **Blue** COUNTY. **Choctaw Nation** **Choctaw Roll** (Not Including Freedmen) CARD NO.
POST OFFICE: Caney, I.T. FIELD NO. 3772

Dawes' Roll No.	NAME	Relationship to Person	AGE	SEX	BLOOD	TRIBAL ENROLLMENT			
						Year	County		No.
10646	₁ King, Sealy ²⁵	First Named	22	F	Full	1896	Blue		7618
	2								
	3								
	4	ENROLLMENT							
	5	OF NOS. I HEREON APPROVED BY THE SECRETARY							
	6	OF INTERIOR FEB 4 1903							
	7								
	8								
	9								
	10								
	11								
	12								
	13								
	14								
	15								
	16								
	17								

TRIBAL ENROLLMENT OF PARENTS

	Name of Father	Year	County	Name of Mother	Year	County
1	Solomon King	Dead	Atoka	Siley King	Dead	Blue
2						
3						
4			Died prior to September 25, 1902;			
5			Not entitled to land or money.			
6			See Indian Office letter of Apr. 26, 1911 G.F. 736-1911			
7						
8						
9						
10						
11						
12						
13						
14					Date of Application for Enrollment:	
15					Aug 23/99	
16						
17						

Choctaw By Blood Enrollment Cards 1898-1914

RESIDENCE:	Blue	COUNTY.		Choctaw Roll	CARD NO.
POST OFFICE:	Caney, I.T.	**Choctaw Nation**		*(Not Including Freedmen)*	FIELD NO. 3773

Dawes' Roll No.	NAME		Relationship to Person First Named	AGE	SEX	BLOOD	TRIBAL ENROLLMENT		
							Year	County	No.
10647	₁ Dana, Charles A	30	First Named	27	M	Full	1896	Blue	3557
10648	₂ " Eliza	30	Wife	27	F	"	1896	"	4321
DEAD.	₃ " Bassie		Dau	2mo	"	"			
10649	₄ Fletcher, Hannah	8	S.Dau	5	"	"	1896	Blue	4322
10650	₅ Dana, Wilburn	16	Bro	13	M	"	1896	"	3560
10651	₆ " Rosie	13	Sister	10	F	"	1896	"	3561
10652	₇ " Henrietta	21	"	18	"	"	1896	"	3559
10653	₈ " Massey	1	Dau	2mo	F	"			
	₉								
	10								
	11	ENROLLMENT							
	12	OF NOS. 1,2,4,5,6,7 and 8 HEREON APPROVED BY THE SECRETARY							
	13	OF INTERIOR FEB 4 1903							
	14	No. 3 HEREON DISMISSED UNDER							
	15	ORDER OF THE COMMISSION TO THE FIVE							
	16	CIVILIZED TRIBES OF MARCH 31, 1905.							
	17								

TRIBAL ENROLLMENT OF PARENTS

	Name of Father	Year	County	Name of Mother	Year	County
₁	Simon Dana	Dead	Blue	Nancy Dana	Dead	Blue
₂	Sampson Nicholas	"	"	Siney Nicholas	"	"
₃	No1			No2		
₄	Solomon Fletcher	Dead	Blue	No2		
₅	Simon Dana	"	"	Nancy Dana	Dead	Blue
₆	" "	"	"	" "	"	"
₇	" "	"	"	" "	"	"
₈	N⁰1			N⁰2		
₉						
10	No1 on 1896 roll as C. A. Dana					
11	No2 " 1896 " " Eliza Fletcher					
	No5 " 1896 " " William Dana					
12	No3 Affidavit of birth to be					
13	supplied:- Filed Nov 2/99				#1 to 7	
14	N⁰8 Born Aug. 8, 1902: enrolled Oct. 2, 1902				Date of Application for Enrollment.	
15	No3 Died Oct 5, 1900: proof of death filed Nov 22 1902				Aug 23/99	
	For child of Nos 1&2 see NB (March 3, 1905) #1346					
16						
17	P.O. Boggy Depot 4/12/05					

Choctaw By Blood Enrollment Cards 1898-1914

RESIDENCE: Jackson   COUNTY. **Choctaw Nation**   **Choctaw Roll**   CARD No.
POST OFFICE: Jackson   *(Not Including Freedmen)*   FIELD No. 3774

Dawes' Roll No.	NAME	Relationship to Person First Named	AGE	SEX	BLOOD	TRIBAL ENROLLMENT		
						Year	County	No.
10655	1 Frazier, Fisher 41	First Named	38	M	Full	1896	Towson	4287
10656	2 " Sarah 43	Wife	40	F	"	1896	"	10343
	3							
	4							
	5	ENROLLMENT						
	6	OF NOS. 1 and 2 HEREON APPROVED BY THE SECRETARY						
	7	OF INTERIOR FEB 4 1903						
	8							
	9							
	10							
	11							
	12							
	13							
	14							
	15							
	16							
	17							

TRIBAL ENROLLMENT OF PARENTS

	Name of Father	Year	County	Name of Mother	Year	County
1	Tobias Frazier	Dead	Jackson		Dead	Jackson
2		"	Towson	Martha Murphey	"	Towson
3						
4						
5						
6			No2 on 1896 roll as Sarah Peter			
7						
8						
9						
10						
11						
12						
13						
14						
15				Date of Application for Enrollment.	Aug 23/99	
16						
17						

Choctaw By Blood Enrollment Cards 1898-1914

RESIDENCE: Blue COUNTY.
POST OFFICE: Bok Chito, I.T.   **Choctaw Nation**

Choctaw Roll (Not Including Freedmen)   CARD NO.   FIELD NO. 3775

Dawes' Roll No.	NAME	Relationship to Person First Named	AGE	SEX	BLOOD	TRIBAL ENROLLMENT Year	County	No.
DEAD.	1 Beames, Julius J		22	M	Full	1896	Blue	1599
10656	2 " Arthur G ¹⁹	Bro	16	"	"	1896	"	1601
10657	3 " Arther W ¹	Nephew	3wks	M	1/2			
I.W. 747	4 " Belle C ⑱	Wife of No2	18	F	I.W.			
	5							
	6	ENROLLMENT						
	7	OF NOS. 2 and 3 HEREON						
	8	APPROVED BY THE SECRETARY OF INTERIOR FEB 4 1903						
	9							
	10	ENROLLMENT						
	11	OF NOS. 4 HEREON APPROVED BY THE SECRETARY						
	12	OF INTERIOR MAY -7 1904						
	13	No. 1 HEREON DISMISSED UNDER						
	14	ORDER OF THE COMMISSION TO THE FIVE						
	15	CIVILIZED TRIBES OF MARCH 31, 1905.						
	16							
	17							

TRIBAL ENROLLMENT OF PARENTS

Name of Father	Year	County	Name of Mother	Year	County
1 Calvin Beams[sic]	Dead	Blue	Eliza Beams		Blue
2 " "	"	"	" "		"
3 Nº2			Belle C Beames		white woman
4 Tom Dougherty[sic]		non-citizen	Rosabelle Daugherty	dead	non-citizen
5					
6					
7					
8					

9 Nº2 is now the husband of Belle C Beames on Choctaw Card #D694. He says the
10 correct spelling of his surname is "Beames" Jan 6, 1902
11 Nº3 Born July 8, 1902: enrolled July 30 1902.
No1 Died November 1901: proof of death filed Nov 22 1902
12 No4 transferred from Choctaw card #D.694
13 See decision of Feby. 27, 1904.
14 For children of No.2 and 4 see NB (Mar 3 '05) #467

Date of Application for Enrollment.

15 Aug 23/99
16 PO Kingston IT 3/25/05
17 Cliff I.T. 11/17/02

175

Choctaw By Blood Enrollment Cards 1898-1914

RESIDENCE: Blue	COUNTY.	**Choctaw Nation**	**Choctaw Roll**	CARD NO.
POST OFFICE: Bennington, I.T.			*(Not Including Freedmen)*	FIELD NO. 3776

Dawes' Roll No.	NAME	Relationship to Person First Named	AGE	SEX	BLOOD	TRIBAL ENROLLMENT Year	County	No.
10658	1 Gardner, Samuel G ³⁸	Named	35	M	1/2	1896	Blue	4936
348	2 " Florence ³³	Wife	30	F	IW	1896	"	14578
10659	3 " Willie ¹¹	Son	8	M	1/4	1896	"	4937
10660	4 " Martin L ⁷	"	4	"	1/4	1896	"	4938
10661	5 " Leroy ¹	"	1 mo	"	1/4			
	6							
	7							
	8	ENROLLMENT OF NOS. 1,3,4 and 5 HEREON APPROVED BY THE SECRETARY						
	9	OF INTERIOR FEB 4 1903						
	10							
	11	ENROLLMENT OF NOS. 2 HEREON						
	12	APPROVED BY THE SECRETARY OF INTERIOR SEP 12 1903						
	13							
	14							
	15							
	16							
	17							

TRIBAL ENROLLMENT OF PARENTS

	Name of Father	Year	County	Name of Mother	Year	County
1	Green Gardner	Dead	Blue	Harriet Gardner	Dead	Blue
2	Henry Wolfe		Non Citz	Mollie Wolfe	"	Non Citz
3	No1			No2		
4	No1			No2		
5	No1			No2		
6						
7			No1 on 1896 roll as Samuel Gardner			
8			No4 " 1896 " " Luther "			
9			Evidence of marriage to be			
10			supplied:- Recd Oct 7/99			
11			No.5 born Dec. 1, 1901: Enrolled Dec. 28, 1901			
12						
13						#1 to 4 inc
14						Date of Application for Enrollment.
15						Aug 23/99
16						
17						

176

RESIDENCE:	Blue	COUNTY.		CARD No.
POST OFFICE:	Caney, I.T.	**Choctaw Nation**	**Choctaw Roll** *(Not Including Freedmen)*	FIELD No. 3777

Dawes' Roll No.	NAME	Relationship to Person	AGE	SEX	BLOOD	TRIBAL ENROLLMENT		
						Year	County	No.
10662	1 Filmore, Gibson ⁵⁵	First Named	52	M	3/4	1896	Blue	4388
10663	2 " Sukey ⁵⁸	Wife	55	F	Full	1896	"	4389
	3							
	4							
	5	ENROLLMENT						
	6	OF NOS. 1 and 2 HEREON APPROVED BY THE SECRETARY						
	7	OF INTERIOR FEB 4 1903						
	8							
	9							
	10							
	11							
	12							
	13							
	14							
	15							
	16							
	17							

TRIBAL ENROLLMENT OF PARENTS

	Name of Father	Year	County	Name of Mother	Year	County
1	Filmore	Dead	Chick Roll	Ish-tu-ney	Dead	Kiamitia
2	Tom Chubbee	"	Skullyville	Are-you-ona	"	Skullyville
3						
4						
5						
6						
7		Surname on 1896 Choctaw roll as "Fillmore"				
8						
9						
10						
11						
12						
13						
14						Date of Application for Enrollment.
15						Aug 23/99
16						
17						

177

Choctaw By Blood Enrollment Cards 1898-1914

RESIDENCE:	Blue	COUNTY.					Choctaw Roll		CARD NO.
POST OFFICE:	Caddo, I.T.	**Choctaw Nation**					*(Not Including Freedmen)*		FIELD NO. 3778

Dawes' Roll No.	NAME		Relationship to Person	AGE	SEX	BLOOD	TRIBAL ENROLLMENT		
							Year	County	No.
10664	1 Nicholas, Wade	22	First Named	19	M	Full	1896	Blue	9798
10665	2 " Sina	21	Wife	18	F	"	1896	"	1719
DEAD.	3 " Willis DEAD.		Son	6wks	M	"			
10666	4 " Roy	1	Son	2mo	M	"			
	5								
	6								
	7	ENROLLMENT							
	8	OF NOS. 1,2 and 4 HEREON APPROVED BY THE SECRETARY							
	9	OF INTERIOR FEB 4 1903							
	10	No. 3 HEREON DISMISSED UNDER ORDER OF THE COMMISSION TO THE FIVE							
	11	CIVILIZED TRIBES OF MARCH 31, 1905.							
	12								
	13								
	14								
	15								
	16								
	17								

TRIBAL ENROLLMENT OF PARENTS

	Name of Father	Year	County	Name of Mother	Year	County
1	Solomon Nicholas	Dead	Blue	Amy Nicholas		Blue
2	Chas Byington	"	"	Chu-tey	Dead	"
3	No1			No2		
4	Nº1			Nº2		
5						
6						
7			No2 on 1896 roll as Sina Byington			
8						
9			No3 Affidavit of birth to be supplied:- Recd Oct 7/99			
10			Nº4 Born April 12, 1902: enrolled June 10, 1902			
11			No3 Died Sept. 11, 1902: proof of death filed Nov 22 1902			
12			For child of Nos 1&2 see NB (Apr 26-06) Card #424			
13						#1 to 3
14						Date of Application for Enrollment.
15						Aug 23/99
16						
17						

Choctaw By Blood Enrollment Cards 1898-1914

RESIDENCE: Blue   COUNTY. **Choctaw Nation**   **Choctaw Roll**   CARD No.
POST OFFICE: Caddo, I.T.   (Not Including Freedmen)   FIELD No. 3779

Dawes' Roll No.	NAME	Relationship to Person	AGE	SEX	BLOOD	TRIBAL ENROLLMENT		
						Year	County	No.
10667	1 Hogan, Wilburn 20	First Named	17	M	Full	1896	Blue	5889
	2							
	3							
	4							
	5							
	6							
	7							
	8							
	9							
	10							
	11							
	12							
	13							
	14							
	15							
	16							
	17							

ENROLLMENT
OF NOS. 1 HEREON
APPROVED BY THE SECRETARY
OF INTERIOR FEB 4 1903

TRIBAL ENROLLMENT OF PARENTS

	Name of Father	Year	County	Name of Mother	Year	County
1	Cephas Hogan	Dead	Blue	Mary Hogan	Dead	Blue
2						
3						
4						
5						
6						
7						
8						
9						
10						
11						
12						
13						
14						Date of Application for Enrollment.
15						Aug 23/99
16						
17						

179

Choctaw By Blood Enrollment Cards 1898-1914

RESIDENCE: Blue   COUNTY. **Choctaw Nation**   **Choctaw Roll** CARD No.
POST OFFICE: Caddo, I.T.   *(Not Including Freedmen)* FIELD No. 3780

Dawes' Roll No.	NAME	Relationship to Person First Named	AGE	SEX	BLOOD	TRIBAL ENROLLMENT		
						Year	County	No.
DEAD.	1 Moore, Nephus	Named	56	M	Full	1896	Blue	8787
DEAD.	2 " Lucy	Wife	42	F	"	1896	"	8788
10668	3 " Elie ¹⁷	Dau	14	"	"	1896	"	8789
10669	4 " Sophina ¹³	"	10	"	"	1896	"	8790
10670	5 Perkins, Shelby ¹³	Ward	10	M	3/4	1896	"	10504
	6							
	7							
	8	ENROLLMENT						
	9	OF NOS. 3,4 and 5 HEREON APPROVED BY THE SECRETARY						
	10	OF INTERIOR FEB 4 1903						
	11	No. 1 and 2 HEREON DISMISSED UNDER						
	12	ORDER OF THE COMMISSION TO THE FIVE						
	13	CIVILIZED TRIBES OF MARCH 31, 1905.						
	14							
	15							
	16							
	17							

TRIBAL ENROLLMENT OF PARENTS

	Name of Father	Year	County	Name of Mother	Year	County
1	A-che-nun-ta	Dead	Red River	Biccy	Dead	Blue
2	Pesa ma kin tubbe	"	Atoka	Ok la te ma	"	Atoka
3	No1			N02		
4	No1			No2		
5	King Perkins	Dead	Blue	Serena Perkins		Jackson
6						
7						
8						
9						
10	No1 on 1896 roll as Naphus More					
11	Surnames of first four appear					
12	on 1896 roll as More					
13	No5 on 1896 roll as Sheby Perkins					
14	No1 died in 1900; proof of death filed Nov 28 1902					
15	No2 " " 1900; " " " " " "			Date of Application for Enrollment.		
16	Correct age of N°3 is 18 years. See testimony of July 10, 1903			Aug 23/99		
17	For child of No.3 see NB (March 3, 1905) #1432					

Choctaw By Blood Enrollment Cards 1898-1914

RESIDENCE:	Blue	COUNTY.							
POST OFFICE:	Boggy Depot, I.T.								

Choctaw Nation

Choctaw Roll *(Not Including Freedmen)*

CARD NO.

FIELD NO. **3781**

Dawes' Roll No.	NAME		Relationship to Person	AGE	SEX	BLOOD	TRIBAL ENROLLMENT		
							Year	County	No.
10671	1 Lewis, Gipson	46	First Named	43	M	Full	1896	Blue	8187
Dead	2 " Susan DEAD.		Wife	40	F	3/4	1896	"	8188
10672	3 " Agnes	15	Dau	13	"	7/8	1896	"	8189
10673	4 " Lenn	7	Son	4	M	7/8	1896	"	8190
10674	5 Byington, Nancy	19	S.Dau	16	F	Full			7179
10675	6 Byington, Rufas	1	Son of Nº5	19mo	M	"			
	7								
	8								
	9	ENROLLMENT							
	10	OF NOS. 1,3,4,5 and 6 HEREON APPROVED BY THE SECRETARY							
	11	OF INTERIOR FEB 4 1903							
	12	No. 2 HEREON DISMISSED UNDER							
	13	ORDER OF THE COMMISSION TO THE FIVE							
	14	CIVILIZED TRIBES OF MARCH 31, 1905.							
	15								
	16								
	17								

TRIBAL ENROLLMENT OF PARENTS

	Name of Father	Year	County	Name of Mother	Year	County
1	John Lewis		Blue	Malis Lewis	Dead	Blue
2	Grant Battiest	Dead	Chick Roll	Letsie Battiest	"	"
3	No1			No2		
4	No1			No2		
5	William James	Dead	Blue	No2		
6	Peter Byington	1896	Atoka	Nº5		
7						
8						
9						
10	No5 was wife of Jefferson Pickens at death July 30, 1904					
11	No4 on 1896 roll as Lane Lewis					
12	Nº5 is now the wife of Peter Byington on Choctaw card #3826. Evidence					
13	of marriage requested Sept. 29, 1902					#1 to 5
14	Nº6 Born April 29, 1901. Enrolled Sept. 29, 1902					Date of Application
	No2 Died Oct 20, 1899; proof of death filed Nov 22 1902					for Enrollment.
15	For child of No.5 see NB (March 3, 1905) #1382					Aug 23/99
16						
17	Laney I.T. 11/17/02					

Choctaw By Blood Enrollment Cards 1898-1914

RESIDENCE: **Blue**
POST OFFICE: **Caddo, I.T.**
COUNTY: **Choctaw Nation**
Choctaw Roll (Not Including Freedmen)
CARD NO. FIELD NO. **3782**

Dawes' Roll No.	NAME	Relationship to Person First Named	AGE	SEX	BLOOD	TRIBAL ENROLLMENT		
						Year	County	No.
10676	1 Tigert, Julia A ²³	First Named	20	F	1/4	1896	Blue	12398
10677	2 Turnbull Inez ²⁵	Sister	22	"	1/4	1896	"	12400
10678	3 Ramsey Lena ²¹	"	18	"	1/4	1896	"	12454
10679	4 Turnbull Simeon ²¹	Bro	18	M	1/4	1896	"	12453
10680	5 Tigert Benjamin Franklin¹	Son	1mo	M	1/8			
10681	6 Ramsey Turner Munroe¹	Nephew	6wks	M	1/8			
	7							
	8 ENROLLMENT OF NOS. 1,2,3,4,5 and 6 HEREON							
	9 APPROVED BY THE SECRETARY OF INTERIOR Feb 4, 1903							
	10							
	11							
	12							
	13							
	14							
	15 For child of No1 see NB (Apr 26-06) Card #367							
	16 " " " " " " (Mar 3, 05) " #1306							
	17 " " " No2 " " " " #1414							

TRIBAL ENROLLMENT OF PARENTS

	Name of Father	Year	County	Name of Mother	Year	County
1	Simeon Turnbull	Dead	Blue	Susan Turnbull	Dead	Cherokee
2	" "	"	"	" "	"	"
3	" "	"	"	" "	"	"
4	" "	"	"	" "	"	"
5	Samuel Tigert		non citizen	No.1		
6	O. A. Ramsey		non citizen	No.3		
7						
8	For child of No3 see NB (Act Mar 3-05) Card #265					
9	Mother of the above parties, Susan Turnbull,					
10	nee Foreman, was a Cherokee. See if she is on Cherokee Rolls For child of No4 see NB (Apr 26'06) Card #157					
11	No 1 is now wife of Samuel Tigert a noncitizen. Evidence of marriage					
12	requested Aug 8, 1901. Filed Aug 20, 1901					
13	No.5 Enrolled Aug 8, 1901					
14	No.3 is now the wife of O.A. Ramsey. A non citz. Evidence of marriage requested Dec. 27, 1901					
15	No.6 born Nov. 14, 1901: Enrolled Dec. 27, 1901					
16	For child of No.1 see NB (Apr 26'06) Card #367					
17	No4 PO Caney I.T. 1/27/06					

Date of Application for Enrollment. Aug 23/99

Date of Application for Enrollment.

No2 P.O. Matoy I.T. 3/27/05

Choctaw By Blood Enrollment Cards 1898-1914

RESIDENCE:	Blue	COUNTY.						CARD No.	
POST OFFICE:	Bok Chito, I.T.	**Choctaw Nation**				**Choctaw Roll** (Not Including Freedmen)		FIELD No. **3783**	

Dawes' Roll No.	NAME	Relationship to Person	AGE	SEX	BLOOD	TRIBAL ENROLLMENT		
						Year	County	No.
10682	1 May, Abner 22	First Named	19	M	Full	1896	Blue	8793
	2							
	3							
	4							
	5							
	6	ENROLLMENT						
	7	OF NOS. 1 HEREON APPROVED BY THE SECRETARY						
	8	OF INTERIOR Feb 4 1903						
	9							
	10							
	11							
	12							
	13							
	14							
	15							
	16							
	17							

TRIBAL ENROLLMENT OF PARENTS

Name of Father	Year	County	Name of Mother	Year	County
1 William May	Dead	Blue	Lucy Battiest	Dead	Blue
2					
3					
4					
5					
6 Father of No.1 is Julius Hampton					
7					
8					
9					
10					
11					
12					
13					
14				Date of Application for Enrollment.	
15				Aug 23/99	
16					
17					

183

Choctaw By Blood Enrollment Cards 1898-1914

RESIDENCE: Blue   COUNTY. **Choctaw Nation**   **Choctaw Roll** *(Not Including Freedmen)*   CARD NO.
POST OFFICE: Boggy Depot, I.T.   FIELD NO. **3784**

Dawes' Roll No.	NAME		Relationship to Person	AGE	SEX	BLOOD	TRIBAL ENROLLMENT		
							Year	County	No.
I.W. 349	1 Dwight, Odile V	53	First Named	50	F	I.W.	1896	Blue	14479
10683	2 " Joseph E	31	Son	28	M	1/2	1893	"	326
15233	3 " Allie	24	Wife of No2	24	F	1/32	1896	"	1538
(No3)p3	See opinion of Atty Gen'l of Feb 18'04 and letter of Secy of Interior of Feb 24'04 in case of James M Buckholts 1896 et al 7-5738								
5									
6	ENROLLMENT								
7	OF NOS. 2	HEREON							
8	APPROVED BY THE SECRETARY OF INTERIOR Feb 4, 1903								
9	ENROLLMENT								
10	OF NOS. 1	HEREON							
11	APPROVED BY THE SECRETARY OF INTERIOR Sep 12 1903								
12	ENROLLMENT								
13	OF NOS. 3	HEREON							
14	APPROVED BY THE SECRETARY OF INTERIOR May 9, 1904								
15									
16									
17									

TRIBAL ENROLLMENT OF PARENTS

	Name of Father	Year	County	Name of Mother	Year	County
1	F. J. Maurer	Dead	Non Citz	Marie Maurer	Dead	Non Citz
2	Edward Dwight	"	Blue	No1		
3	James M Buckholts	1896	"	Jennetta Buckholts		Non Citz
4						
5	No3 Evidence of marriage to No2 filed Nov. 4, 1902					
6	No3 Transferred from Choctaw card #D357					
7	See decision of July 20, 1903 approved by Department Feby 24, 1904 No1 as to marriage, see testimony of					
8	A. Telle					
9	No1 on 1896 Choctaw roll as O.V. Dwight					
10	No2 on 1893 Pay Roll, Page 31, No 326 Blue Co, as J.E. Dwight					
11						
12	No2 on 1896 Choctaw roll, Page 2-363, #13871 as Joseph E Wright					
13	No1 admitted by Dawes Commission in 1896, as an intermarried citizen: Choctaw case #310: no appeal					
14	No.2 is now the husband of Allie Buckholts on Choctaw Card #D357. 11/4/02					Date of Application for Enrollment.
15	For child of Nos 2&3 see NB (Apr 26'06) Card #228					Aug 23/99
16						
17	Wayne I.T.					

184

Choctaw By Blood Enrollment Cards 1898-1914

RESIDENCE:	Blue	COUNTY.							CARD No.	
POST OFFICE:	Caddo, I.T.		**Choctaw Nation**				**Choctaw Roll** (Not Including Freedmen)		FIELD No.	**3785**

Dawes' Roll No.	NAME		Relationship to Person First Named	AGE	SEX	BLOOD	TRIBAL ENROLLMENT		
							Year	County	No.
~~Dead~~ Dead	~~Mitchell, Dukes~~ 1		~~Named~~	~~30~~	~~M~~	~~Full~~	~~1896~~	~~Blue~~	~~8765~~
10684	" Sallie	23	Wife	20	F	"	1896	"	8766
10685	" Isaac	13	Son	10	M	"	1896	"	8767
10686	" Alice	6	Dau	3	F	"	1896	"	8768
	5								
	6								
	7	ENROLLMENT							
	8	OF NOS. 2, 3 and 4 HEREON							
	9	APPROVED BY THE SECRETARY OF INTERIOR Feb 4 1903							
	10								
	11	No1 Died Oct 21, 1900 proof of death filed Nov 22 1902							
	12	No3 lives with Loring Robinson Choc #3763							
	13								
	14								
	15	No. 1 Hereon dismissed under order							
	16	of the Commission to the Five Civilized Tribes of March 31, 1905.							
	17								

TRIBAL ENROLLMENT OF PARENTS

	Name of Father	Year	County	Name of Mother	Year	County
1	~~Stewart Mitchell~~		~~Blue~~	~~Annie Mitchell~~	~~Dead~~	~~Red River~~
2	Simon Dana	Dead	"	Nancy Dana	"	Blue
3	No1			Bessie Mitchell	"	Red River
4	No1			No2		
5						
6						
7	For child of No2 see NB (Apr 26-06) Card #813					
8						
9						
10						
11						
12						
13						
14						
15				Date of Application for Enrollment	Aug 23/99	
16						
17						

Choctaw By Blood Enrollment Cards 1898-1914

RESIDENCE: **Blue**	COUNTY.	**Choctaw Nation**		**Choctaw Roll**	CARD No.	
POST OFFICE: **Caddo, I.T.**				*(Not Including Freedmen)*	FIELD No. **3786**	

Dawes' Roll No.	NAME	Relationship to Person	AGE	SEX	BLOOD	TRIBAL ENROLLMENT		
						Year	County	No.
10687	1 Mitchell, Stewart ~~DIED PRIOR TO SEPTEMBER 25 1902~~	First Named	62	M	Full	1896	Red River	8673
	2							
	3							
	4	ENROLLMENT						
	5	OF NOS. 1 HEREON ~~APPROVED BY THE SECRETARY~~						
	6	OF INTERIOR Feb 4 1903						
	7							
	8							
	9							
	10							
	11							
	12							
	13							
	14							
	15							
	16							
	17							

TRIBAL ENROLLMENT OF PARENTS

	Name of Father	Year	County	Name of Mother	Year	County
1		Dead	Red River	Lucy	Dead	Red River
2						
3						
4						
5						
6	No1 died August 11, 1901 Enrollment cancelled by Department May 2, 1906					
7						
8						
9						
10						
11						
12						
13						
14					Date of Application for Enrollment.	
15					Aug 23/99	
16						
17						

RESIDENCE: Jackson COUNTY.	Choctaw Nation	Choctaw Roll	CARD NO.
POST OFFICE: Bennington, I.T.		(Not Including Freedmen)	FIELD NO. 3787

Dawes' Roll No.	NAME		Relationship to Person First Named	AGE	SEX	BLOOD	TRIBAL ENROLLMENT		
							Year	County	No.
10688	1 Durant, Frank	32	First Named	29	M	Full	1896	Jackson	3485
10689	2 " Eliza	30	Wife	27	F	"	1896	"	3486
10690	3 " Maggie	11	Dau	8	"	"	1896	"	3487
10691	4 " Sampson	10	Son	7	M	"	1896	"	3488
10692	5 " Lizzie	7	Dau	4	F	"	1896	"	3489
10693	6 " Willie	4	Son	1	M	"			
	7								
	8								
	9	ENROLLMENT							
	10	OF NOS. 1,2,3,4,5 and 6 HEREON APPROVED BY THE SECRETARY							
	11	OF INTERIOR Feb 4 1903							
	12								
	13								
	14								
	15								
	16								
	17								

	TRIBAL ENROLLMENT OF PARENTS					
Name of Father	Year	County	Name of Mother	Year	County
1 Besand Durant	Dead	Jackson	Lila Durant		Jackson
2 Eden Frazier	"	"	Betsey Frazier	Dead	"
3	No 1		No 2		
4	No 1		No 2		
5	No 1		No 2		
6	No 1		No 2		
7					
8					
9		No.6 Affidavit of birth to be			
10		supplied Filed Nov 2/99			
11					
12					
13					
14			Date of Application for Enrollment.	Aug 23/99	
15					
16					
17					

Choctaw By Blood Enrollment Cards 1898-1914

RESIDENCE: Jackson COUNTY. **Choctaw Nation** Choctaw Roll CARD No.
POST OFFICE: Bennington, I.T. *(Not Including Freedmen)* FIELD No. 3788

Dawes' Roll No.	NAME	Relationship to Person	AGE	SEX	BLOOD	TRIBAL ENROLLMENT		
						Year	County	No.
10694	1 Durant, Allen ³⁴	First Named	31	M	Full	1896	Jackson	3506
	2							
	3							
	4							
	5							
	6							
	7							
	8							
	9							
	10							
	11							
	12							
	13							
	14							
	15							
	16							
	17							

ENROLLMENT
OF NOS. 1 HEREON
APPROVED BY THE SECRETARY
OF INTERIOR FEB 4 1903

TRIBAL ENROLLMENT OF PARENTS

	Name of Father	Year	County	Name of Mother	Year	County
1	Besand Durant	Dead	Jackson	Lila Durant		Jackson
2						
3						
4						
5						
6						
7	Child of No1 on NB (Apr 26 06) Card #311					
8						
9						
10						
11						
12						
13						
14					Date of Application for Enrollment.	
15					Aug 23/99	
16						
17						

Choctaw By Blood Enrollment Cards 1898-1914

RESIDENCE: Jackson   COUNTY.   **Choctaw Nation**   Choctaw Roll   CARD NO.
POST OFFICE: Jackson, I.T.   (Not Including Freedmen)   FIELD NO. 3789

Dawes' Roll No.	NAME	Relationship to Person Named	AGE	SEX	BLOOD	TRIBAL ENROLLMENT		
						Year	County	No.
10695	1 Jackson, Robert 43	First Named	40	M	Full	1896	Jackson	7137
10696	2 " Sila 25	Wife	22	F	"	1896	Atoka	5940
10697	3 " Micy 1	Dau	14mo	F	"			
	4							
	5							
	6	ENROLLMENT						
	7	OF NOS. 1, 2 and 3 HEREON APPROVED BY THE SECRETARY						
	8	OF INTERIOR FEB 4 1903						
	9							
	10							
	11							
	12							
	13							
	14							
	15							
	16							
	17							

TRIBAL ENROLLMENT OF PARENTS

	Name of Father	Year	County	Name of Mother	Year	County
1	Jackson	Dead	Red River	Jennie	Dead	Red River
2	Jas Harrison		Jackson	Liza A Harrison	"	Jackson
3	Nº1			Nº2		
4						
5						
6						
7	Nº2 on 1896 roll as Sila Harrison					
8	Nº3 Born May 31, 1901: enrolled Aug. 11, 1902.					
9						
10						
11						
12						
13						
14				#1&2		
15				Date of Application for Enrollment.	Aug 23/99	
16						
17						

189

Choctaw By Blood Enrollment Cards 1898-1914

RESIDENCE: **Blue**   COUNTY,   **Choctaw Nation**   **Choctaw Roll**   CARD NO.

POST OFFICE: **Caddo, I.T.**   *(Not Including Freedmen)*   FIELD NO. **3790**

Dawes' Roll No.	NAME	Relationship to Person	AGE	SEX	BLOOD	TRIBAL ENROLLMENT Year	County	No.
10698	1 Frazier, Eliza ~~DIED PRIOR TO SEPTEMBER 25 1902~~	First Named	80	F	Full	1896	Blue	4343
	2							
	3							
	4	ENROLLMENT						
	5	OF NOS. 1 HEREON APPROVED BY THE SECRETARY						
	6	OF INTERIOR Feb 4 1903						
	7							
	8							
	9							
	10							
	11							
	12							
	13							
	14							
	15							
	16							
	17							

TRIBAL ENROLLMENT OF PARENTS

	Name of Father	Year	County	Name of Mother	Year	County
1		Dead	in Mississippi		Dead	in Mississippi
2						
3						
4						
5						
6	No.1 died July 14, 1899; Enrollment cancelled by Department May 2, 1906					
7						
8						
9						
10						
11						
12						
13						
14					Date of Application for Enrollment.	
15					Aug 23/99	
16						
17						

Choctaw By Blood Enrollment Cards 1898-1914

RESIDENCE: Blue COUNTY.									
POST OFFICE: Boggy Depot, I.T.	**Choctaw Nation**				Choctaw Roll (Not Including Freedmen)		CARD NO. FIELD NO. 3791		

Dawes' Roll No.	NAME	Relationship to Person	AGE	SEX	BLOOD	TRIBAL ENROLLMENT		
						Year	County	No.
10699	1 Foster, Joseph ⁴³	First Named	40	M	Full	1896	Blue	4340
	2							
	3							
	4	ENROLLMENT OF NOS. 1 HEREON APPROVED BY THE SECRETARY OF INTERIOR FEB 4 1903						
	5							
	6							
	7							
	8							
	9							
	10							
	11							
	12							
	13							
	14							
	15							
	16							
	17							

TRIBAL ENROLLMENT OF PARENTS

Name of Father	Year	County	Name of Mother	Year	County
1 Wᵐ Foster	Dead	Blue	Ta-lo-a-huna	Dead	Blue
2					
3					
4					
5					
6					
7					
8					
9					
10					
11					
12					
13					
14				Date of Application for Enrollment		
15				Aug 23/99		
16					
17					

191

Choctaw By Blood Enrollment Cards 1898-1914

RESIDENCE: **Blue** COUNTY. **Choctaw Nation** **Choctaw Roll** CARD No.
POST OFFICE: **Boggy Depot, I.T** (Not Including Freedmen) FIELD No. **3792**

Dawes' Roll No.	NAME	Relationship to Person First Named	AGE	SEX	BLOOD	TRIBAL ENROLLMENT Year	TRIBAL ENROLLMENT County	TRIBAL ENROLLMENT No.
DEAD. 1	Harley, Selim	Named	36	M	Full	1896	Blue	5899
DEAD. 2	" Lizzie	Wife	30	F	"	1896	"	5900
10700 3	" Efrena 9	Dau	6	"	"	1896	"	5901
DEAD. 4	" Fannie	"	5	"	"	1896	"	5902
10701 5	" Wysie 5	"	1	"	"			
6								
7								
8	ENROLLMENT OF NOS. 3 and 5 HEREON							
9	APPROVED BY THE SECRETARY							
10	OF INTERIOR FEB 4 1903							
11	No. 1,2 and 4 HEREON DISMISSED UNDER ORDER OF THE COMMISSION TO							
12	THE FIVE CIVILIZED TRIBES OF MARCH 31,							
13								
14								
15								
16								
17								

TRIBAL ENROLLMENT OF PARENTS

	Name of Father	Year	County	Name of Mother	Year	County
1	Dead	Blue			Dead	Blue
2	Thompson Byington	"	Atoka	Melinda Scrimpshire		Choctaw
3	No1			No2		
4	No1			No2		
5	No1			No2		
6						
7						
8						
9						
10	No1 on 1896 roll as Isham Harley					
11	No2 " 1896 " " Lucinda "					
12	No4 " 1896 " " Fina "					
13	No5 Affidavit of birth to be supplied: Recd Oct 7/99					
14	No1 Died May – 1900 proof [sic] death filed Nov 22 1902					Date of Application for Enrollment.
15	No2 Died Feby 28 1900 proof [sic] death filed Nov 22 1902					
	No4 Died July – 1901 proof [sic] death filed Nov 22 1902					Aug 23/99
16						
17						

Choctaw By Blood Enrollment Cards 1898-1914

RESIDENCE: Blue   COUNTY. **Choctaw Nation**   **Choctaw Roll**   CARD NO.

POST OFFICE: Caddo, I.T.   *(Not Including Freedmen)*   FIELD NO. 3793

Dawes' Roll No.	NAME		Relationship to Person	AGE	SEX	BLOOD	TRIBAL ENROLLMENT		
							Year	County	No.
10702	1 Payton, Ned	28	First Named	25	M	Full	1896	Blue	10464
10703	2 " Josephine	27	Wife	24	F	"	1896	Jackson	3502
10704	3 " Harry	3	Son	3mo	M	"			
	4								
	5								
	6	ENROLLMENT							
	7	OF NOS. 1, 2 and 3 HEREON APPROVED BY THE SECRETARY							
	8	OF INTERIOR FEB 4 1903							
	9								
	10								
	11								
	12								
	13								
	14								
	15								
	16								
	17								

TRIBAL ENROLLMENT OF PARENTS

	Name of Father	Year	County	Name of Mother	Year	County
1	Joel Payton	Dead	Blue		Dead	Blue
2	Timothy Dwight	"	Jackson	Minerva Dwight		Jackson
3	No.1			No.2		
4						
5						
6						
7	No2 on 1896 roll as Josephine Dwight					
8	No.3 Enrolled June 11, 1900.					
9	For children of Nos 1 &2 see NB (Mar 3,1905) #605					
10						
11						
12						
13						
14				#1&2		
15				Date of Application for Enrollment.	Aug 23/99	
16						
17						

Choctaw By Blood Enrollment Cards 1898-1914

RESIDENCE: Blue COUNTY. **Choctaw Nation** **Choctaw Roll** CARD NO.
POST OFFICE: Caddo, I.T. (Not Including Freedmen) FIELD NO. 3794

Dawes' Roll No.	NAME	Relationship to Person	AGE	SEX	BLOOD	TRIBAL ENROLLMENT		
						Year	County	No.
10705	1 Myer, Linda ⁴³	First Named	40	F	Full	1896	Blue	10506
10706	2 Wilson, Reason ²²	Son	19	M	"	1896	"	13894
10707	3 " Sarah ¹³	Dau	10	F	"	1896	"	13896
	4							
	5							
	6							
	7							
	8							
	9							
	10							
	11							
	12							
	13							
	14							
	15							
	16							
	17							

ENROLLMENT
OF NOS. 1, 2 and 3 HEREON
APPROVED BY THE SECRETARY
OF INTERIOR FEB 4 1903

TRIBAL ENROLLMENT OF PARENTS

	Name of Father	Year	County	Name of Mother	Year	County
1	James Myer	Dead	Blue	Pe-sa-ten-la-hema	Dead	Blue
2	Abel Wilson		"	No1		
3	" "		"	No1		
4						
5						
6						
7	No1 on 1896 roll as Linda Pickens					
8						
9						
10						
11						
12						
13						
14					Date of Application for Enrollment.	
15					Aug 23/99	
16						
17						

RESIDENCE:	Blue	COUNTY.					Choctaw Roll	CARD No.

Choctaw Nation

(Not Including Freedmen)   FIELD No. 3795

POST OFFICE: Blue, I.T.

Dawes' Roll No.	NAME	Relationship to Person First Named	AGE	SEX	BLOOD	TRIBAL ENROLLMENT		
						Year	County	No.
10708	1 Armby, Simpson 40	First Named	37	M	Full	1896	Blue	411
10709	2 " Martha 43	Wife	40	F	"	1896	Jackson	9780
10710	3 " Dora 12	Dau	9	"	"	1896	Blue	413
	4							
	5							
	6							
	7	ENROLLMENT						
	8	OF NOS. 1, 2 and 3 HEREON APPROVED BY THE SECRETARY						
	9	OF INTERIOR FEB 4 1903						
	10							
	11							
	12							
	13							
	14							
	15							
	16							
	17							

TRIBAL ENROLLMENT OF PARENTS

	Name of Father	Year	County	Name of Mother	Year	County
1	Ben Armby	Dead	Blue	Phoebe Armby	Dead	Blue
2	John Ned	"	Jackson		"	Jackson
3	No1			Nancy Armby	"	Blue
4						
5						
6	No1 on 1896 roll as Sim Armby					
7	No2 " 1896 " " Martha Ned					
8						
9						
10						
11						
12						
13						
14					Date of Application for Enrollment.	
15					Aug 23/99	
16						
17						

Choctaw By Blood Enrollment Cards 1898-1914

RESIDENCE: Blue COUNTY.
POST OFFICE: Caney, I.T.

Choctaw Nation

Choctaw Roll (Not Including Freedmen)

CARD NO.
FIELD NO. 3796

Dawes' Roll No.		NAME		Relationship to Person	AGE	SEX	BLOOD	TRIBAL ENROLLMENT		
								Year	County	No.
10711	1	Talbert, Nicholas	32	First Named	29	M	Full	1896	Blue	12423
10712	2	" Victoria	25	Wife	22	F	"	1896	"	12424
10713	3	" Arthur	9	Son	6	M	"	1896	"	12425
10714	4	" Katie Cristenia	1	Dau	6wk	F	"			
	5									
	6									
	7	ENROLLMENT OF NOS. 1,2,3 and 4 HEREON								
	8	APPROVED BY THE SECRETARY OF INTERIOR FEB 4 1903								
	9									
	10									
	11									
	12									
	13									
	14									
	15									
	16									
	17									

TRIBAL ENROLLMENT OF PARENTS

	Name of Father	Year	County	Name of Mother	Year	County
1	John Talbert	Dead	Blue	Isabelle Talbert		Atoka
2	Impson Jones	"	"	Jincey Jones		Blue
3	No1			No2		
4	No1			No2		
5						
6						
7						
8						
9	Surnames on 1896 roll as Tallbert					
10	No4 Enrolled Sept 10, 1901					
11						
12						
13					Date of Application for Enrollment	For Nos 1 to 3 inclusive
14						
15						Aug 23/99
16						
17						

Choctaw By Blood Enrollment Cards 1898-1914

RESIDENCE: Blue   COUNTY. **Choctaw Nation**   **Choctaw Roll**   CARD NO.
POST OFFICE: Caddo, I.T.   *(Not Including Freedmen)*   FIELD NO. 3797

Dawes' Roll No.	NAME		Relationship to Person First Named	AGE	SEX	BLOOD	TRIBAL ENROLLMENT		
							Year	County	No.
10715	1 Coleman, Norman	35		32	M	Full	1896	Blue	2863
10716	2 " Daly	10	Dau	7	F	"	1896	"	2865
10717	3 " Tennessee	4	Dau	1	F	"			
	4								
	5								
	6	ENROLLMENT							
	7	OF NOS. 1, 2 and 3 HEREON							
	8	APPROVED BY THE SECRETARY OF INTERIOR FEB 4 1903							
	9								
	10								
	11								
	12								
	13								
	14								
	15								
	16								
	17								

TRIBAL ENROLLMENT OF PARENTS

	Name of Father	Year	County	Name of Mother	Year	County
1		Dead			Dead	
2	No 1			Mary Coleman	"	Blue
3	No 1			" "	"	"
4						
5						
6	No 2 on 1896 roll as Dally Coleman					
7						
8	No 3 Affidavit of birth to be supplied: Recd Oct 7/99					
9	For child of No 1 see NB (March 3 1905) #1432					
10						
11						
12						
13						
14					Date of Application for Enrollment.	
15					Aug 23/99	
16						
17						

Choctaw By Blood Enrollment Cards 1898-1914

RESIDENCE: Blue   COUNTY. **Choctaw Nation**   **Choctaw Roll**   CARD NO.
POST OFFICE: Caddo, I.T.   (Not Including Freedmen)   FIELD NO. 3798

Dawes' Roll No.	NAME		Relationship to Person	AGE	SEX	BLOOD	TRIBAL ENROLLMENT		
							Year	County	No.
10718	1 Moore, Loring	26	First Named	23	M	Full	1896	Atoka	8843
10719	2 " Serena	25	Wife	2	F	"	1896	Blue	4366
10720	3 " Suffee	3	Dau	2mo	"	"			
	4								
	5								
	6	ENROLLMENT							
	7	OF NOS. 1, 2 and 3 HEREON APPROVED BY THE SECRETARY							
	8	OF INTERIOR FEB 4 1903							
	9								
	10								
	11								
	12								
	13								
	14								
	15								
	16								
	17								

TRIBAL ENROLLMENT OF PARENTS

	Name of Father	Year	County	Name of Mother	Year	County
1	Nephus Moore		Blue	Ettie Moore	Dead	Blue
2	John Frazier		"	Phoebe Folsom	"	"
3	No1			No2		
4						
5						
6						
7	No1 on 1896 roll as Loring More					
8	No2 " 1896 " " Czarina Frazier					
9						
10						
11						
12						#1&2
13						Date of Application for Enrollment.
14						
15						Aug 23/99
16						No3 enrolled Nov 24/99
17						

Choctaw By Blood Enrollment Cards 1898-1914

RESIDENCE: Jackson COUNTY. **Choctaw Nation**   **Choctaw Roll**   CARD No.
POST OFFICE: Mayhew, I.T.   *(Not Including Freedmen)*   FIELD No. 3799

Dawes' Roll No.	NAME		Relationship to Person	AGE	SEX	BLOOD	TRIBAL ENROLLMENT		
							Year	County	No.
10721	1 Belvin, James	30	First Named	27	M	Full	1896	Jackson	1493
10722	2 " Silway	27	Wife	24	F	"	1896	"	1494
10723	3 " John	5	Son	1	M	"			
	4								
	5								
	6								
	7								
	8								
	9								
	10								
	11								
	12								
	13								
	14								
	15								
	16								
	17								

ENROLLMENT
OF NOS. 1, 2 and 3 HEREON
APPROVED BY THE SECRETARY
OF INTERIOR FEB 4 1903

TRIBAL ENROLLMENT OF PARENTS

Name of Father	Year	County	Name of Mother	Year	County
1 John Belvin	Dead	Jackson	Mary Belvin	Dead	Jackson
2 Esias Nicholas		"	Selina Nicholas	"	"
3 No1			No2		
4					
5					
6					
7					
8 No3 Affidavit of birth to be					
9 supplied:- Filed Dec 14/99					
10					
11					
12					
13					
14				Date of Application for Enrollment.	
15				Aug 23/99	
16					
17 No2 P.O. Boswell Okla					

199

Choctaw By Blood Enrollment Cards 1898-1914

RESIDENCE: Jackson   COUNTY.   **Choctaw Nation**   **Choctaw Roll** *(Not Including Freedmen)*   CARD NO. FIELD NO. **3800**
POST OFFICE: Mayhew, I.T.

Dawes' Roll No.	NAME		Relationship to Person First Named	AGE	SEX	BLOOD	TRIBAL ENROLLMENT		
							Year	County	No.
10724	1	Harmby, James ~~DIED PRIOR TO SEPTEMBER 25, 1902~~	Named	38	M	Full	1896	Jackson	5828
10725	2	" Wilsie 40	Wife	37	F	"	1896	"	5829
10726	3	" Thompson 6	Son	3	M	"	1896	"	5831
10727	4	" Sophina 4	Dau	10mo	F	"			
10728	5	" James Jr ~~DIED PRIOR TO SEPTEMBER 25, 1902~~	Son	11mo	M	"			
	6								
	7								
	8	ENROLLMENT OF NOS. 1,2,3,4 and 5 HEREON APPROVED BY THE SECRETARY OF INTERIOR FEB 4 1903							
	9								
	10								
	11								
	12								
	13								
	14								
	15								
	16								
	17								

TRIBAL ENROLLMENT OF PARENTS

	Name of Father	Year	County	Name of Mother	Year	County
1	Ye-me-ta-homby	Dead	Bok Tuklo	Phillis	Dead	Jackson
2	Chubbee	"	" "	Patsey	"	Bok Tuklo
3	No1			No2		
4	No1			No2		
5	No1			No2		
6						
7						
8			No2 on 1896 roll as Wesley Harmby			
9						
10			No4 Affidavit of birth to be supplied:- Recd Oct 7/99			
11			No5 Enrolled Aug 24, 1901			
12			No. 1 died Oct - 1901: No.5 died March - 1901: Enrollment cancelled by Department July 8, 1904			
13						#1 to 4
14						Date of Application for Enrollment.
15						Aug 23/99
16						
17						

Choctaw By Blood Enrollment Cards 1898-1914

RESIDENCE: Jackson COUNTY. **Choctaw Nation** **Choctaw Roll** CARD NO.
POST OFFICE: Jackson, I.T. *(Not Including Freedmen)* FIELD NO. 3801

Dawes' Roll No.	NAME	Relationship to Person	AGE	SEX	BLOOD	TRIBAL ENROLLMENT		
						Year	County	No.
10729	1 Harmby, Peter ~~DIED PRIOR TO SEPTEMBER 25, 1902~~	First Named	19	M	Full	1896	Jackson	5793
	2							
	3							
	4	ENROLLMENT						
	5	OF NOS. 1 HEREON APPROVED BY THE SECRETARY						
	6	OF INTERIOR FEB 4 1903						
	7							
	8							
	9							
	10							
	11							
	12							
	13							
	14							
	15							
	16							
	17							

TRIBAL ENROLLMENT OF PARENTS

Name of Father	Year	County	Name of Mother	Year	County
1 Henry Harmby	Dead	Jackson	Sally A Harmby	Dead	Jackson
2					
3					
4					
5 No 1 died in the month of October 1901: enrollment cancelled					
6 by the Secretary of Interior – October 5, 1905					
7					
8					
9					
10					
11					
12					
13					
14				Date of Application for Enrollment.	
15				Aug 23/99	
16					
17					

Choctaw By Blood Enrollment Cards 1898-1914

RESIDENCE: Jackson COUNTY. **Choctaw Nation** **Choctaw Roll** CARD NO.
POST OFFICE: Jackson, I.T. *(Not Including Freedmen)* FIELD NO. 3802

Dawes' Roll No.	NAME	Relationship to Person First Named	AGE	SEX	BLOOD	TRIBAL ENROLLMENT Year	TRIBAL ENROLLMENT County	No.
10730	1 Morris, Alfred 23	First Named	20	M	Full	1896	Jackson	8745
	2							
	3							
	4							
	5							
	6							
	7							
	8							
	9							
	10							
	11							
	12							
	13							
	14							
	15							
	16							
	17							

ENROLLMENT
OF NOS. 1 HEREON
APPROVED BY THE SECRETARY
OF INTERIOR FEB 4 1903

TRIBAL ENROLLMENT OF PARENTS

	Name of Father	Year	County	Name of Mother	Year	County
1	Billy Morris	Dead	Jackson	Wilsey Armby		Jackson
2						
3						
4						
5						
6						
7						
8						
9						
10						
11						
12						
13						
14						Date of Application for Enrollment
15						Aug 23/99
16						
17						

Choctaw By Blood Enrollment Cards 1898-1914

RESIDENCE:	Blue	COUNTY.							
POST OFFICE:	Caddo, I.T.								

Choctaw Nation   **Choctaw Roll** *(Not Including Freedmen)*   CARD NO.   FIELD NO. **3803**

Dawes' Roll No.	NAME	Relationship to Person First Named	AGE	SEX	BLOOD	TRIBAL ENROLLMENT Year	County	No.
10731	1 Odell, Mary 45	First Named	42	F	Full	1896	Blue	1660
Dead	2 ~~Benton Charles~~	~~Son~~	~~15~~	~~M~~	~~"~~	~~1896~~	~~"~~	~~1663~~
Dead	3 ~~" Clemon~~	~~"~~	~~15~~	~~"~~	~~"~~	~~1896~~	~~"~~	~~1664~~
10732	4 " James 15	"	12	"	"	1896	"	1665
10733	5 " Edgar 10	"	7	"	"	1896	"	1666
I.W. 1417	6 Odell, W. B.	Husband	48	M	I.W.			
	7							
	8 ENROLLMENT OF NOS. 1, 4 and 5 HEREON APPROVED BY THE SECRETARY OF INTERIOR Feb 4 1903							
	10							
	11							
	12 No. 2 and 3 hereon dismissed under order of the Commission to the Five Civilized Tribes of March 31, 1905.							
	13							
	14							
	15 ENROLLMENT OF NOS. ~ 6 ~~ HEREON APPROVED BY THE SECRETARY OF INTERIOR Jun 12 1905							
	16							
	17							

TRIBAL ENROLLMENT OF PARENTS

	Name of Father	Year	County	Name of Mother	Year	County
1	Brashears Turnbull	Dead	Blue	Jerrico Turnbull		Blue
2	~~Charley Benton~~	~~"~~	~~Sugar Loaf~~	~~No1~~		
3	~~" "~~	~~"~~	~~" "~~	~~No1~~		
4	" "	"	" "	No1		
5	" "	"	" "	No1		
6	James Odell	"	Non Citizen	Mary J Odell	dead	noncitizen
7						
8	Record as to enrollment of No6 forwarded to Department March 14, 1906					
9	Record returned fee opinion of Assistant Attorney General of March 15,1906 in Case of					
10	Omer R Nicholson Nos 1 and 6 were married September 24,1902. ~~No2 on 1896 roll as Charlie Benton~~					
11	No1 is now the wife of W.B. Odell on Choctaw Card #D.805 Sept 24, 1902					
12	No1 was formerly wife of Milton Harkins on Choctaw card #3704 They were divorced Sept 30, 1902					
13	No2 Died Apr. 12,1902: Proof of death filed Nov 10 1902					
14	~~No3 Died in Apr, 1902; Proof of death filed Nov 10 1902~~ Date of Application for Enrollment.					
15	No.6 originally listed for enrollment on Choc. Card #D-805 #1 to 5					
16	Sept 24, 1902: transferred to this card May 15, 1905. See decision of March 28, 1905 Aug 23/99					
17	Cliff I.T. 11/6/02					

203

Choctaw By Blood Enrollment Cards 1898-1914

RESIDENCE: Blue COUNTY. **Choctaw Nation** **Choctaw Roll** (Not Including Freedmen) CARD No. FIELD NO. **3804**
POST OFFICE: Caney, I.T.

Dawes' Roll No.	NAME	Relationship to Person First Named	AGE	SEX	BLOOD	TRIBAL ENROLLMENT Year	County	No.
10734	1 Perkins George L ³⁸	First Named	35	M	Full	1896	Blue	1508
I.W. 1501	2 " Elizabeth ²¹	Wife	18	F	IW	1896	"	14940
10735	3 " Maud A ⁶	Dau	3	"	1/2	1896	"	10509
10736	4 " Lucy ⁴	"	1	"	1/2			
	5							
	6 ENROLLMENT					Notify Riley & Cotner Tishomingo of Decision		
	OF NOS. 1, 3 and 4 HEREON							
	APPROVED BY THE SECRETARY							
	8 OF INTERIOR Feb 4 1903							
	9							

Take no further action relative to enrollment of No2
Protest of Atty for Choctaw and Chickasaw Nations
Jan 23 '04

ENROLLMENT OF NOS. ~~~ 2 ~~~ HEREON APPROVED BY THE SECRETARY OF INTERIOR Nov 27 1905

No2 Granted
Oct 2-1905

TRIBAL ENROLLMENT OF PARENTS

Name of Father	Year	County	Name of Mother	Year	County
1 David Perkins	Dead	Blue	Elsie Perkins	Dead	Blue
2 Daniel Hammock		Non Citz	Tilda Hammock		Non Citz
3 No1			Lillie Perkins		" "
4 No1			No2		
5					
6					
7					
8					
9					
10					

No1 on 1896 roll as G.G. Perkins
No 1-2 Evidence of marriage to be supplied   Rec'd Oct 7/99
No3 Evidence of marriage of parents to be supplied. See testimony of Nicholas Talbert.
No2 now the husband of Mary Perkins on Chickasaw Card #803. Evidence of marriage requested June 25,1902
See testimony of No2 taken Nov 5, 1902

Date of Application for Enrollment. Aug 23/99

_____ I.T.

204

RESIDENCE:	Blue		COUNTY.	**Choctaw Nation**			**Choctaw Roll** _(Not Including Freedmen)_	CARD NO.	
POST OFFICE:	Caddo, I.T.							FIELD NO. 3805	

Dawes' Roll No.	NAME		Relationship to Person First Named	AGE	SEX	BLOOD	TRIBAL ENROLLMENT		
							Year	County	No.
10737	1 Folsom, Jacob	47	First Named	44	M	1/2	1896	Blue	4350
I.W. 158	2 " Mary	41	Wife	38	F	IW	1896	"	14539
10738	3 " Agnes L	21	Dau	18	"	1/4	1896	"	4352
10739	4 " William E	14	Son	11	M	1/4	1896	"	4353
10740	5 " George N	8	"	6	"	1/4	1896	"	4354
10741	6 " Uliss C	6	"	3	"	1/4	1896	"	4355
10742	7 " Ora P	4	Dau	9mo	F	1/4			
	8								
	9	ENROLLMENT							
	10	OF NOS. 1,3,4,5,6 and 7 HEREON APPROVED BY THE SECRETARY							
	11	OF INTERIOR FEB 4 1903							
	12								
	13	ENROLLMENT OF NOS. 2 HEREON							
	14	APPROVED BY THE SECRETARY OF INTERIOR JUN 13 1903							
	15								
	16								
	17								

	TRIBAL ENROLLMENT OF PARENTS						
Name of Father	Year	County		Name of Mother	Year	County	
1 Daniel Folsom	Dead	Blue		Adaline Folsom	Dead	Non Citz	
2 John H Parks	"	Non Citz		Eliza Hensley	"	"	
3	No1			No2			
4	No1			No2			
5	No1			No2			
6	No1			No2			
7	No1			No2			
8							
9	No2 evidence of marriage to be						
10	supplied:- Recd Oct 7/99						
11	No1 as to marriage of parents, see testimony of Arabella Gardner						
12	No3 on 1896 roll as Agnes Folsom						
13	No4 " 1896 " " Wm Ed "					Date of Application for Enrollment.	
14	No7 Affidavit of birth to be supplied" - Received Aug 23/99			No5 on 1896 Roll as Geo M Folsom			
15	For child of No1 see NB (Act Mar 3-05) Card #266			Aug 23/99			
16	" " " No3 " " " " " " #1205						
17	Caney I.T. 11/17/02						

205

Choctaw By Blood Enrollment Cards 1898-1914

RESIDENCE: Blue	COUNTY.					Choctaw Roll	CARD NO.	
POST OFFICE: Academy, I.T.	**Choctaw Nation**					(Not Including Freedmen)	FIELD NO. 3806	

Dawes' Roll No.	NAME	Relationship to Person First Named	AGE	SEX	BLOOD	TRIBAL ENROLLMENT Year	County	No.
10743	1 Gardner Daniel H ²⁸	Named	25	M	full	1896	Blue	4928
10744	2 " Othena ¹	Dau	6mo	F	1/2			
I.W. 1558	3 " Mimie	Wife	25	F	IW			
	4							
	5 ENROLLMENT							
	OF NOS. 1 and 2 HEREON							
	6 APPROVED BY THE SECRETARY							
	7 OF INTERIOR Feb 4 1903							
	8							
	9							
	10							
	11							
	12 ENROLLMENT							
	OF NOS. ~~~ 3 ~~~ HEREON							
	APPROVED BY THE SECRETARY							
	OF INTERIOR Aug 2-1906							
	15							
	16							
	17							

TRIBAL ENROLLMENT OF PARENTS

	Name of Father	Year	County	Name of Mother	Year	County
1	Green Gardner	Dead	Blue	Arabella C Gardner		Blue
2	No1			Minnie Gardner		non-citz
3	Calvin J Holman		noncitizen	Elizabeth Holman		noncitizen
4						
5						
6						
7						
8						
9	No3 placed hereon under order of Commissioner to Five Civilized Tribes of January 11, 1906					
10	holding that application was made for her enrollment within the time provided					
11	by the act of Congress approved July 1, 1902 (32 Stat. 641)					
	Full name of No1 is Daniel Harris Gardner.					
12	No.1 is now the husband of Minnie Gardner, noncitizen, evidence of					
13	marriage filed Aug 26, 1901.					
	No2 Born April 30, 1901: Enrolled Nov. 13, 1901					
14	For child of Nos 1&3 see NB (Apr 26-06) Card #362				No 3	
15	" " " Nos 1&3 " " (Mar 3-05) " #1268				Granted Apr 24 1906	
16					#1	
17	P.O. Bokchito IT 1/23/05			Date of Application for Enrollment.	Aug 23/99	

Choctaw By Blood Enrollment Cards 1898-1914

RESIDENCE: Blue COUNTY.
POST OFFICE: Academy, I.T.

Choctaw Nation

Choctaw Roll
(Not Including Freedmen)

CARD No.
FIELD No. 3807

Dawes' Roll No.	NAME	Relationship to Person First Named	AGE	SEX	BLOOD	TRIBAL ENROLLMENT Year	County	No.
10745	1 Gardner, Arabella C 51	Named	48	F	Full	1896	Blue	4876
10746	2 " Robert L 23	Son	20	M	"	1896	"	4879
10747	3 " Willington L 17	"	14	"	"	1896	"	4880
10748	4 " Dona S 20	Dau	17	F	"	1896	"	4881
10749	5 " Bessie A 16	"	13	"	"	1896	"	4882
10750	6 " Jesse G 12	Son	9	M	"	1896	"	4883
VOID.	7 Thompson, Selena	G.Dau	8	F	1/2	1893	"	500
	8							
	9							
	10	ENROLLMENT OF NOS. 1,2,3,4,5 and 6 HEREON						
	11	APPROVED BY THE SECRETARY						
	12	OF INTERIOR FEB 4 1903						
	13							
	14							
	15							
	16							
	17							

TRIBAL ENROLLMENT OF PARENTS

	Name of Father	Year	County	Name of Mother	Year	County
1	Daniel Folsom	Dead	Blue	Lasiney Folsom	Dead	Blue
2	Green Gardner	"	"	No1		
3	" "	"	"	No1		
4	" "	"	"	No1		
5	" "	"	"	No1		
6	" "	"	"	No1		
7	Thos. Thompson		Chick Roll	Isabella Thompson	Dead	Blue
8						
9						
10	No2 on 1896 roll as Robt. L. Gardner					
11	No4 " " 1896 " " Dora S. "					
12	No7 on 1893 Pay Roll, Page 47, — For child of No.2 see NB (March 3, 1904) #849			On Choctaw Card #334.		
13						
14					Date of Application for Enrollment.	
15					Aug 23/99	
16						
17	P.O. Jackson I.T. 4/10/05					

Choctaw By Blood Enrollment Cards 1898-1914

RESIDENCE: **Blue** COUNTY. **Choctaw Nation** Choctaw Roll CARD NO.
POST OFFICE: Caddo, I.T. (Not Including Freedmen) FIELD NO. **3808**

Dawes' Roll No.	NAME	Relationship to Person First Named	AGE	SEX	BLOOD	TRIBAL ENROLLMENT		
						Year	County	No.
10751	1 Carnes, Willie 24	First Named	21	M	Full	1896	Blue	2980
	2							
	3							
	4	ENROLLMENT						
	5	OF NOS. 1 HEREON APPROVED BY THE SECRETARY						
	6	OF INTERIOR FEB 4 1903						
	7							
	8							
	9							
	10							
	11							
	12							
	13							
	14							
	15							
	16							
	17							

TRIBAL ENROLLMENT OF PARENTS

	Name of Father	Year	County	Name of Mother	Year	County
1	Eli Carnes	Dead	Blue	Margaret Tumby		Atoka
2						
3						
4						
5						
6						
7						
8						
9						
10						
11						
12						
13						
14						
15				Date of Application for Enrollment.		Aug 23/99
16						
17	Sulphur, I.T. (P.O. Beulah, Okla. personal notice 7/24/11)					

208

NAME	Relationship to Person First Named	AGE	SEX	BLOOD	TRIBAL ENROLLMENT		
					Year	County	No.
1 Gardner, Edward N ³⁰	Named	27	M	Full	1896	Blue	4877
2 " Rosetta ²³	Wife	20	F	I.W.			
3 " Iona ³	Dau	4mo	F	9/16			
4 " Dona Lee ¹	Dau	6wks	F	9/16			
5							
6							
7							
8							
9							
10							
11							
12							
13							
14							
15							
16							
17							

ENROLLMENT OF NOS. 1, 3 and 4 HEREON APPROVED BY THE SECRETARY OF INTERIOR FEB 4 1903

ENROLLMENT OF NOS ~~~ 2 ~~~ HEREON APPROVED BY THE SECRETARY OF INTERIOR OCT 21 1904

TRIBAL ENROLLMENT OF PARENTS

Name of Father	Year	County	Name of Mother	Year	County
1 Green Gardner	Dead	Blue	Arabella S Gardner		Blue
2 Saml Riddle		Choctaw	Martha Rebble[sic]		Non-citizen
3 No.1			No.2		
4 Nº1			Nº2		
5					
6					
7 Now Denied in 96 Case #686 as a citizen by blood					
8 No.2 Admitted by U.S. Court, Central Dist.					
9 Aug 30, '97. Court case No.8, as Rosetta Riddle.					
10 As to residence see her testimony; also					
11 see enrollment of Saml B. Riddle, her					
12 father. Transferred from Choctaw 3954, June 4, 1900					
13 No.3 Enrolled June 4, 1900		Date of Application for Enrollment	#1		
14 Nº4 Born June 27, 1902; enrolled Aug. 8, 1902					
15 No2 Denied by C.C.C. March 21 '04 as a citizen by blood					Aug 23/99
16 For child of Nos 1&2 see NB (Apr 26-06) Card #595				No.2 " 25, 1899	
17 Bokchito I.T 5/19/04					

209

Choctaw By Blood Enrollment Cards 1898-1914

RESIDENCE: **Blue** COUNTY.
POST OFFICE: **Academy, I.T.**

Choctaw Nation

Choctaw Roll
(Not Including Freedmen)

CARD NO.
FIELD NO. **3810**

Dawes' Roll No.	NAME	Relationship to Person First Named	AGE	SEX	BLOOD	TRIBAL ENROLLMENT		
						Year	County	No.
10755	1 Riddle, Mary A 26	First Named	23	F	Full	1896	Blue	4878
10756	2 " Thelma D 5	Dau	2	"	1/2			
10757	3 " Bartis G 3	Son	2mo	M	1/2			
~~Dead~~	4 " ~~Una M~~ dead	~~Dau~~	~~2mo~~	~~F~~	~~1/2~~			
	5							
	6	ENROLLMENT						
	7	OF NOS. 1, 2 and 3 HEREON						
	8	APPROVED BY THE SECRETARY OF INTERIOR Feb 4 1903						
	9	No. 4 Hereon dismissed under order						
	10	of the Commission to the Five Civilized						
	11	Tribes of March 31, 1905.						
	12							
	13							
	14							
	15							
	16							
	17							

TRIBAL ENROLLMENT OF PARENTS

	Name of Father	Year	County	Name of Mother	Year	County
1	Green Gardner	Dead	Blue	Arabella Gardner		Blue
2	J. T. Riddle		Non Citz	No1		
3	" " "		" "	No1		
4	" " "		" "	~~No1~~		
5						
6						
7						
8			No1 On 1896 roll as Mary A. Gardner			
9			No4 born Aug 23d, 1901. Enrolled Nov. 13, 1901			
10			No4 died Sept 21, 1902 proof of death filed Nov 24, 1902			
11						
12			Is No1 the wife of James T. Riddle in Choctaw #3896?			
13			For child of No1 see N.B. (Apr 26 '06) Card #257			
			" " " " " (Mar 3-1905) " #252			
14						
15				Date of Application for Enrollment.		Aug 23/99
16						
17	P.O. Bokchito, I.T. 4/5/05					

210

Choctaw By Blood Enrollment Cards 1898-1914

RESIDENCE: Blue   COUNTY. **Choctaw Nation**   **Choctaw Roll**   CARD NO.
POST OFFICE: Caddo, I.T.   *(Not Including Freedmen)*   FIELD NO. 3811

Dawes' Roll No.	NAME	Relationship to Person First Named	AGE	SEX	BLOOD	TRIBAL ENROLLMENT		
						Year	County	No.
DEAD.	1 Frazier, Johnson		56	M	Full	1896	Blue	4364
10758	2 " Louisa ³⁹	Wife	36	F	"	1896	"	4365
	3							
	4	ENROLLMENT						
	5	OF NOS. 2 HEREON APPROVED BY THE SECRETARY						
	6	OF INTERIOR FEB 4 1903						
	7	No. 1 HEREON DISMISSED UNDER						
	8	ORDER OF THE COMMISSION TO THE FIVE CIVILIZED TRIBES OF MARCH 31, 1905.						
	9							
	10							
	11							
	12							
	13							
	14							
	15							
	16							
	17							

TRIBAL ENROLLMENT OF PARENTS

	Name of Father	Year	County	Name of Mother	Year	County
1	Jones Frazier		Blue		Dead	Blue
2	James Makinley	Dead	"	Mary Makinley	"	"
3						
4						
5						
6						
7	No 1 Died March 4, 1902; proof of death filed Nov 22 1902					
8						
9						
10						
11						
12						
13						
14						
15				Date of Application for Enrollment.	Aug 23/99	
16						
17						

Choctaw By Blood Enrollment Cards 1898-1914

RESIDENCE: **Blue**   COUNTY. **Choctaw Nation**   **Choctaw Roll**   CARD No. ▮▮▮
POST OFFICE: **Bok Chito, I.T.**   *(Not Including Freedmen)*   FIELD No. **3812**

Dawes' Roll No.	NAME	Relationship to Person First Named	AGE	SEX	BLOOD	TRIBAL ENROLLMENT		
						Year	County	No.
DEAD.	1 Pickens, Sarah DEAD.	Named	63	F	Full	1896	Blue	10501
See 5347	2 Garland, Jack	G.Son	17	M	"	1896	"	4905
10759	3 " James 16	"	13	"	"	1896	"	4906
10760	4 " Aurilla 14	G.Dau	11	F	"	1896	"	4907
	5							
	6							
	7	ENROLLMENT						
	8	OF NOS. 3 and 4 HEREON APPROVED BY THE SECRETARY						
	9	OF INTERIOR FEB 4 1903						
	10	No. 1 HEREON DISMISSED UNDER						
	11	ORDER OF THE COMMISSION TO THE FIVE CIVILIZED TRIBES OF MARCH 31, 1905.						
	12							
	13							
	14							
	15							
	16							
	17							

TRIBAL ENROLLMENT OF PARENTS

	Name of Father	Year	County	Name of Mother	Year	County
1	John Garland	Dead	Towson	E-a-le-hoke	Dead	Towson
2	Levi Garland	"	Blue	Liffie Garland	"	Blue
3	" "	"	"	" "	"	"
4	" "	"	"	" "	"	"
5						
6						
7		No3 on 1896 roll as Jim Garland				
8		No4 " 1896 " " Orilla "				
9						
10		No.1 died November 16th, 1899 See testimony of No.2				
11		No.2 transferred to Choctaw card #5347 with his				
12		wife, November 28th, 1900.				
13						
14						
15				Date of Application for Enrollment	Aug 23/99	
16						
17						

Choctaw By Blood Enrollment Cards 1898-1914

Dawes' Roll No.	NAME	Relationship to Person	AGE	SEX	BLOOD	TRIBAL ENROLLMENT		
						Year	County	No.
10761	1 Lewis, John ⁸⁰	First Named	77	M	Full	1896	Blue	8204
	2							
	3							
	4							
	5							
	6							
	7							
	8							
	9							
	10							
	11							
	12							
	13							
	14							
	15							
	16							
	17							

ENROLLMENT
OF NOS. 1 HEREON
APPROVED BY THE SECRETARY
OF INTERIOR FEB 4 1903

TRIBAL ENROLLMENT OF PARENTS

Name of Father	Year	County	Name of Mother	Year	County
1 E-la-oi-tink-batabe	Dead	Skullyville		Dead	
2					
3					
4					
5					
6 On 1896 roll as John Lowis[sic]					
7					
8					
9					
10					
11					
12					
13					
14					
15			Date of Application for Enrollment.		Aug 23/99
16					
17					

Choctaw By Blood Enrollment Cards 1898-1914

RESIDENCE: Jackson COUNTY.
POST OFFICE: Jackson, I.T.

Choctaw Nation

Choctaw Roll
(Not Including Freedmen)

CARD NO.
FIELD NO. 3814

Dawes' Roll No.	NAME	Relationship to Person First Named	AGE	SEX	BLOOD	TRIBAL ENROLLMENT		
						Year	County	No.
10762	1 Pistokache, Cornelius [21]	First Named	18	M	Full	1896	Jackson	10461
	2							
	3							
	4							
	5							
	6							
	7							
	8							
	9							
	10							
	11							
	12							
	13							
	14							
	15							
	16							
	17							

ENROLLMENT
OF NOS. 1 HEREON
APPROVED BY THE SECRETARY
OF INTERIOR FEB 4 1903

TRIBAL ENROLLMENT OF PARENTS

	Name of Father	Year	County	Name of Mother	Year	County
1	Morris Pistokcha[sic]	Dead	Jackson	Yim-me	Dead	Jackson
2						
3						
4						
5						
6	On 1896 roll as Cornelius Pistokachi					
7						
8						
9	No1 is now the husband of Adeline Byington on Choctaw Card 3826					
10					Nov 22 1902	
11						
12						
13						
14					Date of Application for Enrollment.	
15					Aug 23/99	
16						
17						

Choctaw By Blood Enrollment Cards 1898-1914

RESIDENCE: Blue	COUNTY.								
POST OFFICE: Caddo, I.T.	**Choctaw Nation**					**Choctaw Roll** (Not Including Freedmen)		CARD No. FIELD No. 3815	

Dawes' Roll No.	NAME		Relationship to Person First Named	AGE	SEX	BLOOD	TRIBAL ENROLLMENT		
							Year	County	No.
14812	1 Wright, Joseph	23		20	M	Full	1896	Blue	13851
14813	2 " Mary	24	Wife	21	F	"	1896	Atoka	8274
14814	3 " Daniel	2	Son	2	M	"			
	4								
	5								
	6								
	7								
	8	ENROLLMENT OF NOS. 1, 2 and 3 HEREON APPROVED BY THE SECRETARY OF INTERIOR MAY 20 1903							
	9								
	10								
	11								
	12								
	13								
	14								
	15								
	16								
	17								

TRIBAL ENROLLMENT OF PARENTS

Name of Father	Year	County	Name of Mother	Year	County
1 Allen Wright	Dead	Blue	Betsey Robinson		Blue
2 Watkins LeFlore		Atoka	Seliney LeFlore	Dead	Atoka
3 No.1			No.2		
4					
5					
6					
7 No2 on 1896 roll as Mary LeFlore, also on					
8 1896 roll as Mary Carnes, Page 70, No 2967,					
9 Atoka Co., No.3 Born Oct 23 1900; Evidence of Birth filed Dec 23 1902					
10					
11					
12					
13				Date of Application for Enrollment.	
14					
15				Aug 23/99	
16					
17 Caney I.T. 11/18/02					

215

Choctaw By Blood Enrollment Cards 1898-1914

RESIDENCE: **Blue**   COUNTY. **Choctaw Nation**   **Choctaw Roll** *(Not Including Freedmen)*   CARD NO.
POST OFFICE: **Caddo, I.T.**   FIELD NO. **3816**

Dawes' Roll No.	NAME		Relationship to Person First Named	AGE	SEX	BLOOD	TRIBAL ENROLLMENT		
							Year	County	No.
10763	1 LeFlore, Forbis F	35	First Named	32	M	1/8	1896	Blue	8178
I.W. 350	2 " Phoebe E	30	Wife	27	F	IW	1896	"	14777
10764	3 " Loraine	8	Dau	5	"	1/16	1896	"	8179
10765	4 " Dreda	7	"	4	"	1/16	1896	"	8180
10766	5 " Forbis E	6	Son	3	M	1/16	1896	"	8181
	6								
	7								
	8	ENROLLMENT OF NOS. 1,3,4 and 5 HEREON							
	9	APPROVED BY THE SECRETARY OF INTERIOR FEB 4 1903							
	10								
	11	ENROLLMENT OF NOS. 2 HEREON							
	12	APPROVED BY THE SECRETARY OF INTERIOR SEP 12 1903							
	13								
	14								
	15								
	16								
	17								

TRIBAL ENROLLMENT OF PARENTS

	Name of Father	Year	County	Name of Mother	Year	County
1	Forbis LeFlore	Dead	Blue	Mary LeFlore		Intermarried
2	William Kays		Non Citz	Margaret A Kays		Non Citz
3	No1			No2		
4	No1			No2		
5	No1			No2		
6						
7						
8						
9						
10	No1 on 1896 roll as Forbis LeFlore					
11	No3 " 1896 " " Loraine "					
12	No2 " 1896 " " Phoebe "					
13	No1 as to marriage of parents, see testimony of Peter Maytubby					
14	No2 was admitted in 1896 as an intermarried citizen					Date of Application for Enrollment.
15	by Dawes Commission: Choctaw Case #1228: No appeal.					Aug 23/99
16						
17						

216

RESIDENCE: Chickasaw Natn	COUNTY.	Choctaw Nation		Choctaw Roll	CARD No.	
POST OFFICE: Marlow, I.T.				(Not Including Freedmen)	FIELD No. **3817**	

Dawes' Roll No.	NAME Antlers, I.T.	Relationship to Person Named	AGE	SEX	BLOOD	TRIBAL ENROLLMENT		
						Year	County	No.
10767	1 Dillard, Gill 34	First Named	31	M	1/8	1896	Chick Dist	3640
10768	2 " Bessie 13	Dau	10	F	1/16	1896	" "	3651
10769	3 " Grover 8	Son	5	M	1/16	1896	" "	3652
10770	4 " Clara E 6	Dau	3	F	1/16	1896	" "	3653
I.W. 1259	5 " Myrtle 20	Wife	17	"	I.W.			
10771	6 " Velma 2	Dau	2wks	"	1/16			
10772	7 " Malcolm C 1	Son	10mo	M	1/16			
	8							
	9							
	10 ENROLLMENT							
	11 OF NOS. 1,2,3,4,6 and 7 HEREON APPROVED BY THE SECRETARY							
	12 OF INTERIOR Feb 4 1903							
	13							
	14 ENROLLMENT							
	15 OF NOS. 5 HEREON APPROVED BY THE SECRETARY							
	16 OF INTERIOR Dec 30 1904							
	17							

TRIBAL ENROLLMENT OF PARENTS

	Name of Father	Year	County	Name of Mother now Simpson	Year	County
1	Hamp Dillard	Dead	Non Citz	Eliz. Dillard		Chick Dist
2	No1			Mary Dillard	Dead	Non Citz
3	No1			" "	"	" "
4	No1			" "	"	" "
5	Charles Corbin		Non Citz	Ella Corbin	"	" "
6	No1			No5		
7	No1			No5		
8						
9						
10	No2 on 1896 roll as Elizabeth Dillard					
11	No4 " 1896 " " Clara "					
12						
13	Evidence of marriage of parents of					
14	above three children to be supplied; See			#1 to 4		
15	testimony of No1 and Ed Simpson			Date of Application for Enrollment.	Aug 23/99	
16	No.7 Born August 12th 1901: Enrolled June 25th 1902			No5 enrolled Dec 7/99 No		
17	No6 enrolled 6/5/1900			ticket issued		

Choctaw By Blood Enrollment Cards 1898-1914

RESIDENCE: **Blue**
POST OFFICE: Caddo, I.T.

COUNTY. **Choctaw Nation**

Choctaw Roll
(Not Including Freedmen)

CARD NO.
FIELD NO. **3818**

Dawes' Roll No.		NAME		Relationship to Person	AGE	SEX	BLOOD	TRIBAL ENROLLMENT		
								Year	County	No.
14377	1	Dorset, John	25	First Named	22	M	Full	1896	Wade	3351
	2									
	3									
	4									
	5									
	6									
	7									
	8									
	9									
	10									
	11									
	12									
	13									
	14									
	15									
	16									
	17									

ENROLLMENT
OF NOS. 1 HEREON
APPROVED BY THE SECRETARY
OF INTERIOR Apr 11 1903

TRIBAL ENROLLMENT OF PARENTS

	Name of Father	Year	County	Name of Mother	Year	County
1	John Dorset	Dead	in Louisiana	Peggy Dorset	Dead	in Louisiana
2						
3						
4						
5						
6						
7						
8						
9						
10						
11						
12						
13						
14						
15						
16						
17						

No.1 claims to have been admitted to citizenship in the Choctaw
Nation by Act of Council passed in October 1895
No1 admitted in 1896 by Dawes Commission in
Choctaw Case #321. No appeal
For child of No1 see NB (Apr 26-06) Card #592
" " " " " " (Mar 3 1905) " #609

Date of Application for Enrollment.
Aug 23/99

Choctaw By Blood Enrollment Cards 1898-1914

RESIDENCE: Blue   COUNTY. **Choctaw Nation**   **Choctaw Roll**   CARD NO.
POST OFFICE: Caddo, I.T.   *(Not Including Freedmen)*   FIELD NO. 3819

Dawes' Roll No.	NAME		Relationship to Person	AGE	SEX	BLOOD	TRIBAL ENROLLMENT		
							Year	County	No.
10773	1 Lewis, Silas	27	First Named	24	M	Full	1896	Blue	8241
10774	2 " Silvy	41	Wife	38	F	"	1896	"	8242
	3								
	4								
	5								
	6	ENROLLMENT OF NOS. 1 and 2 HEREON							
	7	APPROVED BY THE SECRETARY OF INTERIOR FEB 4 1903							
	8								
	9								
	10								
	11								
	12								
	13								
	14								
	15								
	16								
	17								

TRIBAL ENROLLMENT OF PARENTS

	Name of Father	Year	County	Name of Mother	Year	County
1	Absalom Lewis	Dead	Blue	Nancy Lewis	Dead	Blue
2	Tobachee Wright	"	Jackson	Ok-la-chee	"	Jackson
3						
4						
5						
6						
7						
8						
9						
10						
11						
12						
13						
14						
15				Date of Application for Enrollment	Aug 23/99	
16						
17						

Choctaw By Blood Enrollment Cards 1898-1914

RESIDENCE: **Blue** COUNTY.
POST OFFICE: **Caddo, I.T.**

Choctaw Nation

Choctaw Roll (Not Including Freedmen)

CARD No.
FIELD No. **3820**

Dawes' Roll No.	NAME		Relationship to Person First Named	AGE	SEX	BLOOD	TRIBAL ENROLLMENT		
							Year	County	No.
10775	1 Robinson, Wallace	27	First Named	24	M	Full	1896	Blue	10929
10776	2 " Sina	25	Wife	22	F	"	1896	"	10930
10777	3 " Stulger E	7	Son	4	M	"	1896	"	10931
DEAD	4 " Gilbert DEAD		"	1	"	"			
	5								
	6								
	7								
	8	ENROLLMENT							
	9	OF NOS. 1, 2 and 3 HEREON APPROVED BY THE SECRETARY							
	10	OF INTERIOR FEB 4 1903							
	11	No. 4 HEREON DISMISSED UNDER							
	12	ORDER OF THE COMMISSION TO THE FIVE CIVILIZED TRIBES OF MARCH 31, 1905.							
	13								
	14								
	15								
	16								
	17								

TRIBAL ENROLLMENT OF PARENTS

	Name of Father	Year	County	Name of Mother	Year	County
1	Robinson Makinley	Dead	Jackson	Phillis Makinley	Dead	Jackson
2	James Elum	"	Blue	Seliney Elum	"	Blue
3	No1			No2		
4	No1			No2		
5						
6						
7						
8	No2 on 1896 roll as Sanie Robinson					
9	No3 " 1896 " " Asan "					
10	No4 Affidavit of birth to be supplied:-					
11						
12	No.4 Died Sept. 4, 1899; Proof of death filed Nov 7, 1902					
13						
14					Date of Application for Enrollment.	
15					Aug 23/99	
16						
17						

Choctaw By Blood Enrollment Cards 1898-1914

RESIDENCE:	Blue	COUNTY.								

RESIDENCE: **Blue** COUNTY. **Choctaw Nation**   **Choctaw Roll** (Not Including Freedmen)   CARD No.
POST OFFICE: **Caddo, I.T.**   FIELD No. **3821**

Dawes' Roll No.	NAME	Relationship to Person First Named	AGE	SEX	BLOOD	TRIBAL ENROLLMENT		
						Year	County	No.
I.W.977	1 Williams, Mary 61	First Named	59	F	IW	1896	Blue	15188
	2							
	3							
	4							
	5							
	6							
	7							
	8							
	9							
	10 See Petitions No. W 104 - 105							
	11							
	12							
	13							
	14							
	15	ENROLLMENT OF NOS. 1 HEREON APPROVED BY THE SECRETARY OF INTERIOR SEP 22 1904						
	16							
	17							

TRIBAL ENROLLMENT OF PARENTS

	Name of Father	Year	County	Name of Mother	Year	County
1	Thos. Parker	Dead	Non Citz	Anna Parker	Dead	Non Citz
2						
3						
4						
5						
6	No1 See Decision of July 19 '04					
7						
8	As to marriage, see testimony of Loring S.W. Folson[sic].					
9	Admitted by Dawes Com. Case No 957,					
10	as Mrs. Mary Williams. No appeal.					
11						
12						
13						
14					Date of Application for Enrollment.	
15					Aug 23/99	
16						
17						

Choctaw By Blood Enrollment Cards 1898-1914

Dawes' Roll No.	NAME		Relationship to Person	AGE	SEX	BLOOD	TRIBAL ENROLLMENT			
							Year	County		No.
10778	1 King, Jesse	24	First Named	21	M	Full	1896	Blue		7619
	2									
	3									
	4									
	5	ENROLLMENT								
	6	OF NOS. 1 HEREON APPROVED BY THE SECRETARY								
	7	OF INTERIOR Feb 4 1903								
	8									
	9									
	10									
	11									
	12									
	13									
	14									
	15									
	16									
	17									

TRIBAL ENROLLMENT OF PARENTS

	Name of Father	Year	County	Name of Mother	Year	County
1	Solomon King	Dead	Atoka	Mary King	Dead	Blue
2						
3						
4						
5						
6						
7	No1 is now the husband of Alice Nicholas on Choc #3452					
8						
9						
10						
11						
12						
13						
14					Date of Application for Enrollment.	
15					Aug 23/99	
16						
17						

Choctaw By Blood Enrollment Cards 1898-1914

RESIDENCE: Blue COUNTY.
POST OFFICE: Boggy Depot, I.T.

Choctaw Nation

Choctaw Roll
(Not Including Freedmen)

CARD NO.
FIELD NO. **3823**

Dawes' Roll No.	NAME	Relationship to Person	AGE	SEX	BLOOD	TRIBAL ENROLLMENT Year	County	No.
10779	1 Hall, Eliza ⁵³	First Named	50	F	Full	1896	Blue	5860
10780	2 " Roberson ¹⁹	Son	16	M	"	1896	"	5861
10781	3 Byington Elizabeth ²³	Dau	20	F	"	1896	"	4341
10782	4 Byington Thompson ¹	GrSon	7mo	M	"			
	5							
	6							
	7	ENROLLMENT						
	8	OF NOS. 1,2,3 and 4 HEREON APPROVED BY THE SECRETARY						
	9	OF INTERIOR Feb 4 1903						
	10							
	11							
	12							
	13							
	14							
	15							
	16							
	17							

TRIBAL ENROLLMENT OF PARENTS

	Name of Father	Year	County	Name of Mother	Year	County
1	Ok-pu-la-ha-ya	Dead	Blue	Sophia	Dead	Blue
2	Roberson Hall	"	"	No1		
3	" "	"	"	No1		
4	Benjamin Byington	1896	Atoka	Nº3		
5						
6						
7						
8						
9	Nº3 is now the wife of Benjamin Byington on Choctaw card #4891. Evidence of					
10	marriage requested Sept. 4, 1902					
11	Nº4 Born Feby. 13, 1901: enrolled Sept. 4, 1902					
12						
13					#1 to 3 inc	
14					Date of Application for Enrollment.	
15					Aug 23/99	
16						
17						

Choctaw By Blood Enrollment Cards 1898-1914

RESIDENCE:	Blue	COUNTY:						CARD NO.	
POST OFFICE:	Caddo, I.T.		**Choctaw Nation**			Choctaw Roll (Not Including Freedmen)		FIELD No. 3824	

Dawes' Roll No.	NAME		Relationship to Person First Named	AGE	SEX	BLOOD	TRIBAL ENROLLMENT		
							Year	County	No.
I.W. 790	1 Stewart, Bettie	31	First Named	28	F	IW	1896	Blue	15058
10783	2 " Minnie B	10	Dau	7	"	1/4	1896	"	11594
10784	3 " Samuel E	8	"	5	"	1/4	1896	"	11595
	4								
	5								
	6								
	7								
	8	ENROLLMENT OF NOS. 2 and 3 HEREON APPROVED BY THE SECRETARY							
	9	OF INTERIOR FEB 4 1903							
	10								
	11	ENROLLMENT OF NOS. 1 HEREON							
	12	APPROVED BY THE SECRETARY							
	13	OF INTERIOR MAY 9 1904							
	14								
	15								
	16								
	17								

TRIBAL ENROLLMENT OF PARENTS

	Name of Father	Year	County	Name of Mother	Year	County
1	Wade Hampton	Dead	Non Citz	Louisa Hampton	Dead	Non Citz
2	S. W. Stewart	"	Blue	No1		
3	" " "	"	"	No1		
4						
5						
6	No1 denied in 96 Case #782					
7	No1 on 1896 roll as Bettie Steward					
8	No3 " 1896 " " Esther Samuel Stewart					
	No.1 admitted by U.S. Court, Central District, Indian territory					
9	July 13th, 1897, in Court case #114, Bettie Stewart vs. Choctaw Nation					
10	Judgment of U.S. Ct. admitting No1 vacated and set aside by Decree of Choctaw Chickasaw Citizenship Court Dec' 17'02					
11	No1 now in C.C.C.C. case #92					
12	No1 admitted by the C.C.C.C. Case #92 March 9 01					
13						
14						
15					Aug 23/99	
16						
17						

Choctaw By Blood Enrollment Cards 1898-1914

RESIDENCE: Blue	COUNTY. **Choctaw Nation**		**Choctaw Roll**		CARD NO.	
POST OFFICE: Caddo, I.T.			*(Not Including Freedmen)*		FIELD NO. **3825**	

Dawes' Roll No.	NAME	Relationship to Person First Named	AGE	SEX	BLOOD	TRIBAL ENROLLMENT		
						Year	County	No.
10785	1 Turnbull, Turner B. ⁵¹	First Named	48	M	Full	1896	Blue	12391
10786	2 " Adeline D ⁴¹	Wife	38	F	"	1896	"	12392
10787	3 " Elizabeth ²¹	Dau	18	"	"	1896	"	12393
10788	4 " Timothy ¹⁸	Son	15	M	"	1896	"	12394
10789	5 " Walter J ¹⁶	"	13	"	"	1896	"	12395
10790	6 " Charles C ¹³	"	10	"	"	1896	"	12396
10791	7 " William P ¹¹	"	8	"	"	1896	"	12397
10792	8 " Jane L ⁹	Dau	6	F	"	1896	"	12399
	9							
	10							
	11	ENROLLMENT OF NOS. 1,2,3,4,5,6,7 and 8 HEREON						
	12	APPROVED BY THE SECRETARY						
	13	OF INTERIOR Feb 4 1903						
	14							
	15							
	16							
	17							

TRIBAL ENROLLMENT OF PARENTS

	Name of Father	Year	County	Name of Mother	Year	County
1	T. B. Turnbull	Dead	Blue	Jerrico Turnbull	Dead	Blue
2	Timothy Dwight	"	Jackson	Minerva Dwight		Jackson
3	No 1			No 2		
4	No 1			No 2		
5	No 1			No 2		
6	No 1			No 2		
7	No 1			No 2		
8	No 1			No 2		
9						
10						
11	No5 on 1896 roll as Walter Turnbull					
12	No6 " 1896 " " Chas. C. "					
13	No7 " 1896 " " Wᵐ P. "					
14					Date of Application for Enrollment.	
15					Aug 23/99	
16						
17						

Choctaw By Blood Enrollment Cards 1898-1914

RESIDENCE: Atoka COUNTY. **Choctaw Nation** Choctaw Roll CARD NO.
POST OFFICE: Boggy Depot, I.T. *(Not Including Freedmen)* FIELD NO. **3826**

Dawes' Roll No.	NAME	Relationship to Person First Named	AGE	SEX	BLOOD	TRIBAL ENROLLMENT		
						Year	County	No.
1079	1 Byington, Peter 19	First Named	16	M	Full	1896	Atoka	1802
DEAD	2 " Henry DEAD	Bro	15	"	"	1896	"	1800
10794	3 Pistokache Adeline 16	Sister	13	F	"	1896	"	1801
DEAD	4 " Mary DEAD	"	9	"	"	1896	"	1803
10795	5 Pistokache William Pain	Nephew	11m	M	"			
	6							
	7							
	8							
	9	ENROLLMENT OF NOS. HEREON APPROVED BY THE SECRETARY OF INTERIOR						
	10							
	11							
	12 No. 2 and 4 hereon dismissed under							
	13 order of the Commission to the Five							
	14 Civilized Tribes of March 31, 1905.							
	15							
	16							
	17							

TRIBAL ENROLLMENT OF PARENTS

Name of Father		Year	County	Name of Mother		Year	County
1 Thompson Byington		Dead	Atoka	Melinda Byington			Atoka
2 " "		"	"	" "			"
3 " "		"	"	" "			"
4 " "		"	"	" "			"
5 Cornelius Pistockche[sic]				No3			
6							
7							
8							
9							
10							
11	Nº1 is now husband of Nancy James on Choctaw card #3781 Sept 29, 1902						
12	No3 is now the wife of Cornelius Pistokcha on Choctaw Card #3814 Nov 22, 1902						
13	No5 Born January 10 1902. Enrolled Nov 22, 1902						
14	No2 Died Feby 16, 1901. Proof of death filed Nov 22 1902					#1 to 4 Date of Application for Enrollment.	
	No4 Died Feby 13, 1900. Proof of death filed Nov 22 1902						
15						Aug 23/99	
16							
17	No2 In jail at Atoka 9/14/02						

Choctaw By Blood Enrollment Cards 1898-1914

RESIDENCE: Blue   COUNTY. **Choctaw Nation**   **Choctaw Roll** *(Not Including Freedmen)*   CARD No.

POST OFFICE: Caddo, I.T.   FIELD No. **3827**

Dawes' Roll No.	NAME	Relationship to Person First Named	AGE	SEX	BLOOD	TRIBAL ENROLLMENT		
						Year	County	No.
10796	1 Chateau, Martin ²³	First Named	20	M	Full	1896	Kiamitia	2699
	2							
	3							
	4	ENROLLMENT						
	5	OF NOS. 1 HEREON						
	6	APPROVED BY THE SECRETARY OF INTERIOR Feb 4 1903						
	7							
	8							
	9							
	10							
	11							
	12							
	13							
	14							
	15							
	16							
	17							

TRIBAL ENROLLMENT OF PARENTS

	Name of Father	Year	County	Name of Mother	Year	County
1	Dan Smallwood	Dead	Blue	Asa A Smallwood	Dead	Kiamitia
2						
3						
4						
5						
6						
7			On 1896 roll as Martin Chantou			
8						
9			For child of No1 see NB (Mar 3, 05) Card #253			
10						
11						
12						
13					Date of Application for Enrollment.	
14						
15					Aug 23/99	
16						
17	P.O. Caney I T 11/12/04					

P.O. Atoka I.T. 3/29/05

Choctaw By Blood Enrollment Cards 1898-1914

RESIDENCE: Blue	COUNTY.					CARD No.
POST OFFICE: Caddo, I.T.	**Choctaw Nation**		Choctaw Roll (Not Including Freedmen)			FIELD No. 3828

Dawes' Roll No.	NAME	Relationship to Person First Named	AGE	SEX	BLOOD	TRIBAL ENROLLMENT Year	County	No.
10797	1 Robinson, Lewis 23	First Named	20	M	Full	1896	Blue	10925
	2							
	3							
	4							
	5	ENROLLMENT OF NOS. 1 HEREON APPROVED BY THE SECRETARY OF INTERIOR FEB 4 1903						
	6							
	7							
	8							
	9							
	10							
	11							
	12							
	13							
	14							
	15							
	16							
	17							

TRIBAL ENROLLMENT OF PARENTS

	Name of Father	Year	County	Name of Mother	Year	County
1	Lewis Robinson	Dead	Blue	Phillis Robinson	Dead	Blue
2						
3						
4						
5						
6	On 1896 roll as Louis Roberson					
7						
8						
9						
10						
11						
12						
13						
14						Date of Application for Enrollment.
15						Aug 23/99
16						
17						

RESIDENCE: Blue   COUNTY. **Choctaw Nation**   **Choctaw Roll** (Not Including Freedmen)   CARD NO.

POST OFFICE: Caddo, I.T.   FIELD NO. 3829

Dawes' Roll No.	NAME	Relationship to Person First Named	AGE	SEX	BLOOD	TRIBAL ENROLLMENT Year	County	No.
DEAD.	1 Lewis, Solomon DEAD.		54	M	Full	1896	Blue	8227
10798	2 Bond Sallie ²⁸	Dau	25	F	"	1896	"	8229
10799	3 Lewis Jiman ²⁵	Son	22	M	"	1896	"	8230
DEAD.	4 " Adeline DEAD.	Dau	16	F	"	1896	"	8231
10800	5 Bond Marvin	Son of Nº2	15mo	M	"			
	6							
	7	ENROLLMENT						
	8	OF NOS. 2, 3 and 5 HEREON APPROVED BY THE SECRETARY OF INTERIOR FEB 4 1903						
	9	No. 1 and 4 HEREON DISMISSED UNDER ORDER OF THE COMMISSION TO THE FIVE CIVILIZED TRIBES OF MARCH 31, 1905.						
	10							
	11							
	12							
	13							
	14							
	15							
	16							
	17							

TRIBAL ENROLLMENT OF PARENTS

	Name of Father	Year	County	Name of Mother	Year	County
1	Un-chi-ubbee	Dead	Jacks Fork	Milh-ta-ho-na	Dead	Red River
2	No1			Phoebe Lewis	"	Blue
3	No1			" "	"	" "
4	No1			" "	"	" "
5	Redmond Bond	1896	Atoka	Nº2		
6						
7						
8	No3 on 1896 roll as Jimson Lewis					
9	Nº2 is the wife of Redmond Bond on Choctaw card #1782					
10	Nº5 Born July 24, 1901, enrolled Oct. 22, 1902					
11	Nº1 Died in October 1899, proof of death filed Oct. 22 1902					
12	Nº4 Died in September 1899, proof of death filed Oct. 22 1902					
13	For children of No2 see NB (Mar 3 1905) #528					
14						#1 to 4
15						DATE OF APPLICATION FOR ENROLLMENT.
16						Aug 23/99
17	P.O. Duncan IT 4/27/05					

Choctaw By Blood Enrollment Cards 1898-1914

RESIDENCE: Blue   COUNTY. **Choctaw Nation**   **Choctaw Roll**   CARD NO.
POST OFFICE: Caddo, I.T.   *(Not Including Freedmen)*   FIELD NO. 3830

Dawes' Roll No.	NAME	Relationship to Person First Named	AGE	SEX	BLOOD	TRIBAL ENROLLMENT Year	County	No.
10801	1 Hayes, Henry B ^32	First Named	29	M	Full	1896	Blue	5874
DEAD.	2 " Rhoda ~~DEAD~~	~~Wife~~	~~29~~	~~F~~	~~"~~	~~1896~~	~~"~~	~~5875~~
10802	3 " Edmond A ^6	Son	2	M	"			
10803	4 " Susan ^4	Dau	5mo	F	"			
10804	5 " Cornelia ^1	Dau	1mo	F	"			
	6							
	7							
	8	ENROLLMENT OF NOS. 1,3,4 and 5 HEREON APPROVED BY THE SECRETARY OF INTERIOR FEB 4 1903						
	9							
	10							
	11	No. 2 HEREON DISMISSED UNDER ORDER OF THE COMMISSION TO THE FIVE CIVILIZED TRIBES OF MARCH 31, 1905.						
	12							
	13							
	14							
	15							
	16							
	17							

TRIBAL ENROLLMENT OF PARENTS

	Name of Father	Year	County	Name of Mother	Year	County
1	Cornelius Hayes	Dead	Blue	Sallie Hayes	Dead	Blue
2	~~Charles Armby~~		"	~~Betsy Armby~~		"
3	No 1			No 2		
4	No 1			No 2		
5	No.1			No.2		
6						
7	No 1 on 1896 roll as Henry Hayes					
8						
9	Nos 3-4 affidavits of birth to be supplied.- Recd Oct 7/99					
10	No 5 Enrolled May 17, 1901					
11	N°2 Died June 28, 1902 proof of death filed Nov 22 1902					
12						
13						#1 to 4
14						Date of Application for Enrollment.
15						Aug 23/99
16						
17						

Choctaw By Blood Enrollment Cards 1898-1914

RESIDENCE: Blue   COUNTY. **Choctaw Nation**   **Choctaw Roll** *(Not Including Freedmen)*   CARD No.

POST OFFICE: Caddo, I.T.   FIELD No. 3831

Dawes' Roll No.	NAME		Relationship to Person First Named	AGE	SEX	BLOOD	TRIBAL ENROLLMENT		
							Year	County	No.
10805	1 Wilson, Abel	41	First Named	38	M	Full	1893	Blue	1156
10806	2 " Mary	24	Wife	21	F	"	1893	"	600
10807	3 " Rosa	6	Dau	2	"	"			
10808	4 " Isaac	4	Son	8mo	M	"			
	5								
	6	ENROLLMENT							
	7	OF NOS. 1,2,3 and 4 HEREON APPROVED BY THE SECRETARY							
	8	OF INTERIOR FEB 4 1903							
	9								
	10								
	11								
	12								
	13								
	14								
	15								
	16								
	17								

TRIBAL ENROLLMENT OF PARENTS

	Name of Father	Year	County	Name of Mother	Year	County
1	Saul Wilson	Dead	Jackson	Phoebe Wilson	Dead	Jackson
2	James Myer	"	Blue		"	Blue
3	No1			No2		
4	No1			No2		
5						
6						
7	qFor child of Nos 1 and 2 see NB (Apr 26 '06) No. 938					
8	No1 on 1893 Pay Roll, Page 113, No 1156, Blue Co					
9	No2 " 1893 " " 57 " 600, " " as Mary Hogan.					
10	Nos 3-4 affidavits of birth to be					
11	supplied:- Recd Oct 7/99					
12						
13	For child of Nos 1&2 see NB (Mar 3-1905) Card #254					
14						
15				Date of Application for Enrollment.	Aug 23/99	
16						
17						

231

RESIDENCE:	Blue	COUNTY.					CARD NO.
POST OFFICE:	Bok Chito, I.T.	**Choctaw Nation**		*(Not Including Freedmen)* **Choctaw Roll**			FIELD NO. 3832

Dawes' Roll No.	NAME	Relationship to Person Named	AGE	SEX	BLOOD	TRIBAL ENROLLMENT		
						Year	County	No.
10809	1 Baker, Johnson 57	First Named	54	M	Full	1896	Blue	1676
10810	2 " Lottie 71	Wife	68	F	"	1896	"	1677
10811	3 Anderson Elsie 22	Dau	19	"	"	1896	"	1679
10812	4 Anderson Tandy Lee 1	Gr Son	2mo	M	"			
	5							
	6							
	7	ENROLLMENT						
	8	OF NOS. 1,2,3 and 4 HEREON APPROVED BY THE SECRETARY						
	9	OF INTERIOR FEB 4 1903						
	10							
	11							
	12							
	13							
	14							
	15							
	16							
	17							

TRIBAL ENROLLMENT OF PARENTS

	Name of Father	Year	County	Name of Mother	Year	County
1	Ho-te-chubbee	Dead	Towson	Yo-te-ma	Dead	Towson
2	Phille-ca-tubbee	"	Bok Tuklo	Sealey	"	Bok Tuklo
3	No1			Sibbie Baker		Blue
4	Frank Anderson	1896	Blue	Nº3		
5						
6						
7						
8						
9	No2 on 1896 roll as Sallie Baker					
10						
11	No3 It is claimed that mother, Sibbie Baker, was a Chickasaw					
12	Nº3 is now the wife of Frank Anderson on Choctaw card #3750, evidence of marriage filed Aug 4, 1902.					
13	Nº4 Born May 18, 1902: enrolled Aug 4, 1902					
14	For child of No3 see N.B. (Act Mar 3-05) #255.					
15						#1,2 &3 Aug 23/99
16						Date of Application for Enrollment.
17						

232

Choctaw By Blood Enrollment Cards 1898-1914

RESIDENCE:	Blue	COUNTY.							
POST OFFICE:	Bok Chito, I.T.	**Choctaw Nation**				Choctaw Roll *(Not Including Freedmen)*		CARD NO. FIELD NO. **3833**	

Dawes' Roll No.	NAME		Relationship to Person Named	AGE	SEX	BLOOD	TRIBAL ENROLLMENT		
							Year	County	No.
10813	₁ Robinson, David	41	First Named	38	M	1/2	1896	Blue	10926
I.W. 352	₂ " Allie May	30	Wife	26	F	I.W.	1896	"	14983
10814	₃ " Jessie M	6	Dau	3	"	1/4	1896	"	10928
10815	₄ " Jerome	4	Son	1	M	1/4			
10816	₅ " Edward	1	Son	3wks	M	1/4			
	₆								
	₇								
	₈	ENROLLMENT OF NOS. 1,3,4 and 5 HEREON APPROVED BY THE SECRETARY OF INTERIOR Feb 4 1903							
	₉								
	₁₀								
	₁₁	ENROLLMENT OF NOS. 2 HEREON APPROVED BY THE SECRETARY OF INTERIOR Sep 12 1903							
	₁₂								
	₁₃								
	₁₄								
	₁₅								
	₁₆								
	₁₇								

TRIBAL ENROLLMENT OF PARENTS

	Name of Father	Year	County	Name of Mother	Year	County
₁	Solomon Robinson	Dead	Wade	Eliz. Robinson		Nashoba
₂	Dan Walker		Non Citz	Annie Walker	Dead	Non Citz
₃	No.1			No.2		
₄	No.1			No.2		
₅	No.1			No.2		
₆						
₇						
₈						
₉						
₁₀		No.1 on 1896 roll as David Roberson				
		No.2 " 1896 " " Ollie May Robinson				
₁₁		No.3 " 1896 " " Jessie May Roberson				
₁₂		As to marriage, see testimony of No.1				
₁₃		and Lewis Robinson				
		No.4 Affidavit of birth to be				
₁₄		supplied; Recd Oct 7/99			Date of Application for Enrollment.	
₁₅		No.2 admitted as an intermarried citizen by Dawes Commission in 1896,			Aug 23/99	
₁₆		Choctaw case #681; no appeal				
		No.3 admitted as a citizen by blood by Dawes Commission in 1896,				
₁₇		Choctaw case #681; no appeal No 5 Enrolled June 27 1901				

For child of No.1 see NB (Act Mar 3' 05) Card #275

Choctaw By Blood Enrollment Cards 1898-1914

RESIDENCE: **Blue**   COUNTY. **Choctaw Nation**   **Choctaw Roll**   CARD No.

POST OFFICE: **Caddo, I.T.**   *(Not Including Freedmen)*   FIELD No. **3834**

Dawes' Roll No.	NAME		Relationship to Person First Named	AGE	SEX	BLOOD	TRIBAL ENROLLMENT		
							Year	County	No.
10817	1 Wright, Milton	32	First Named	29	M	Full	1896	Blue	13861
10818	2 " Fannie	23	Wife	20	F	"	1896	"	13862
10819	3 " Edna	3	Dau	2mo	"	"			
	4								
	5								
	6								
	7	ENROLLMENT							
	8	OF NOS. 1, 2 and 3 HEREON APPROVED BY THE SECRETARY							
	9	OF INTERIOR Feb 4 1903							
	10								
	11								
	12								
	13								
	14								
	15								
	16								
	17								

TRIBAL ENROLLMENT OF PARENTS

	Name of Father	Year	County	Name of Mother	Year	County
1	Allen Wright	Dead	Blue	Betsey Wright		Blue
2	Ben Washington	"	"	Sally A Washington	Dead	Jackson
3	No1			No2		
4						
5						
6						
7						
8						
9						
10						
11						
12						
13						
14					Date of Application for Enrollment.	
15					Aug 23/99	
16				No3 enrolled Dec 16/99		
17						

234

Choctaw By Blood Enrollment Cards 1898-1914

RESIDENCE: Blue   COUNTY. **Choctaw Nation**   **Choctaw Roll** No.
POST OFFICE: Academy, I.T.   *(Not Including Freedmen)* No. 3835

Dawes' Roll No.	NAME	Relationship to Person First Named	AGE	SEX	BLOOD	Year	County	No.
14815	1 Kelly, Laura 50	First Named	47	F	1/4	1896	Blue	7623
10820	2 Turnbull, Robert 22	Son	19	M	1/8	1896	"	12412
10821	3 Moore Rosa 18	Dau	15	F	1/8	1896	"	12413
10822	4 Turnbull Edna 16	Dau	13	F	1/8	1896	"	12414
10823	5 Kelly, Emmet J 11	Son	8	M	1/8	1896	"	7624
10824	6 " Viola A 9	Dau	6	F	1/8	1896	"	7625
10825	7 Moore John E 1	Gr Son	1wk	M	1/16			

ENROLLMENT OF NOS. 2,3,4,5,6 and 7 HEREON APPROVED BY THE SECRETARY OF INTERIOR FEB 4 1903

ENROLLMENT OF NOS. 1 HEREON APPROVED BY THE SECRETARY OF INTERIOR MAY 20 1903

TRIBAL ENROLLMENT OF PARENTS

Name of Father	Year	County	Name of Mother		
1 Stephen Buckley	Dead	Non Citz	Orlena Buckley	Dead	Blue
2 Edmond Turnbull	"	Chickasaw	No1		
3 " "	"	"	No1		
4 " "	"	"	No1		
5 Robert Kelly		Non Citz	No1		
6 " "		" "	No1		
7 Robert F Moore		" "	Nº3		

No5 on 1896 roll as Emmet Kelly
No6 " 1896 " " Viola "
Nº3 is now the wife of Robert F Moore Non-Citz: Evidence of marriage filed Aug 21, 1902
Nº7 Born Aug. 13, 1902: enrolled Aug. 21, 1902
No4 Female: correct name Edna Turnbull; correction made under Departmental letter of Nov. 16, 1903 (D.C. 32219-1903)
For child of No.3 see NB (Mar 3, 1903) #629
No3 Bok Chito 11/22/02

#1 to 6
Date of Application for Enrollment. Aug 23/99

235

Choctaw By Blood Enrollment Cards 1898-1914

RESIDENCE: **Blue**   COUNTY. **Choctaw Nation**   **Choctaw Roll** CARD NO.
POST OFFICE: **Caddo, I.T.**   *(Not Including Freedmen)*   FIELD NO. **3836**

Dawes' Roll No.	NAME		Relationship to Person First Named	AGE	SEX	BLOOD	TRIBAL ENROLLMENT		
							Year	County	No.
10826	1 Fryer, Adeline	22	First Named	19	F	1/4	1896	Blue	4351
10827	2 " Edith	3	dau	2wks	"	1/8			
10828	3 " Oliver B	2	Son	1mo	M	1/8			
	4								
	5								
	6	ENROLLMENT							
	7	OF NOS. 1, 2 and 3 HEREON							
	8	APPROVED BY THE SECRETARY OF INTERIOR FEB 4 1903							
	9								
	10								
	11								
	12								
	13								
	14								
	15								
	16								
	17								

TRIBAL ENROLLMENT OF PARENTS

	Name of Father	Year	County	Name of Mother	Year	County
1	Jacob Folsom		Blue	Mary Folsom		Intermarried
2	Bert Fryer		Non Citz	No1		
3	A. J. Fryer			No1		
4						
5						
6						
7			On 1896 roll as Adeline Folsom			
8						
9			As to proof of marriage of parents, see enrollment of Jacob Folsom.			
10			No.3 Enrolled February 26, 1901			
11						
12						
13						
14				#1		
15				DATE OF APPLICATION FOR ENROLLMENT. Aug 23/99		
16				No2 enrolled Oct 7/99		
17						

236

Choctaw By Blood Enrollment Cards 1898-1914

RESIDENCE:	Blue	COUNTY.					Choctaw Roll	CARD No.	
POST OFFICE:	Caddo, I.T.	**Choctaw Nation**					(Not Including Freedmen)	FIELD No. 3837	

Dawes' Roll No.	NAME	Relationship to Person	AGE	SEX	BLOOD	TRIBAL ENROLLMENT		
						Year	County	No.
10829	1 Benton Theodore 21	First Named	18	M	Full	1896	Blue	1662
	2							
	3							
	4	ENROLLMENT						
	5	OF NOS. 1 HEREON APPROVED BY THE SECRETARY						
	6	OF INTERIOR FEB 4 1903						
	7							
	8							
	9							
	10							
	11							
	12							
	13							
	14							
	15							
	16							
	17							

TRIBAL ENROLLMENT OF PARENTS

Name of Father	Year	County	Name of Mother	Year	County
1 Chas Benton	Dead	Sugar Loaf	Mary Benton		Blue
2					
3					
4					
5					
6					
7					
8					
9					
10					
11					
12					
13					
14				Date of Application for Enrollment.	
15				Aug 23/99	
16					
17					

237

Choctaw By Blood Enrollment Cards 1898-1914

RESIDENCE: **Blue**

POST OFFICE: **Caddo, I.T.**

Choctaw Nation   **Roll** *(Not Including Freedmen)*

CARD No.

FIELD No. **3838**

Dawes' Roll No.	NAME		Relationship to Person First Named	AGE	SEX	BLOOD	TRIBAL ENROLLMENT		
							Year	County	No.
DEAD	1 Peters, Wesley	DEAD		26	M	3/4	1896	Blue	10502
I.W. 831	2 Peters, Delia	㉙	Wife	25	F	IW	1896	"	14947
10830	3 " Elisha	5	Son	3	M	3/8	1896	"	10503
10831	4 " William T	3	"	4mo	"	3/8			
	5								
	6								
	7	ENROLLMENT OF NOS. 3 and 4 HEREON APPROVED BY THE SECRETARY OF INTERIOR FEB 4 1903							
	8								
	9								
	10								
	11	ENROLLMENT OF NOS. 2 HEREON APPROVED BY THE SECRETARY OF INTERIOR MAY 21 1904							
	12								
	13								
	14	No. 1 HEREON DISMISSED UNDER ORDER OF THE COMMISSION TO THE FIVE CIVILIZED TRIBES OF MARCH 31, 1905.							
	15								
	16								
	17								

TRIBAL ENROLLMENT OF PARENTS

	Name of Father	Year	County	Name of Mother	Year	County
1	Isom Peters	Dead	Kiamitia	Eliz. Peters	Dead	Kiamitia
2	Sylvester Roberson		Non Citz	Sophronia Roberson		Non Citz
3	No1			No2		
4	No1			No2		
5						
6						
7						
8						
9						
10						
11	No4 Affidavit of birth to be					
12	supplied: Recd Oct 7/99					
13	No1 Died September 11, 1900. Proof of death filed Feby 27 1901 Evidence of marriage between William Peters and					
14	Adelia Smith filed Jany 3, 1903				Date of Application for Enrollment.	
15					Aug 23/99	
16						
17						

238

Choctaw By Blood Enrollment Cards 1898-1914

RESIDENCE:	Jackson	COUNTY.							CARD NO.	
POST OFFICE:	Jackson, I.T.	**Choctaw Nation**				**Choctaw Roll** *(Not Including Freedmen)*			FIELD NO. 3839	

Dawes' Roll No.	NAME		Relationship to Person	AGE	SEX	BLOOD	TRIBAL ENROLLMENT		
							Year	County	No.
10832	1 Bully, Anderson	35	First Named	32	M	Full	1896	Jackson	1533
10833	2 " Sibbie	43	Wife	40	F	"	1896	"	1534
	3								
	4								
	5								
	6	ENROLLMENT							
	7	OF NOS. 1 and 2	HEREON						
	8	APPROVED BY THE SECRETARY OF INTERIOR FEB 4 1903							
	9								
	10								
	11								
	12								
	13								
	14								
	15								
	16								
	17								

TRIBAL ENROLLMENT OF PARENTS

	Name of Father	Year	County	Name of Mother	Year	County
1	William Bully	Dead	Kiamitia	Hannah Bully	Dead	Kiamitia
2	Jim Crowder	"	"	Liza Crowder	"	"
3						
4						
5						
6						
7			For children of No.1 see NB (Mar 3 1905) #447			
8						
9						
10						
11						
12						
13						
14						
15				Date of Application for Enrollment.		Aug 23/99
16						
17						

Choctaw By Blood Enrollment Cards 1898-1914

RESIDENCE: Jackson COUNTY.
POST OFFICE: Crowder, I.T.

Choctaw Nation

Choctaw Roll Card No.
(Not Including Freedmen) Field No. 3840

Dawes' Roll No.	NAME		Relationship to Person First Named	AGE	SEX	BLOOD	TRIBAL ENROLLMENT		
							Year	County	No.
10834	1 Cochnauer, Nicholas	46	First Named	43	M	1/4	1896	Jackson	2800
10835	2 " Bettie	27	Wife	24	F	3/4	1896	"	2801
10836	3 " William	11	Son	8	M	1/2	1896	"	2802
10837	4 " Melvina	9	Dau	6	F	1/2	1896	"	2803
10838	5 " Mary C	6	"	3	"	1/2	1896	"	2804
10839	6 " Zenie J	3	"	4mo	"	1/2			
	7								
	8								
	9	ENROLLMENT							
	10	OF NOS. 1,2,3,4,5 and 6 HEREON APPROVED BY THE SECRETARY							
	11	OF INTERIOR FEB 4 1903							
	12								
	13								
	14								
	15								
	16								
	17								

TRIBAL ENROLLMENT OF PARENTS

	Name of Father	Year	County	Name of Mother	Year	County
1	David Cochnauer	Dead	Blue	Mahala Cochnauer	Dead	Non Citz
2	Roger Nelson	"	Jackson	Ce-sa-tuna	"	Blue
3	No1			No2		
4	No1			No2		
5	No1			No2		
6	No1			No2		
7						
8						
9						
10			No1 on 1896 roll as Nicholas Cocheuan			
11			No2 " 1896 " " Bettie "			
12			No3 " 1896 " " William "			
13			No4 " 1896 " " Melvina "			
			No5 " 1896 " " Mary "			
14			No1 Evidence of marriage of parents to		Date of Application for Enrollment.	
15			be supplied:		Aug 23/99	
16			No6 Affidavit of birth to be supplied Filed Nov 2/99			
17			For child of No1 see NB (Mar 3' 05) Card #267			

240

Choctaw By Blood Enrollment Cards 1898-1914

RESIDENCE: Jackson COUNTY. **Choctaw Nation** **Choctaw Roll** CARD No.
POST OFFICE: Jackson, I.T. *(Not Including Freedmen)* FIELD No. **3841**

Dawes' Roll No.	NAME	Relationship to Person	AGE	SEX	BLOOD	TRIBAL ENROLLMENT		
						Year	County	No.
10840 1	Harrison, Margaret 26	First Named	23	F	1/8	1896	Blue	5851
10841 2	Crowder, Flossie L 10	Dau	7	"	1/4	1896	"	2912
10842 3	Harrison, Benjamin W 7	Son	4	M	1/16	1896	"	5852
10843 4	" William H 5	"	2	"	1/16			
10844 5	" Neter L 4	Dau	1	F	1/16			
10845 6	" Mary V 3	Dau	5mo	F	1/16			
10846 7	" Fannie R 1	Dau	5mo	F	1/16			
8								
9								
10	ENROLLMENT							
11	OF NOS. 1,2,3,4,5,6,7 HEREON APPROVED BY THE SECRETARY							
12	OF INTERIOR Feb 4 1903							
13								
14								
15								
16								
17								

TRIBAL ENROLLMENT OF PARENTS

	Name of Father	Year	County	Name of Mother	Year	County
1	D. M. Cochnaner		Blue	Mary A Cochnaner	Dead	Non Citz
2	Bolin Crowder		Jackson	No1		
3	B. W. Harrison		Non Citz	No1		
4	" " "		" "	No1		
5	" " "		" "	No1		
6	" " "		" "	No.1		
7	" " "		" "	Nº1		
8						
9						
10			No1 on 1896 roll as Flossie F Crowder			
11			No3 " 1896 " " Benjamin Harrison			
12			No1 " 1896 " " Margaret Harris as to marriage of parents, see testimony of			
13			Douglad M. and Nicholas Cochnaner			
14			No4-5 Affidavits of birth to be		Date of Application for Enrollment.	
15			supplied:- Recd Oct 7/99		Aug 23/99	
16			No.6 Enrolled Aug 22d, 1900			
17			Nº7 Born Dec 12, 1901 enrolled May 7, 1902 For child of No1 see NB (March 3, 1905) #1204			

Choctaw By Blood Enrollment Cards 1898-1914

RESIDENCE: Blue   COUNTY. **Choctaw Nation**   **Choctaw Roll**   CARD NO.
POST OFFICE: Bennington, I.T.   *(Not Including Freedmen)*   FIELD NO. **3842**

Dawes' Roll No.	NAME	Relationship to Person First Named	AGE	SEX	BLOOD	TRIBAL ENROLLMENT		
						Year	County	No.
10847	1 Brackett, Laura A ²⁸	First Named	25	F	1/8	1896	Blue	1561
10848	2 " Myrtle M ⁸	Dau	5	"	1/16	1896	"	1562
10849	3 " Daniel M 5	Son	2	M	1/16			
DEAD.	4 " ~~Sarah D~~ DEAD.	~~Dau~~	~~7mo~~	~~F~~	~~1/16~~			
10850	5 " Phidelia A ²	Dau	6mo	F	1/16		"	
10851	6 " Cora Lee ¹	Dau	5mo	F	1/16			
	7							
	8							
	9	ENROLLMENT						
	10	OF NOS. 1,2,3,5 and 6 HEREON						
	11	~~APPROVED BY THE SECRETARY~~ OF INTERIOR FEB 4 1903						
	12	No 4 HEREON DISMISSED UNDER						
	13	ORDER OF THE COMMISSION TO THE FIVE						
	14	CIVILIZED TRIBES OF MARCH 31, 1905.						
	15	No4 died Feb 4, 1900; proof of						
	16	death filed Nov 29 1902						
	17							

TRIBAL ENROLLMENT OF PARENTS

	Name of Father	Year	County	Name of Mother	Year	County
1	D. M. Cochnauer		Blue	Mary A Cochnauer	Dead	Non Citz
2	H. A. Brackett		Non Citz	No1		
3	" " "		" "	No1		
4	" " "		" "	~~No1~~		
5	" " "		" "	No.1		
6	" " "		" "	Nº1		
7						
8						
9						
10	No2 on 1896 roll as Myrh M Brackett					
11	No1 as to evidence of marriage of					
12	parents, see testimony of Dougald M Cochnauer					
13	Nos 3-4 Affidavits of birth to be					
14	supplied:-- Recd Oct 7/99				#1 to 4	
15	For child of No.1 see NB (March 3, 1905) #751 ~~No5 Enrolled May 6, 1902~~			Date of Application for Enrollment		Aug 23/99
16	Nº6 Born May 2, 1901, enrolled Oct. 13, 1902.					
17						

Choctaw By Blood Enrollment Cards 1898-1914

RESIDENCE: Chickasaw Nation ~~COUNTY~~. **Choctaw Nation**

POST OFFICE: McGee, I.T.

Choctaw Roll CARD No.
(Not Including Freedmen)   FIELD No. 3843

Dawes' Roll No.	NAME	Relationship to Person First Named	AGE	SEX	BLOOD	TRIBAL ENROLLMENT		
						Year	County	No.
DEAD. 1	~~Roberts, Annie B.~~	~~Named~~	~~23~~	~~F~~	~~1/8~~	~~1893~~	~~Kiamitia~~	Page 119 #78
15582 2	" Myrtle M ¹⁰	Dau	7	"	1/16	"	"	Page 119 #79
15583 3	" Estala ⁵	"	20mo	"	1/16			
15584 4	" Mary E ³	"	2mo	"	1/16			
DEAD. 5	~~" Coleman~~	~~Son~~	~~1mo~~	~~M~~	~~1/16~~			
I.W. 1219 6	Roberts, George W ³⁰	Husband	30	M	I.W.	No. 1 and 5 HEREON DISMISSED UNDER ORDER OF THE COMMISSION TO THE FIVE CIVILIZED TRIBES OF MARCH 31, 1905.		
7								
8	ENROLLMENT OF NOS. ~6~ HEREON APPROVED BY THE SECRETARY OF INTERIOR DEC 12 1904							
9								
10	No.6 remarried to No.1 under Choctaw Law							
11	July 20, 1899.							
12	No.6 Transferred from Choctaw card #D-252 Nov 26, 1904. See decision of Nov 3,1904							
13								
14	ENROLLMENT OF NOS. 2 3 and 4 HEREON APPROVED BY THE SECRETARY OF INTERIOR SEP 22 1904							
15								
16	~~Not restored to roll by Departmental authority of January 10,1909 (sub. 5-51.)~~							
17	~~Enrollment of Nos. cancelled by order of Department March 4, 1907~~							

TRIBAL ENROLLMENT OF PARENTS

	Name of Father	Year	County	Name of Mother	Year	County
1	~~Boswell~~	~~Dead~~	~~Non Citz~~	~~Ellen Boswell~~	~~Dead~~	~~Choctaw~~
2	Geo. W Roberts		white man	No 1		
3	" " "		" "	No 1		
4	" " "		" "	No 1		
5	~~" " "~~		~~" "~~	~~No 1~~		
6	Frank Roberts	dead	Non Citz	Susan Roberts	dead	non citizen
7						
8						
9	Nos 1-2 were admitted by Dawes Com			No.6 admitted by Com in 96 case #659		
10	Case No 659. No appeal			No.6 was denied by United States Court in Indian Territory Central Dist		
11	No1 was admitted as Annie Belle Roberts No2 " " " Myrtle May "			July 13,1896, Court case #218.		
12	As to residence, see testimony of Geo.			Two sets of appeal papers filed in this case, Dawes Commission		
13	W. Roberts.			#659: case #151 dismissed by		
14	No3 Affidavit of birth to be supplied. Recd Oct 7/99			attorney for appellant.		
15	N⁰5 Born March 22,1901: enrolled April 22,1902.			Date of Application for Enrollment. #1 to 3 inc Aug 23/99		
16	N⁰1 Died April 24,1902. proof of death filed Oct 14 1902			No4 enrolled Oct 7/99		
17	N⁰5 Died Aug 7,1902. proof of death filed Oct 14 1902					

No.6 originally listed for enrollment on Choctaw card #D-352 Aug 23/99

Choctaw By Blood Enrollment Cards 1898-1914

RESIDENCE: **Blue**
POST OFFICE: **Caddo, I.T.**
COUNTY: **Choctaw Nation**
Choctaw Roll *(Not Including Freedmen)*
CARD NO. FIELD NO. **3844**

Dawes' Roll No.	NAME		Relationship to Person First Named	AGE	SEX	BLOOD	TRIBAL ENROLLMENT Year	County	No.
14378	1 LeFlore, Louis C	45	First Named	42	M	1/8	1896	Blue	8171
I.W.791	2 " Keturah	36	Wife	33	F	I.W.			
14379	3 " Rosa	16	Dau	13	"	1/16	1896	Blue	8172
14380	4 " Michael	14	Son	11	M	1/16	Blue	"	8173
14381	5 " Josephine	12	Dau	9	F	1/16	Blue	"	8174
14382	6 " Helen	9	"	6	"	1/16	Blue	"	8175
14383	7 " Campbell	6	Son	3	M	1/16	Blue	"	8176
	8 ENROLLMENT								
	9 OF NOS. 2 HEREON APPROVED BY THE SECRETARY								
	10 OF INTERIOR May 9 1904								
	11 Certified copy of certificate of marriage between								
	12 Nos 1and 2 Also affidavit of Ruby Saunders, a								
	13 witness to said marriage and affidavit of Green								
	14 McCurtain as to tribal enrollment of Nos 1, 3 4 5 6 and								
	7 received and filed Nov. 19, 1902								
	15 ENROLLMENT								
	16 OF NOS. 1 3 4 5 6 and 7 HEREON APPROVED BY THE SECRETARY								
	17 OF INTERIOR Apr 11 1903								

TRIBAL ENROLLMENT OF PARENTS

	Name of Father	Year	County	Name of Mother	Year	County
1	Louis LeFlore	Dead	in Mississippi	Josephine LeFlore		Non Citz
2	R. B. Coleman		Non Citz	Mary Coleman		" "
3	No1			No2		
4	No1			No2		
5	No1			No2		
6	No1			No2		
7	No1			No2		

8 * No2 Denied by the Dawes Com. in 96 Choctaw Cit Case #1232 * Judgment of US Court C.D.
9 Nos 1-3-4-5 were admitted by Act of Choctaw   admitting No2 vacated and
10 Council. No1 approved October 13, 1893.   set aside by Decree of
As to residence, see testimony of No1   Choctaw-Chickasaw Decr
11 No1 Evidence of marriage of parents   17 '02 No2 admitted by
12 to be supplied.   Choctaw-Chickasaw
13 * No2 was admitted by U.S. Court Central   Citizenship Court Feb 1st
Dist. Aug 24/97 Case No 55   As to her   1904 Case #18
14 residence, see testimony of No1   Date of Application for Enrollment.
15 Nos 1,3,4,5,6&7 admitted by Dawes Com #1247   Aug 24/99
16 No appeal

244

Choctaw By Blood Enrollment Cards 1898-1914

RESIDENCE:	Blue	COUNTY.	**Choctaw Nation**	**Choctaw Roll**	CARD NO.	
POST OFFICE:	Caddo, I.T.			(Not Including Freedmen)	FIELD NO. 3845	

Dawes' Roll No.	NAME	Relationship to Person First Named	AGE	SEX	BLOOD	TRIBAL ENROLLMENT Year	County	No.
14384	1 LeFlore, Abbott 43		40	M	1/8	1896	Blue	8177
	2							
	3							
	4	ENROLLMENT						
	5	OF NOS. I HEREON APPROVED BY THE SECRETARY						
	6	OF INTERIOR APR 11 1903						
	7							
	8							
	9							
	10							
	11							
	12							
	13							
	14							
	15							
	16							
	17							

TRIBAL ENROLLMENT OF PARENTS

	Name of Father	Year	County	Name of Mother	Year	County
1	Louis LeFlore	Dead	in Mississippi	Josephine LeFlore		Non Citz
2						
3						
4						
5						
6						
7						
8						
9						
10		On 1896 roll as Albert LeFlore				
11		As to residence, see testimony of Louis C. LeFlore				
12		As to marriage of parents, see				
13		enrollment of Louis C. LeFlore				
14		Admitted by Act of Choctaw			Date of Application for Enrollment	
15		Council, No 1, approved Oct 13/93			Aug 24/99	
16		No1 admitted by Dawes Com in 1896 Case No 1247				
17		No appeal.				

245

Choctaw By Blood Enrollment Cards 1898-1914

RESIDENCE: **Blue** COUNTY. **Choctaw Nation** (Not Including Freedmen) CARD NO.
POST OFFICE: Caddo, I.T. **Choctaw Roll** FIELD NO. **3846**

Dawes' Roll No.	NAME	Relationship to Person First Named	AGE	SEX	BLOOD	TRIBAL ENROLLMENT		
						Year	County	No.
I.W.832	1 Goddard, James M (31)	First Named	28	M	IW			
14385	2 " Felicia (39)	Wife	36	F	1/8	1896	Blue	8183
	3							
	4	ENROLLMENT						
	5	OF NOS. 2 HEREON APPROVED BY THE SECRETARY						
	6	OF INTERIOR APR 11 1903						
	7							
	8	ENROLLMENT						
	9	OF NOS. 1 HEREON APPROVED BY THE SECRETARY						
	10	OF INTERIOR MAY 21 1904						
	11							
	12							
	13							
	14							
	15							
	16							
	17							

TRIBAL ENROLLMENT OF PARENTS

	Name of Father	Year	County	Name of Mother	Year	County
1	James Goddard		Non Citz	Fannie Goddard		Non Citz
2	Louis LeFlore	Dead	in Mississippi	Josephine LeFlore		" "
3						
4						
5						
6						
7						
8						
9						
10			No2 On 1896 roll as Filicia Landers			
11			No2 Admitted by Act of Choctaw			
12			Council No1 approved Oct 13/93 as			
13			Felicia Landers			
			As to residence, see testimony			
14			of No1			Date of Application for Enrollment.
15			As to marriage of parents of No2, see			Aug 24/99
16			enrollment of Louis C. LeFlore			
			No2 was admitted by Dawes Com in 1896			
17			case No 1247 as Felicia Landers. No appeal.			

246

Choctaw By Blood Enrollment Cards 1898-1914

RESIDENCE: Jackson   COUNTY.   **Choctaw Nation**   **Choctaw Roll**   CARD NO.
POST OFFICE: Bennington, I.T.   *(Not Including Freedmen)*   FIELD NO. **3847**

Dawes' Roll No.	NAME	Relationship to Person	AGE	SEX	BLOOD	TRIBAL ENROLLMENT		
						Year	County	No.
10852	1 Polk, Mary ^33	First Named	30	F	Full	1896	Jackson	10465
10853	2 " Loren ^15	Son	12	M	1/2	1896	"	10466
10854	3 " Joseph ^10	"	7	"	1/2	1896	"	10467
	4							
	5							
	6	ENROLLMENT						
	7	OF NOS. 1,2 and 3 HEREON APPROVED BY THE SECRETARY						
	8	OF INTERIOR Feb 4 1903						
	9							
	10							
	11							
	12							
	13							
	14							
	15							
	16							
	17							

TRIBAL ENROLLMENT OF PARENTS

	Name of Father	Year	County	Name of Mother	Year	County
1	Jno. A. Taleboleh	Dead	Kiamitia		Dead	Kiamitia
2	Cephus K. Polk		Chick Roll	No1		
3	" " "		" "	No1		
4						
5						
6						
7						
8						
9						
10	No1 on 1896 roll as Mary Poke					
11	No2 " 1896 " " Lorena "					
12	No3 " 1896 " " Joseph "					
	No.1 on Choctaw 1896 roll as Mary Anderson, page #9; #351					
13						
14						
15				Date of Application for Enrollment.		Aug 24/99
16						
17						

Choctaw By Blood Enrollment Cards 1898-1914

| RESIDENCE: Jackson COUNTY. | POST OFFICE: Bennington, I.T. | **Choctaw Nation** | Choctaw Roll (Not Including Freedmen) | CARD NO. FIELD NO. **3848** |

Dawes' Roll No.	NAME	Relationship to Person First Named	AGE	SEX	BLOOD	TRIBAL ENROLLMENT		
						Year	County	No.
10855	1 Anderson, Willie E 36	Named	33	M	Full	1896	Jackson	363
10856	2 " Sarah 43	Wife	40	F	"	1896	"	364
10857	3 " Walter 14	Son	11	M	"	1896	"	365
10858	4 Carnes, Ellen 19	S.Dau	16	F	"	1896	"	2789
10859	5 " James 11	S.Son	8	M	"	1896	"	2791
	6							
	7							
	8	ENROLLMENT						
	9	OF NOS. 1,2,3,4 and 5 HEREON APPROVED BY THE SECRETARY						
	10	OF INTERIOR Feb 4 1903						
	11							
	12							
	13							
	14							
	15							
	16							
	17							

TRIBAL ENROLLMENT OF PARENTS

	Name of Father	Year	County	Name of Mother	Year	County
1	Eastman Anderson	Dead	Jackson	Eliz. Anderson	Dead	Jackson
2		"	"		"	"
3	No1			Leanna Anderson	"	"
4	Ben Carnes	Dead	Jackson	No2		
5	Tillis Carnes	"	"	No2		
6						
7						
8						
9	No1 on 1896 roll as W. E. Anderson					
10	No4 " 1896 " " Ellen Carnes					
11	No5 " 1896 " " James "					
	Nos 1 and 2 have separated					
12						
13	For child of No4 see NB (Apr 26-06) Card #637					#1 to 5 inc
14					Date of Application for Enrollment.	
15					Aug 24/99	
16						
17						

248

RESIDENCE:	Jackson	COUNTY.	**Choctaw Nation**			Choctaw Roll	CARD No.	
POST OFFICE:	Bennington, I.T.					(Not Including Freedmen)	FIELD No. 3849	

Dawes' Roll No.		NAME	Relationship to Person Named	AGE	SEX	BLOOD	TRIBAL ENROLLMENT		
							Year	County	No.
10860	1	Smallwood, Daniel ⁵²	First Named	49	M	Full	1896	Blue	11614
DEAD	2	" Mattie DEAD	Wife	22	F	"	1896	"	11615
10861	3	" Benjamin ⁶	Son	3	M	"	1896	"	11616
	4								
	5								
	6	ENROLLMENT							
	7	OF NOS. 1 and 3 HEREON							
	8	APPROVED BY THE SECRETARY OF INTERIOR Feb 4 1903							
	9								
	10	No.2 hereon dismissed under order of							
	11	the Commission to the Five Civilized							
	12	Tribes of March 31, 1905.							
	13								
	14								
	15								
	16								
	17								

TRIBAL ENROLLMENT OF PARENTS

	Name of Father	Year	County	Name of Mother	Year	County
1	Ben Smallwood	Dead	Atoka	Siney Leflore	Dead	Kiamitia
2	Robinson Battiest	"	Jackson		"	Jackson
3	No1			No2		
4						
5						
6						
7	No2 on 1896 roll as Matie[sic] Smallwood					
8						
9						
10	No2 died January 10 1902: proof of death filed Dec 1 1902					
11						
12						
13						
14					Date of Application for Enrollment.	
15					Aug 24/99	
16						
17						

Choctaw By Blood Enrollment Cards 1898-1914

RESIDENCE: Jackson   COUNTY.   **Choctaw Nation**   **Choctaw Roll**   CARD No.
POST OFFICE: Jackson, I.T.   *(Not Including Freedmen)*   FIELD No. **3850**

Dawes' Roll No.	NAME	Relationship to Person First Named	AGE	SEX	BLOOD	TRIBAL ENROLLMENT		
						Year	County	No.
10862	1 Frazier Thomas 33	First Named	30	M	Full	1896	Atoka	4481
10863	2 " Serena 33	Wife	30	f	"	1896	"	4482
15053	3 " Susan 7	Dau	4	"	"			
10864	4 " Thompson 4	Son	1	M	"			
10865	5 " Mary 2	Dau	2	F	"			
	6							
	7							
	8	ENROLLMENT OF NOS. 1,2,4 and 5 HEREON						
	9	APPROVED BY THE SECRETARY OF INTERIOR Feb 4 1903						
	10							
	11	ENROLLMENT						
	12	OF NOS. ~~~3~~~ HEREON APPROVED BY THE SECRETARY						
	13	OF INTERIOR Feb 16 1904						
	14							
	15							
	16							
	17							

11/21/33 See Testimony 10863-15053

TRIBAL ENROLLMENT OF PARENTS

	Name of Father	Year	County	Name of Mother	Year	County
1	Simon Frazier	Dead	Jackson	Marsie Peter		Atoka
2		"	"	Bicey Wilson		Jackson
3	No1			No2		
4	No1			No2		
5	No1			No2		
6						
7						
8						
9						
10						
11	No2 on 1896 roll as Semmilling Frazier					
12						
13	Nos 3-4: Affidavits of birth to be supplied:- Filed Nov 2/99					#1 to 4
14	No5 born Oct. 23, 1900; Proof of birth filed Dec.r 23,1902					
15	Correct given name of Nº3 is Susan. See affidavits of No1			Date of Application for Enrollment.		Aug 24/99
16	Edmund Billy & Thomas Wade filed Nov 13, 1903					
17	Boswell City I.T.					

Choctaw By Blood Enrollment Cards 1898-1914

<table>
<tr><td>RESIDENCE: Chickasaw Nation</td><td>COUNTY.</td><td rowspan="2">Choctaw Nation</td><td>Choctaw Roll</td><td>CARD No.</td></tr>
<tr><td>POST OFFICE: Healdton, I.T.</td><td></td><td>(Not Including Freedmen)</td><td>FIELD No. 3851</td></tr>
</table>

Dawes' Roll No.	NAME	Relationship to Person Named	AGE	SEX	BLOOD	TRIBAL ENROLLMENT Year	County	No.
10866	1 Lowery, Thomas M Sr 58	First Named	55	M	1/4	1896	Atoka	8310
I.W. 159	2 " Crecy A 50	Wife	47	F	I.W.	1896	"	14786
10867	3 " Thomas M Jr 58	Son	19	M	1/8	1896	"	8311
10868	4 " Effie A 14	Dau	11	F	1/8	1896	"	8313
10869	5 " Nevada 12	"	9	"	1/8	1896	"	8314
10870	6 " Joseph H 9	Son	6	M	1/8	1896	"	8312
10871	7 " Miller Emmett 1	G.Son	10da	"	1/16			
I.W. 1418	8 " Florena 19	Wife of No3	19	F	I.W.			
	9							
	10 ENROLLMENT OF NOS. 1,3,4,5,6 and 7 HEREON APPROVED BY THE SECRETARY							
	11 OF INTERIOR FEB 4 1903							
	12							
	13 ENROLLMENT OF NOS. 2 HEREON							
	14 APPROVED BY THE SECRETARY							
	15 OF INTERIOR JUN 13 1903							
	16 ENROLLMENT OF NOS. 8 HEREON							
	17 APPROVED BY THE SECRETARY OF INTERIOR JUN 12 1905							

TRIBAL ENROLLMENT OF PARENTS

	Name of Father	Year	County	Name of Mother	Year	County
1	B H Lowery	Dead	Non-Citizen	Lucy Lowery	Dead	Tobucksy
2	Geo Chatman	"	"		"	Non-Citizen
3	No1			No2		
4	No1			No2		
5	No1			No2		
6	No1			No2		
7	No1			Florence Lowery		White
8	C. S. Carbin		noncitizen	Ella Carbin	Dead	noncitizen
9						
10	No1 on 1896 Roll as Thos M Lowery Sr					
11	" 2 " 1896 " " Cressy A "					
12	" 3 " 1896 " " Thos M Jr Wife of No3 on Card D517 Oct 25/99					
13	" 4 " 1896 " " Effie H "					
14	" 6 " 1896 " " Jos H "					
15	" 7 Born Dec 9 1901: Enrolled Dec 28 1901					
16	No2 was admitted by Dawes Commission in 1896 as an intermarried citizen Choctaw Case #1208 No appeal					
17	Decision of Commission of May 2, 1903 refusing No8 reversed by Secretary of Interior January 12, 1905 No 8 transferred from Choctaw Card D517 February 10, 1905			Date of Application for Enrollment. Aug 24/99		

Choctaw By Blood Enrollment Cards 1898-1914

RESIDENCE: Jackson COUNTY.
POST OFFICE: Mayhew, I.T.
Choctaw Nation
Choctaw Roll (Not Including Freedmen)
CARD NO.
FIELD NO. 3852

Dawes' Roll No.	NAME		Relationship to Person	AGE	SEX	BLOOD	TRIBAL ENROLLMENT		
							Year	County	No.
10872	1 Tucker, Romulus	45	First Named	42	M	Full	1896	Jackson	12382
10873	2 " Sissie	19	Dau	16	F	"	1896	"	12384
10874	3 " Minnie	18	"	15	"	"	1896	"	12385
10875	4 " Jane	13	"	10	"	"	1896	"	12386
10876	5 " Betsie	8	"	5	"	"	1896	"	12387
14816	6 Frazier, Harriet	1	Gr Dau	8mo	"	"			
	7								
	8	ENROLLMENT OF NOS. 1,2,3,4 and 5 HEREON							
	9	APPROVED BY THE SECRETARY							
	10	OF INTERIOR FEB 4 1903							
	11								
	12	ENROLLMENT							
	13	OF NOS. 6 HEREON APPROVED BY THE SECRETARY							
	14	OF INTERIOR MAY 20 1903							
	15								
	16								
	17								

TRIBAL ENROLLMENT OF PARENTS

	Name of Father	Year	County	Name of Mother	Year	County
1	Levi Tucker	Dead	Blue	Beckey Tucker	Dead	Jackson
2	No1			Amy Tucker	"	"
3	No1			" "	"	"
4	No1			" "	"	"
5	No1			" "	"	"
6	Sweeny Frazier	1896	Jackson	Nº3		
7						
8						
9			No2 on 1896 roll as Sinie Tucker			
10			No3 married Sweeney[sic] Frazier 7- #3767			
11			Nº6 Born April 24, 1902; enrolled Dec. 24, 1902.			
12						
13						#1 to 5
14						Date of Application for Enrollment.
15						Aug 24/99
16	No1 Boswell, 12/2/02					
17						

Choctaw By Blood Enrollment Cards 1898-1914

RESIDENCE:	Blue	COUNTY.				CARD No.		
POST OFFICE:	Bok Chito, I.T.	**Choctaw Nation**		Choctaw Roll *(Not Including Freedmen)*		FIELD No. 3853		

Dawes' Roll No.	NAME	Relationship to Person First Named	AGE	SEX	BLOOD	TRIBAL ENROLLMENT Year	County	No.
Void 1	Beams, Eliza	Named	40	F	Full	1896	Blue	1598
Void 2	" Ephraim W	Son	10	M	"	1896	"	1602
3								
4								
5								
6								
7	*cancelled see 4759*							
8								
9								
10								
11								
12								
13								
14								
15								
16								
17								

TRIBAL ENROLLMENT OF PARENTS

	Name of Father	Year	County	Name of Mother	Year	County
1	Sam'l Houston	Dead	Blue	Eliz. Houston	Dead	Blue
2	Calvin Beams	"	"	No 1		
3						
4						
5						
6						
7	See Choctaw Card No 3684 for Calvin S.					
8	Beams, and Choctaw Card No 3775 for					
9	Julius J. and Arthur G. Beams, the other					
10	children of No1, above.					
11						
12						
13						
14				Date of Application for Enrollment.		
15				Aug 24/99		
16						
17						

CANCELLED

253

Choctaw By Blood Enrollment Cards 1898-1914

RESIDENCE: Blue COUNTY.								
POST OFFICE: Boggy Depot, I.T	**Choctaw Nation**					Choctaw Roll *(Not Including Freedmen)*	CARD No. FIELD No. 3854	

Dawes' Roll No.	NAME	Relationship to Person	AGE	SEX	BLOOD	TRIBAL ENROLLMENT		
						Year	County	No.
15234	1 Buckholts, William 85	First Named	82	M	1/8	1896	Chick Dist	2015
	2							
	3							
	4							
	5 ~~In opinion of Atty. Genl. of Feb 18 '04 and letter of Secy. of Interior of Feb 24 '04 in case of James M Buckholts et al 7-5738~~							
	7 See copy of Act authorizing							
	8 Supreme Court to admit to Citizenship							
	9 and Act of Supreme Court admitting ~~William Buckholts, R. T. Jones, and~~							
	10 John Null, filed herewith.							
	11							
	12							
	13							
	14							
	15 ENROLLMENT OF NOS. ~~ 1 ~~ HEREON APPROVED BY THE SECRETARY OF INTERIOR MAY 9 1904							
	16							
	17							

TRIBAL ENROLLMENT OF PARENTS						
Name of Father	Year	County	Name of Mother	Year	County	
1 W. H. Buckholts	Dead	Non Citz	Eliz Buckholts	Dead	in Alabama	
2						
3						
4						
5 On 1896 roll as William Buckholtz						
6						
7 Admitted by Supreme Court, October Term of						
8 1872, with R. T. Jones and John Null. No other names being mentioned in the record.						
9 William L Buckholtz is 50 years old and						
10 W.E. Buckholtz, his son. Both are on						
11 page 50, Nos 2049 and 2050 respectively.						
12						
13						
14					Date of Application for Enrollment.	
15					Aug 24/99	
16						
17						

RESIDENCE:	Blue	COUNTY.							

Choctaw Nation — RESIDENCE: Blue COUNTY. POST OFFICE: Boggy Depot, I.T. — Choctaw Roll (Not Including Freedmen) — CARD NO. / FIELD NO. 3855

Dawes' Roll No.	NAME	Relationship to Person First Named	AGE	SEX	BLOOD	TRIBAL ENROLLMENT Year	County	No.
[I.W.] 1333	1 Jones, Rodham T ⁷⁴	First Named	71	M	IW	1896	Blue	14703
15235	2 " Lurena Elizabeth ⁶⁰	Wife	57	F	1/16	1896	"	7171
15236	3 " Thomas J ²⁹	Son	26	M	1/32	1896	"	7173
15237	4 " Marcus A ²⁷	"	24	"	1/32	1896	"	7174
15238	5 " Rodham F ²⁵	"	22	"	1/32	1896	"	7175
15239	6 " Elbert M ²¹	"	18	"	1/32	1896	"	7176
15240	7 Hinchey, Lula C ¹⁵	Dau	13	F	1/32	1896	"	7177
15241	8 Hinchey, Ora Luraney ¹	Gr Dau	2wks	F	1/64			
	See opinion or Atty Genl of Feb 18 '04 and letter of Secy of Interior Feb 24 '04							
	10 No2 is daughter of Wᵐ							
	11 Buckholts, but not included in							
	12 Act of Supreme Court Oct. 1872.							
	13							
	14 Evidence of marriage of							
	15 parents of No2 waived by							
	16 Commissioner MᶜKennon.							
	17							

TRIBAL ENROLLMENT OF PARENTS

	Name of Father	Year	County	Name of Mother	Year	County
1	Benj Jones	Dead	Non Citz	Mary Jones		Non Citz
2	Wᵐ Buckholts		Blue	Matilda Buckholts	Dead	" "
3	No1			No2		
4	No1			No2		
5	No1			No2		
6	No1			No2		
7	No1			No2		ENROLLMENT OF NOS. 2-3-4-5-6-7 and 8 HEREON APPROVED BY THE SECRETARY OF INTERIOR MAY 9 1904
8	C. F. Hinchey		non-citizen	Nº7		
9	No1 was admitted by Supreme Court					
10	October 1872. For child of No.3 see N.B. Apr 26,1906) Card No. 15 814					
	No2 on 1896 roll as Elizabeth Jones					
11	No3 " 1896 " Jeff "					
12	No4 " 1896 " Louie "			ENROLLMENT OF NOS. 1 HEREON APPROVED BY THE SECRETARY OF INTERIOR MAR 14 1905		#1 to 7 inc Date of Application for Enrollment
13	No5 " 1896 " Roddy "					
14	No6 " 1896 " Elbert "					
	No7 " 1896 " Lula "					
15	Nº8 Born July 22, 1902: enrolled Aug 4, 1902					Aug 24/99
16	Nº7 is now the wife of C.F. Hinchey a non-citizen. Evidence of marriage filed Aug 4,1902.					
17	P.O. Wapanucka I.T. 9/1/04					

Choctaw By Blood Enrollment Cards 1898-1914

RESIDENCE: Blue COUNTY. **Choctaw Nation** Choctaw Roll CARD NO.
POST OFFICE: Boggy Depot, I.T. *(Not Including Freedmen)* FIELD NO. 3856

Dawes' Roll No.	NAME	Relationship to Person First Named	AGE	SEX	BLOOD	TRIBAL ENROLLMENT Year	County	No.
I.W. 1334 1	Buckholts, Temmy 38	First Named	35	F	IW	1896	Blue	14339
15242 2	" Robert E L 18	Son	15	M	1/32	1896	"	1576
15243 3	" Enis E 15	"	12	"	1/32	1896	"	1577
15244 4	" Ida 10	Dau	7	F	1/32	1896	"	1578
15245 5	" Rhoda 6	"	3	"	1/32	1896	"	1579
	See opinion of Atty Genl of Feb 18 '04 and letter of Secy of Interior of Feb 24 '04 in case of James Buckholts et al 7-5738							
8								
9								
10								
11	ENROLLMENT OF NOS. 2-3-4 and 5 HEREON							
12	APPROVED BY THE SECRETARY OF INTERIOR MAY 9 1904							
13								
14								
15	See affidavit of E.O. Loomis M.D. relative							
16	to mental and physical condition of N°1 filed							
17	Jany 2, 1903.							

TRIBAL ENROLLMENT OF PARENTS

	Name of Father	Year	County	Name of Mother	Year	County
1	Tim Truelove	Dead	Non Citz	Alice Truelove	Dead	Non Citz
2	N.O. Buckholtz[sic]	"	Blue	No1		
3	" " "	"	"	No1		
4	" " "	"	"	No1		
5	" " "	"	"	No1		
6						
7	No.1 formerly wife of N.O. Buckholts, 1896, Blue, No 1575					
8	who died in 1896					
9	No2 on 1896 roll as R.E.L. Buckholts					
10						
11	N.O. Buckholts, father of above children now deceased, not included in Act of					
12	Supreme Court, admitting father; Wm Buckholts, Oct. 1872				ENROLLMENT OF NOS. 1 HEREON	
13					APPROVED BY THE SECRETARY OF INTERIOR MAR 14 1905	
14	As to marriage of No1, see testimony				Date of Application for Enrollment.	
15	of Wm Buckholts				Aug 24/99	
16	No.1 admitted as an intermarried citizen in 1896: Choctaw case #947; no appeal					
17	P.O. Madill I.T.					

Choctaw By Blood Enrollment Cards 1898-1914

RESIDENCE:	Blue	COUNTY.					CARD NO.		
POST OFFICE:	Caddo, I.T.	**Choctaw Nation**			Choctaw Roll *(Not Including Freedmen)*		FIELD NO. **3857**		

Dawes' Roll No.	NAME	Relationship to Person First Named	AGE	SEX	BLOOD	TRIBAL ENROLLMENT		
						Year	County	No.
1	Landers, James		21	M	1/8			
2								
3								
4	Denied Citizenship by the Choctaw and Chickasaw							
5	Citizenship Court Case #80, April 18-'04							
6	See Petition jacket C-67							
7								
8								
9	In I. W. Pet #67							
10								
11								
12								
13								
14								
15								
16								
17	For record see 7-3858 also See Pet #C-67							

TRIBAL ENROLLMENT OF PARENTS

	Name of Father	Year	County	Name of Mother	Year	County
1	Jas. Landers	Dead	Non Citz	Martha Landers	Dead	Choctaw
2						
3						
4						
5	No1 Denied in 96 Case #268					
6	Admitted by U S. Court, Central Dist.,					
7	Aug 30/97, Case No 86					
8	As to residence, see his testimony					
9	Judgement[sic] of U S Ct admitting No1 vacated and set aside by					
10	Decree of Choctaw Chickasaw Citizenship Court Decr 17 '02					
11	No.1 now in C.C.C.C. Case #80					
12						
13						
14					Date of Application for Enrollment.	
15					Aug 24/99	
16						
17						

Choctaw By Blood Enrollment Cards 1898-1914

RESIDENCE: Blue	COUNTY.								
POST OFFICE: Caddo, I.T.									

Choctaw Nation

Choctaw Roll (Not Including Freedmen)

CARD No.

FIELD NO. 3858

Dawes' Roll No.	NAME	Relationship to Person First Named	AGE	SEX	BLOOD	TRIBAL ENROLLMENT		
						Year	County	No.
✓ ✓	1 Gideon, Nellie J		30		1/8			
	2							
	3							
	4							
	5							
	6							
	7							
	8							
	9							
	10							
	11							
	12	petition jacket C-6						
	13							
	14							
	15							
	16							
	17							

TRIBAL ENROLLMENT OF PARENTS

	Name of Father	Year	County	Name of Mother	Year	County
1	Jas. Landers	Dead	Non Citz	Martha Landers	Dead	Choctaw
2						
3						
4						
5						
6	No1 Denied in 96 Case #268					
7	Admitted by U.S. Court, Central Dist					
8	Aug 30/97, Case No 86. As to residence see testimony of husband, David C. Gideon,					
9	Card No D359					
10	Judgement[sic] of U.S. Ct admitting No2 vacated and set aside by Decree of Choctaw Chickasaw Cit Court Decr 17 '02					
11	No1 now in C.C.C.C. Case #80					
12						
13						
14					Date of Application for Enrollment	
15					Aug 24/99	
16						
17	P.O. 2901 Lucas Ave, St. Louis, MO 12/20/06			See Petition #C-67		

258

RESIDENCE: Blue COUNTY. **Choctaw Nation** **Choctaw Roll** CARD NO.
POST OFFICE: Caddo, I.T. *(Not Including Freedmen)* FIELD NO. 3859

Dawes' Roll No.	NAME		Relationship to Person	AGE	SEX	BLOOD	TRIBAL ENROLLMENT		
							Year	County	No.
DEAD.	Goode, Melvina	DEAD	First Named	36	F	1/2	1896	Blue	4931
10877	" James	21	Son	18	M	3/4	1896	"	4932
10878	3 Jones Virginia	18	Dau	15	F	1/4	1896	"	4933
10879	4 Goode David	17	Son	14	M	1/4	1896	"	4934
10880	5 " Minnie	7	Dau	4	F	1/4	1896	"	4935
10881	6 " Willie F	5	Son	2	M	1/4			
10882	7 Jackson, Rosa	17	Wart	14	F	Full	1896	Blue	7227
10883	8 Jones, Osborn Allen	1	Gr Son	10mo	M	3/8			
	9 Not P.O. Boswell OK								
	10	ENROLLMENT							
	11	OF NOS. 2,3,4,5,6,7 and 8 HEREON APPROVED BY THE SECRETARY							
	12	OF INTERIOR FEB 4 1903							
	13 No. 1 HEREON DISMISSED UNDER								
	14 ORDER OF THE COMMISSION TO THE FIVE								
	15 CIVILIZED TRIBES OF MARCH 31, 1905.								
	16 For child of No3 see NB (Apr 26-06) Card #329								
	17 " children " " " " (Mar 3-05) " #1318								

TRIBAL ENROLLMENT OF PARENTS

	Name of Father	Year	County	Name of Mother	Year	County
1	John Carnes	Dead	Bok Tuklo	Lizzie Carnes	Dead	Bok Tuklo
2	Ed Killingsworth		Tobucksy	No1		
3	John Goode		Non Citz	No1		
4	" "		" "	No1		
5	" "		" "	No1		
6	" "		" "	No1		
7	Calvin Jackson	Dead	Jackson	Isabelle Jackson	Dead	Jackson
8	Osborne Jones	1896	"	N°3		
9						
10	No1 on 1896 roll as Melvinay Goode					
11	No3 " 1896 " " Virgie "					
12	No7 " 1896 " " Rose Jackson					
13	No6 Affidavit of birth to be supplied:- Recd Oct 7/99				Date of Application for Enrollment.
14	No1 died January 10, 1901; proof of death filed Dec 8, 1902				Aug 24/99
15	N°8 Born Feby 6, 1902. Enrolled Dec. 24, 1902				
16	No3 is the wife of Osborne Jones on Choctaw Card #5534 — 12/1/02				
17	No7 is duplicate of No6 on Choctaw care 1831 Sissie Jackson approved roll #5211 Enrollment cancelled under Departmental authority of May 23, 1905 (I.T.D. 9206-1906) DC 21511-1906				

259

Choctaw By Blood Enrollment Cards 1898-1914

RESIDENCE: Jackson COUNTY. **Choctaw Nation** Choctaw Roll CARD NO.
POST OFFICE: Bennington I.T. *(Not Including Freedmen)* FIELD NO. **3860**

Dawes' Roll No.	NAME		Relationship to Person First Named	AGE	SEX	BLOOD	TRIBAL ENROLLMENT		
							Year	County	No.
10884	₁ Matoy, Mary A	58	First Named	55	F	3/8	1896	Blue	8804
10885	₂ Zion Susan	21	Dau	18	"	3/16	1896	"	8805
10886	₃ Matoy Ora	17	"	14	"	3/16	1896	"	8806
10887	₄ Zion, Earie	1	Gr.Dau	4mo	F	3/32			
I.W. 1419	₅ Matoy, William M		Husband	56	M	IW			
	₆								
	₇	ENROLLMENT							
	₈	OF NOS. 1,2,3 and 4 HEREON APPROVED BY THE SECRETARY							
	₉	OF INTERIOR Feb 4 1903							
	10								
	11	ENROLLMENT							
	12	OF NOS. ~~~ 5 ~~~ HEREON APPROVED BY THE SECRETARY							
	13	OF INTERIOR Jun 12 1905							
	14								
	15								
	16								
	17								

TRIBAL ENROLLMENT OF PARENTS

	Name of Father	Year	County	Name of Mother	Year	County
₁	Daniel Folsom	Dead	Blue	Lucinda Folsom	Dead	Blue
₂	William Matoy		Cherokee	No1		
₃	" "		"	No1		
₄	W. E. Zion		non-citz	N°2		
₅						
₆						
₇						
₈						
₉						
10	No3 on 1896 roll as Oray Matoy					
11	N°2 is now the wife of W.E. Zion a non-citizen. Evidence of marriage filed Sept. 8, 1902					
12	N°4 Born May 17, 1902; enrolled Sept 8, 1902					
13	No.5 placed on this card Jany 7 1905 in accordance with decision					1 to 8
14	of Commission of that date holding that application was made within time prescribed by Act of Congress, approved July 1, 1902.					
15	For child of No3 see NB (Apr 26-06) Card #811			Date of Application for Enrollment.		Aug 24/99
16	" " " " " " (Mar 3 '05) " #268					
17	" " " No2 " " " " #1374					

Choctaw By Blood Enrollment Cards 1898-1914

Dawes' Roll No.	NAME	Relationship to Person	AGE	SEX	BLOOD	TRIBAL ENROLLMENT		
						Year	County	No.
10888	1 Matoy, Albert 26	First Named	23	M	3/16	1896	Blue	8764
	2							
	3							
	4							
	5							
	6							
	7							
	8							
	9							
	10							
	11							
	12							
	13							
	14							
	15							
	16							
	17							

ENROLLMENT
OF NOS. 1 HEREON
APPROVED BY THE SECRETARY
OF INTERIOR Feb 4 1903

TRIBAL ENROLLMENT OF PARENTS

Name of Father	Year	County	Name of Mother	Year	County
1 William Matoy		Cherokee	Mary Matoy		Blue
2					
3					
4					
5					
6					
7					
8					
9					
10					
11					
12					Date of Application for Enrollment.
13					
14					Aug 24/99
15					
16					
17					

Choctaw By Blood Enrollment Cards 1898-1914

RESIDENCE:	Blue		COUNTY.				Choctaw Roll		CARD NO.	
POST OFFICE:	Bok Chito, I.T.		**Choctaw Nation**				*(Not Including Freedmen)*		FIELD NO. **3862**	

Dawes' Roll No.	NAME		Relationship to Person	AGE	SEX	BLOOD	TRIBAL ENROLLMENT		
							Year	County	No.
10891	1 Beames, Josiah	51	First Named	48	M	1/2	1896	Blue	1604
I.W. 352	2 " Minnie	24	Wife	21	F	IW	1896	"	14326
10892	3 " Leonara I	17	Dau	14	"	1/4	1896	"	1605
10893	4 " David W	7	Son	4	M	1/4	1896	"	1606
10894	5 " Henry C	5	Son	2	"	1/4			
10895	6 " Levi L	4	"	8mo	"	1/4			
10896	7 " George W	2	Son	2mo	M	1/4			
	8								
	9								
	10								
	11	ENROLLMENT OF NOS. 1,3,4,5,6 and 7 HEREON							
	12	APPROVED BY THE SECRETARY							
	13	OF INTERIOR Feb 4 1903							
	14	ENROLLMENT							
	15	OF NOS. 2 HEREON							
	16	APPROVED BY THE SECRETARY OF INTERIOR Sep 12 1903							
	17								

TRIBAL ENROLLMENT OF PARENTS

	Name of Father	Year	County	Name of Mother	Year	County
1	Jas. Beams[sic]	Dead	Blue	Amy Beams	Dead	Blue
2	James Sauls		Non Citz	Eliz. Sauls	"	Non Citz
3	No1			Mary Beams	"	Cherokee
4	No1			No2		
5	No1			No2		
6	No1			No2		
7	No1			No2		
8						
9						
10	No2 – evidence of marriage to be					
11	supplied:- Recd Oct 7/99					
12	No3 – on 1896 roll as Leonora Beams					
13	No3 – evidence of marriage of parents					
14	filed. See if Mary, mother who was			Date of Application for Enrollment.		
15	a Cherokee, is on rolls of that Nation					
16	Nos 5-6 Affidavits of birth to be			For Nos 1 to 6 Incl Aug 24/99		
17	supplied:- Recd Oct 7/99					
	No.7 Enrolled November 17th, 1900					
	Nos 2 and 4 admitted by Dawes Commission 1896 case #887; No appeal					

For child of Nos 1&2 see NB (Apr 26-06) Card #207

Choctaw By Blood Enrollment Cards 1898-1914

RESIDENCE:	Blue	COUNTY.			Choctaw Roll	CARD No.
POST OFFICE:	Bok Chito, I.T.	**Choctaw Nation**			(Not Including Freedmen)	FIELD No. 3863

Dawes' Roll No.	NAME	Relationship to Person First Named	AGE	SEX	BLOOD	TRIBAL ENROLLMENT Year	County	No.
10897	1 Beames, Edmond	22	19	M	1/4	1896	Blue	1603
	2							
	3							
	4							
	5	ENROLLMENT OF NOS. 1 HEREON APPROVED BY THE SECRETARY OF INTERIOR FEB 4 1903						
	6							
	7							
	8							
	9							
	10							
	11							
	12							
	13							
	14							
	15							
	16							
	17							

TRIBAL ENROLLMENT OF PARENTS

	Name of Father	Year	County	Name of Mother	Year	County
1	Chas. Beams[sic]	Dead	Blue	Nancy Beams	Dead	Cherokee
2						
3						
4						
5			As to marriage of parents and residence			
6			of mother, see testimony of Josiah Beams			
7						
8			No.1 is a duplicate of Edmond Beams, Choctaw card #3422			
9			approved roll of Choctaws by blood #9764			
10			Enrollment of No.1 cancelled by Secretary of Interior, Aug. 24, 1904: see Departmental letter of that date (I.T.D.6704-1904) D.C. No 30951-1904			
11						
12						
13						
14						
15				Date of Application for Enrollment.	Aug 24/99	
16						
17						

Choctaw By Blood Enrollment Cards 1898-1914

RESIDENCE: Blue   COUNTY. **Choctaw Nation**   **Choctaw Roll**   CARD No.
POST OFFICE: Caddo, I.T.   *(Not Including Freedmen)*   FIELD No. 3864

Dawes' Roll No.		NAME		Relationship to Person	AGE	SEX	BLOOD	TRIBAL ENROLLMENT		
								Year	County	No.
10889	1	Sharkey, Israel	32	First Named	29	M	Full	1896	Blue	11618
10890	2	" Louisa	21	Wife	18	F	"	1896	"	12421
	3									
	4									
	5	ENROLLMENT								
	6	OF NOS. 1 and 2	HEREON APPROVED BY THE SECRETARY							
	7	OF INTERIOR	FEB 4 1903							
	8									
	9									
	10									
	11									
	12									
	13									
	14									
	15									
	16									
	17									

TRIBAL ENROLLMENT OF PARENTS

	Name of Father	Year	County	Name of Mother	Year	County
1	Sharkey	Dead	Jackson	Lottie Jackson	Dead	Jackson
2	Eastman Tehomba		Blue	Louisa Frazier		Blue
3						
4						
5						
6						
7	No2 on 1896 roll as Louisa Tehomba					
8	For child of Nos 1&2 see NB (Apr 26-06) Card #686					
9	" children " " " " " " (Mar 3-05) " #1168					
10						
11						
12						
13						
14						Date of Application for Enrollment.
15						Aug 24/99
16						
17	PO Caney IT 4/8/05					

264

Choctaw By Blood Enrollment Cards 1898-1914

RESIDENCE: Jackson COUNTY. **Choctaw Nation** | **Choctaw Roll** (Not Including Freedmen) | CARD NO.
POST OFFICE: Bennington, I.T. | | FIELD NO. 3865

Dawes' Roll No.	NAME	Relationship to Person First Named	AGE	SEX	BLOOD	TRIBAL ENROLLMENT		
						Year	County	No.
10898	1 Strickland Alfred ³⁸	First Named	35	M	1/4	1896	Jackson	11567
	2							
	3							
	4	ENROLLMENT						
	5	OF NOS. 1 HEREON APPROVED BY THE SECRETARY						
	6	OF INTERIOR FEB 4 1903						
	7							
	8							
	9							
	10							
	11							
	12							
	13							
	14							
	15							
	16							
	17							

TRIBAL ENROLLMENT OF PARENTS

	Name of Father	Year	County	Name of Mother	Year	County
1	Chas Strickland	Dead	Chick Roll	Emily Strickland	Dead	Jackson
2						
3						
4						
5						
6						
7						
8						
9						
10						
11						
12						
13						
14					Date of Application for Enrollment.	
15					Aug 24/99	
16						
17						

265

Choctaw By Blood Enrollment Cards 1898-1914

| RESIDENCE: Blue | COUNTY. | Choctaw Nation | Choctaw Roll | CARD No. |
| POST OFFICE: Caddo, I.T. | | | (Not Including Freedmen) | FIELD No. **3866** |

Dawes' Roll No.	NAME		Relationship to Person	AGE	SEX	BLOOD	TRIBAL ENROLLMENT		
							Year	County	No.
10899	1 Carnes, Andrew J	25	First Named	22	M	Full	1896	Blue	2867
I.W.353	2 " Myrtle	23	Wife	20	F	I.W.	1896	Jackson	14418
10900	3 " Charles A	5	Son	1½	M	1/2			
10901	4 " Odee	3	"	1mo	"	1/2			
	5								
	6	ENROLLMENT							
	7	OF NOS. 1, 3 and 4 HEREON APPROVED BY THE SECRETARY							
	8	OF INTERIOR Feb 4 1903							
	9								
	10	ENROLLMENT							
	11	OF NOS. 2 HEREON APPROVED BY THE SECRETARY							
	12	OF INTERIOR Sep 12 1903							
	13								
	14								
	15								
	16								
	17								

TRIBAL ENROLLMENT OF PARENTS

	Name of Father	Year	County	Name of Mother	Year	County
1	Eli Carnes	Dead	Blue	Maggie Tumley		Atoka
2	Kit Sparks		Non Citz	Mary J Sparks	Dead	Non Citz
3	No1			No2		
4	No1			No2		
5						
6						
7			No3 affidavit of birth to be			
8			supplied:- Recd Oct 7/99			
9			For child of Nos 1&2 see NB (Apr 26/06) Card #353			
10						
11						
12						
13						
14					#1 to 3	
15					Date of Application for Enrollment.	Aug 24/99
16					No4 enrolled Nov 2/99	
17	Hickory I.T. 1/10/03					

Choctaw By Blood Enrollment Cards 1898-1914

RESIDENCE: Jackson   COUNTY.   **Choctaw Nation**   Choctaw Roll   CARD NO.
POST OFFICE: Jackson, I.T.   (Not Including Freedmen)   FIELD NO. **3867**

Dawes' Roll No.	NAME			Relationship to Person First Named	AGE	SEX	BLOOD	TRIBAL ENROLLMENT		
								Year	County	No.
10902	1	Sanders, Robert	25		22	M	Full	1893	Kiamitia	7
10903	2	" Frances	20	Wife	17	F	"	1896	Jackson	11562
DEAD	3	" Abner DEAD		Son	5mo	M	"			
15768	4	" Solomon	1	Son	1	M	"			
	5									
	6	ENROLLMENT								
	7	OF NOS. 1 and 2 HEREON APPROVED BY THE SECRETARY								
	8	OF INTERIOR Feb 4 1903								
	9									
	10	ENROLLMENT								
	11	OF NOS. ~~ 4 ~~~~ HEREON APPROVED BY THE SECRETARY								
	12	OF INTERIOR Dec 28 1904								
	13	No.3 hereon dismissed under order of								
	14	the Commission to the Five Civilized								
	15	Tribes of March 31, 1905.								
	16									
	17									

TRIBAL ENROLLMENT OF PARENTS

	Name of Father	Year	County	Name of Mother	Year	County
1	Solomon Sanders	Dead	Kiamitia	Sally Sanders	Dead	Kiamitia
2	John Scott		Jackson	Sibbie Scott		Jackson
3	No1			No2		
4	No.1			Susan Sanders		Kiamitia
5						
6						
7			For child of Nos 1 and 2 see NB (Apr 26,06) No. 787			
8			No1 on 1893 Pay Roll, Page 1, No7 Kiamitia			
9			Co as Robt Alexander			
10			No2 on 1896 roll as Frances Scott			
11			No3 Affidavit of birth to be			
12			supplied:- For child of No.1 see NB (March 3,1905) #1079			
			No.1 on 1896 Choctaw roll as Robert Sounder page 297 #11529			
13			No.3 died Aug, 1899: proof of death filed Dec 6 1902			#1 to 3 inc
	No.4 was born Aug 29, 1902 application was made for his enrollment at					
14	Antlers, I.T. Dec 3,1902 by Robert Sanders: No.4 placed on this card					Date of Application for Enrollment
15	Dec.9,1904. Mother of No.4 is Susan Willis. No.1 on Choctaw					Aug 24/99
	card #1771, Choctaw roll number 5021. Dec. 9, 1904					
16						
17						

267

Choctaw By Blood Enrollment Cards 1898-1914

RESIDENCE: Blue   County   Choctaw Nation   Choctaw Roll   CARD NO.

POST OFFICE: Bok Chito, I.T.   (not including Freedmen)   FIELD NO. 3868

Dawes' Roll No.	NAME	Relationship to Person First Named	AGE	SEX	BLOOD	TRIBAL ENROLLMENT		
						Year	County	No.
10904	1 Harrison, Rufus 25		22	M	Full	1896	Blue	5869
	2							
	3							
	4							
	5							
	6							
	7							
	8							
	9							
	10							
	11							
	12							
	13							
	14							
	15							
	16							
	17							

ENROLLMENT OF NOS. 1 HEREON APPROVED BY THE SECRETARY OF INTERIOR FEB 4 1903

TRIBAL ENROLLMENT OF PARENTS

	Name of Father	Year	County	Name of Mother	Year	County
1	Gilbert Harrison	Dead	Towson	Elizabeth Harrison	Dead	Towson
2						
3						
4						
5						
6						
7						
8						
9						
10						
11						
12						
13						
14						Date of Application for Enrollment
15						Aug 24/99
16						
17	P.O. Wade I.T. 9/28/08					

Choctaw By Blood Enrollment Cards 1898-1914

RESIDENCE:	Blue	COUNTY.							
POST OFFICE:	Blue, I.T.								

Choctaw Nation

Choctaw Roll (Not Including Freedmen)

CARD NO.
FIELD NO. 3869

Dawes' Roll No.	NAME	Relationship to Person	AGE	SEX	BLOOD	TRIBAL ENROLLMENT		
						Year	County	No.
10905	1 Fullomme, Gibson ⁴⁸	First Named	45	M	Full	1896	Blue	4386
	2							
	3							
	4							
	5	ENROLLMENT OF NOS. 1 HEREON						
	6	APPROVED BY THE SECRETARY OF INTERIOR FEB 4 1903						
	7							
	8							
	9							
	10							
	11							
	12							
	13							
	14							
	15							
	16							
	17							

TRIBAL ENROLLMENT OF PARENTS

	Name of Father	Year	County	Name of Mother	Year	County
1	Fullomme	Dead	Blue	Ho-te-mo-na	Dead	Blue
2						
3						
4						
5						
6	No 1 "Died prior to September 25, 1902; not entitled to land or money" See					
7	Indian Office Letter of March 17, 1908. (I.T. 15414-1908)					
8						
9						
10						
11						
12						
13						
14					Date of Application for Enrollment.	
15					Aug 24/99	
16						
17						

Choctaw By Blood Enrollment Cards 1898-1914

RESIDENCE: **Blue** COUNTY. **Choctaw Nation** **Choctaw Roll** CARD NO.
POST OFFICE: **Caddo, I.T.** *(Not Including Freedmen)* FIELD NO. **3870**

Dawes' Roll No.	NAME	Relationship to Person First Named	AGE	SEX	BLOOD	TRIBAL ENROLLMENT Year	TRIBAL ENROLLMENT County	TRIBAL ENROLLMENT No.
DEAD	₁ Tehomba, Eastman DEAD 45	First Named	42	M	Full	1896	Blue	12420
10906	₂ " Annis 13	Dau	10	F	"	1896	"	12422
10907	₃ Holton, Anderson 15	Ward	12	M	"	1896	"	5873
	₄							
	₅							
	₆ ENROLLMENT							
	₇ OF NOS. 2 and 3 HEREON APPROVED BY THE SECRETARY							
	₈ OF INTERIOR Feb 4 1903							
	₉							
	₁₀ No -1- Dismissed							
	₁₁ May 19 1905							
	₁₂							
	₁₃							
	₁₄							
	₁₅							
	₁₆							
	₁₇							

TRIBAL ENROLLMENT OF PARENTS

Name of Father	Year	County	Name of Mother	Year	County
₁ Casson Tehomba	Dead	Blue	Liza Tehomba	Dead	Blue
No1			Simpsey Tehomba	"	"
₃ Felix Holton	Dead	Blue	Edna Holton	"	"
₄					
₅					
₆					
₇ No3 on 1896 roll as Anderson Holson					
₈					
₉ No1 died August 8, 1902: proof of death filed Nov 28 1902					
₁₀					
₁₁ Notify Chas E McPherron, Caddo of decision					
₁₂					
₁₃ No2 now Annie Folson 2/27/08					
₁₄				Date of Application for Enrollment.	
₁₅				Aug 24/99	
₁₆					
₁₇					

Choctaw By Blood Enrollment Cards 1898-1914

RESIDENCE: Blue   COUNTY.
POST OFFICE: Bok Chito, I.T.

Choctaw Nation

Choctaw Roll (Not Including Freedmen)

CARD NO.
FIELD NO. 3871

Dawes' Roll No.	NAME	Relationship to Person	AGE	SEX	BLOOD	TRIBAL ENROLLMENT Year	County	No.
10908	1 Wesley, Davis ³¹	First Named	28	M	Full	1896	Blue	13892
	2							
	3							
	4	ENROLLMENT						
	5	OF NOS. 1 HEREON APPROVED BY THE SECRETARY						
	6	OF INTERIOR FEB 4 1903						
	7							
	8							
	9							
	10							
	11							
	12							
	13							
	14							
	15							
	16							
	17							

TRIBAL ENROLLMENT OF PARENTS

	Name of Father	Year	County	Name of Mother	Year	County
1	McIntosh	Dead	Cedar	Margaret Wesley	Dead	Cedar
2						
3						
4						
5						
6						
7						
8						
9						
10						
11						
12						
13						
14						
15			Date of application for enrollment		Aug 24/99	
16						
17						

Choctaw By Blood Enrollment Cards 1898-1914

RESIDENCE: Blue   COUNTY.
POST OFFICE: Caddo, I.T.

Choctaw Nation

Choctaw Roll
(Not Including Freedmen)

CARD NO.
FIELD NO. 3872

Dawes' Roll No.	NAME		Relationship to Person First Named	AGE	SEX	BLOOD	TRIBAL ENROLLMENT		
							Year	County	No.
I.W.354	1 Hull, Joseph L	46	First Named	43	M	IW	1896	Blue	14645
10909	2 " Lena B	28	Wife	25	F	3/4	1896	"	5848
10910	3 " Luther S	9	Son	6	M	3/8	1896	"	5849
10911	4 " Loda L	7	"	4	"	3/8	1896	"	5850
10912	5 " Vivia B	6	Dau	2	F	3/8			
10913	6 " Gussie V	3	"	1mo	"	3/8			
	7								
	8	ENROLLMENT							
	9	OF NOS. 2,3,4,5 and 6 HEREON ~~APPROVED BY THE SECRETARY~~							
	10	OF INTERIOR FEB 4 1903							
	11	ENROLLMENT							
	12	OF NOS. 1 HEREON ~~APPROVED BY THE SECRETARY~~							
	13	OF INTERIOR SEP 12 1903							
	14								
	15								
	16								
	17								

TRIBAL ENROLLMENT OF PARENTS

	Name of Father	Year	County	Name of Mother	Year	County
1	Cyrus Hull		Non Citz	Sarah J Hull		Non Citz
2	Caleb Impson	Dead	Blue	Melina Freeny		Blue
3	No1			No2		
4	No1			No2		
5	No1			No2		
6	No1			No2		
7						
8						
9			No1 on 1896 roll as Joseph S Hull			
10			No2 " 1896 " " Lena Belle "			
11			~~No.1 admitted as an intermarried citizen by Dawes Commission in 1896; Choctaw Case #200: No appeal.~~			
12						
13						
14						Date of Application for Enrollment
15						Aug 24/99
16						
17						

Choctaw By Blood Enrollment Cards 1898-1914

RESIDENCE: Blue   COUNTY.   Choctaw Roll   CARD NO.
POST OFFICE: Caddo, I.T.   **Choctaw Nation**   (Not Including Freedmen)   FIELD NO. 3873

Dawes' Roll No.	NAME	Relationship to Person First Named	AGE	SEX	BLOOD	TRIBAL ENROLLMENT		
						Year	County	No.
1	Bryant, Mattie E	Named	25	F	1/8			
2	" Miriam L	Dau	1mo	F	1/16			
3	" Mary R	Dau	1 wk	F	1/16			
4								
5								
6	No1 Denied by C.C.C.C. as							
7	Mattie E Bryant (nee Smith) or Mattie E Smith							
8				No				
9								
10	2-3- DISMISSED NOV 12 1904							
11								
12								
13								
14	DENIED CITIZENSHIP BY THE CHOCTAW AND							
15	CHICKASAW CITIZENSHIP COURT							
16								
17								

TRIBAL ENROLLMENT OF PARENTS

	Name of Father	Year	County	Name of Mother	Year	County
1	W.H.P. Smith	Dead	Non Citz	Mary A Loving		Choctaw
2	James R Bryant		noncitizen	No1		
3	J. R. Bryant		"	No1		
4						
5						
6						
7						
8	No1 Denied in 96 Case #546					
9	Admitted by U.S. Court, Central Dist June 19/99, Case No 71; a Mattie E					
10	Smith					
11	As to residence, see her testimony					
12	Nos 1,2 and 3 now in C.C.C.C. Case #107					
13	Daughter Mary R., born Dec 13/99 on Card No D-545					
14	No2 Born March 15, 1901; enrolled April 22, 1902					Date of Application for Enrollment.
15	No3 born December 13 1899; transferred to this card May 24, 1902					Aug 24/99
16	Nos 2 and 3 dismissed by C.C.C.C [remainder illegible]					
17						

273

Choctaw By Blood Enrollment Cards 1898-1914

<table>
<tr><td>RESIDENCE:</td><td>Jackson</td><td>COUNTY.</td><td rowspan="2">Choctaw Nation</td><td>Choctaw Roll</td><td>CARD No.</td></tr>
<tr><td>POST OFFICE:</td><td>Mayhew, I.T.</td><td></td><td>(Not Including Freedmen)</td><td>FIELD No. 3874</td></tr>
</table>

Dawes' Roll No.		NAME	Relationship to Person First Named	AGE	SEX	BLOOD	TRIBAL ENROLLMENT		
							Year	County	No.
10914	1	Moseley, Wilson ²⁴	First Named	21	M	Full	1896	Jackson	8744
IW1606	2	" Daisy	Wife	24	F	I.W.			
	3								
	4								
	5	ENROLLMENT							
	6	OF NOS. 1 HEREON APPROVED BY THE SECRETARY							
	7	OF INTERIOR Feb 4 1903							
	8	ENROLLMENT							
	9	OF NOS. ~ 2 ~ HEREON APPROVED BY THE SECRETARY							
	10	OF INTERIOR Feb 12 1907							
	11								
	12								
	13								
	14								
	15								
	16								
	17								

TRIBAL ENROLLMENT OF PARENTS

	Name of Father	Year	County	Name of Mother	Year	County
1	Morris Moseley	Dead	Blue	Mary Moseley	Dead	Blue
2	Dan Sanders			Ella Sanders	dead	
3						
4						
5						
6						
7			No1 placed hereon under order of the Commissioner to the Five			
8			Civilized Tribes of Oct 19-1906 holding that application was made			
9			for her enrollment within the time provided by the Act of Congress			
10			Approved April 26-1906 (34 Stats 137)			
11						
12						
13					Date of Application for Enrollment.	
14						
15					Aug 24/99	
16						
17						

Choctaw By Blood Enrollment Cards 1898-1914

RESIDENCE: Jackson COUNTY. **Choctaw Nation** **Choctaw Roll** CARD NO.
POST OFFICE: Bennington, I.T. *(Not Including Freedmen)* FIELD NO. **3875**

Dawes' Roll No.	NAME	Relationship to Person First Named	AGE	SEX	BLOOD	TRIBAL ENROLLMENT		
						Year	County	No.
10915	1 Riddle, Dolphus A ⁴³	First Named	40	M	1/2	1896	Blue	10956
I.W. 355	2 " Ella ³⁸	Wife	33	F	I.W	1896	"	14987
10916	3 " Oscar ¹⁵	Son	12	M	1/4	1896	"	10957
10917	4 " Jesse G ⁶	"	3	"	1/4	1896	"	10959
	5							
	6							
	7	ENROLLMENT						
	8	OF NOS. 1,3 and 4 HEREON						
	9	APPROVED BY THE SECRETARY OF INTERIOR Feb 4 1903						
	10							
	11	ENROLLMENT OF NOS. 2 HEREON						
	12	APPROVED BY THE SECRETARY OF INTERIOR Sep 12 1903						
	13							
	14							
	15							
	16							
	17							

TRIBAL ENROLLMENT OF PARENTS

	Name of Father	Year	County	Name of Mother	Year	County
1	Edmond Riddle	Dead	Skullyville	Jincy Riddle	Dead	Skullyville
2	Wᵐ Richard		Non Citz	Susan Richard	"	Non Citz
3	No.1			No.2		
4	No.1			No.2		
5						
6						
7						
8			No. 1 on 1896 roll as D.A. Riddle			
9			No.4 " 1896 " " Green "			
10			No.2 As to marriage see testimony of Arabella Gardner and Mary Matoy			
11						
12						
13						
14					Date of Application for Enrollment.	
15					Aug 24/99	
16						
17	PO. Banty I.T. 3/16/03					

275

Choctaw By Blood Enrollment Cards 1898-1914

RESIDENCE: Blue   COUNTY.   **Choctaw Nation**   **Choctaw Roll**   CARD NO.

POST OFFICE: Caddo, I.T.   *(Not Including Freedmen)*   FIELD NO. 3876

Dawes' Roll No.	NAME	Relationship to Person First Named	AGE	SEX	BLOOD	TRIBAL ENROLLMENT		
						Year	County	No.
10918	1 Robinson, George 25	First Named	22	M	Full	1896	Blue	10940
	2							
	3							
	4							
	5							
	6							
	7							
	8							
	9							
	10							
	11							
	12							
	13							
	14							
	15							
	16							
	17							

ENROLLMENT OF NOS. 1 HEREON APPROVED BY THE SECRETARY OF INTERIOR FEB 4 1903

TRIBAL ENROLLMENT OF PARENTS

	Name of Father	Year	County	Name of Mother	Year	County
1	Jas. Robinson	Dead	Blue	Ceowmey Robinson	Dead	Blue
2						
3						
4						
5						
6	No 1 on 1896 roll as George Roberson					
7	No 1 is now the husband of Lucy A. Myer on Chow #3648					
8						
9						
10						
11						
12						
13						
14					Date of Application for Enrollment.	
15					Aug 24/99	
16						
17						

276

Choctaw By Blood Enrollment Cards 1898-1914

RESIDENCE:	Blue	COUNTY:					CARD NO.	
POST OFFICE:	Nida, I.T.	**Choctaw Nation**			Choctaw Roll (Not Including Freedmen)		FIELD NO. **3877**	

Dawes' Roll No.	NAME	Relationship to Person First Named	AGE	SEX	BLOOD	TRIBAL ENROLLMENT		
						Year	County	No.
1	Horne, Edward J	Named	47	M	1/4			
2	" Joan	Wife	37	F	1/8			
3	" Isedora	Dau	19	"	3/16			
4	" Victoria D	"	16	"	3/16			
5	" James O	Son	14	M	3/16			
6	" Charles S	"	12	"	3/16			
7	" Commie E	Dau	10	F	3/16			
8	" Mary E	"	8	"	3/16			
9	" Sarah E	"	4	"	3/16			
Dis 10	" Joe Ellen	"	2	"	3/16			
11	" Juel	"	6mo	"	3/16			
12	Pyle, Cecil Smith	G.Son	5mo	M	3/32			
13	" Thelma Horne	"	2wks	"	3/32			
14	Davis, J. P.	"	4mo	"	3/32			
15	Nos 1 to 14 incl now in C.C.C.C. Case #83 M							
	All but No10 was admitted by U.S. Court, Central District Aug 4-1896 Case No29							
16	No1 was admitted as E.J. Horne, No2 admitted as Icy Do Horne, No7 admitted as Commie Horne As to residence and birth of child Oct 27/97 see testimony of No.1							
17	No4 is now the wife of Cecil C Pyle March 16 1901 Evidence of marriage filed May 29" 1901 No3 is now the wife Eggel Davis a non citizen Evidence of marriage filed Aug 5" 1902							

	Name of Father	Year	County	Name of Mother	Year	County
1	E. G Horne		Non Citizen	Mary Horne	Dead	Choctaw
2	J. B. Smith	Dead	" "			"
3	No1			No2		
4	No1			No2		
5	No1			No2		
6	No1			No2		
7	No1			No2		
8	No1			No2		
9	No1			No2		
10	No1			No2		
11	No1			No2		
12	Cecil C. Pyle		Non-Citizen	No4		
13	" " "		" "	No4		
14	Eggel Davis		" "	No3		
15	Nos1 to 9 incl Denied in 96 Case #1410					
16	No11 Enrolled May 24" 1900 " 12 Enrolled May 29" 1901					
17	" 13 Born July 16 1901 Enrolled Aug 5" 1902					
	" 14 Born April 4" 1902: Enrolled Aug 5" 1902					

DISMISSED

MAY 25 1904

Aug 24/99

Choctaw By Blood Enrollment Cards 1898-1914

RESIDENCE: Atoka	COUNTY.		Choctaw Roll	CARD NO.
POST OFFICE: Atoka, I.T.	**Choctaw Nation**		(Not Including Freedmen)	FIELD No. 3878

Dawes' Roll No.	NAME		Relationship to Person First Named	AGE	SEX	BLOOD	TRIBAL ENROLLMENT		
							Year	County	No.
I.W. 748	1 Mathews,	Andrew J ㊷	First Named	39	M	IW			
DEAD	2 "	Silway DEAD	Wife	27	F	Full	1893	Atoka	746
10919	3 "	Sarah E 14	Dau	11	"	1/32			8858
10920	4 "	Eliza 12	"	9	"	1/32			8859
10921	5 "	Annie 6	"	3	"	1/2			8287
	6								
	No1 See Decision of March 2 '04								
	8								
	9 ENROLLMENT OF NOS. 3, 4 and 5 HEREON APPROVED BY THE SECRETARY OF INTERIOR Feb 4 1903								
	10								
	11								
	12								
	13 No5 now living with Harrison								
	14 Gibson on Choctaw card #1753								
	15								
	16 # Decision Prepared 11/13/03								
	17								

TRIBAL ENROLLMENT OF PARENTS

	Name of Father	Year	County	Name of Mother	Year	County
1	Jas Mathews	Dead	Non Citz	Eliz Mathews	Dead	Non Citz
2	Gibson	"	Atoka	Eliza Gibson	"	Atoka
3	No1			Nancy Mathews	"	"
4	No1			" "	"	"
5	Dave Lawrence			No2		
6						
7						
8	Father of No.5 is Dave Lawrence					
9	#5 on 1896 Choctaw roll page 206 #8287 as Sophy Lawrence					
10	#2 died in spring of 1900					
11	No1 Admitted by Dawes Com, Case No 1297		No appeal			
12	as A. J. Mathews					
	Surname on 1896 roll as Mathes					
13	No2 on 1893 Pay Roll, Page 72, No 746					
14	Atoka Co., as Silway Lewis	No.2 hereon dismissed under				
	No5 Affidavit of birth to be	order of the Commission to the				
15	supplied: Recd Oct 7/99	Five Civilized Tribes of March 31 1905				
16	No.2 Died about April 11 1900. Evidence of death filed May 17, 1901					
	Nº2 also on 1896 Choctaw census roll page 121 #4964 as Malinda Gipson					
17	For child of No3 see NB (Act Mar 3-05) Card #269					

ENROLLMENT OF NOS. 1 HEREON APPROVED BY THE SECRETARY OF INTERIOR May 7 1904

Date of Application for Enrollment.
Aug 24/99

Choctaw By Blood Enrollment Cards 1898-1914

RESIDENCE: Blue   COUNTY. **Choctaw Nation**   **Choctaw Roll**   CARD NO.
POST OFFICE: Caddo, I.T.   *(Not Including Freedmen)*   FIELD NO. **3879**

Dawes' Roll No.	NAME		Relationship to Person	AGE	SEX	BLOOD	TRIBAL ENROLLMENT		
							Year	County	No.
10922	1 Lewis, Bacey	36	First Named	33	F	Full	1896	Blue	8238
10923	2 " Rachel	3	Dau	6mo	"	"			
10924	3 Hokubbi, Sisley	20	Niece	17	"	"	1896	Blue	4407
10925	4 Hokubbi Silmy	1	Dau of No3	10mo	F	"			
	5								
	6								
	7	ENROLLMENT							
	8	OF NOS. 1,2,3 and 4 HEREON APPROVED BY THE SECRETARY							
	9	OF INTERIOR Feb 4 1903							
	10								
	11								
	12								
	13								
	14								
	15								
	16								
	17								

TRIBAL ENROLLMENT OF PARENTS

	Name of Father	Year	County	Name of Mother	Year	County
1	Harris Fletcher	Dead	Blue	Sally Fletcher	Dead	Blue
2	Abel Lewis	Dead	Blue	No1		
3	Jackson Fletcher	"	"	Sarah Fletcher	Dead	Blue
4	Peter Hokabi	1893	Atoka	No3		
5						
6						
7						
8						
9						
10						
11						
12	No3 is now the wife of Peter Hokabi on Choctaw card #4188. Evidence of					
13	marriage requested Aug. 2, 1902					#1 to 3 inc
14	No4 Born Sept. 11, 1901: enrolled Aug. 2, 1902					Date of Application for Enrollment.
15	For child of No3 see NB (Act Mar 3-05) Card #270					Aug 24/99
16						
17	Caney I.T.					

Lewis I.T. 7/14/07 = Now Tushka, Okla.

Choctaw By Blood Enrollment Cards 1898-1914

Dawes' Roll No.	NAME	Relationship to Person First Named	AGE	SEX	BLOOD	TRIBAL ENROLLMENT Year	County	No.
10926	1 Paddock, Reuben W 24	First Named	21	M	1/16	1896	Blue	10475
10927	2 " John S 17	Bro	14	"	1/16	1896	"	10477
10928	3 Simmons Eliza E 17	Sister	14	F	1/16	1896	"	10476
10929	4 Paddock, Annie E 14	"	11	"	1/16	1896	"	10478
10930	5 Simmons, Minnie May 2	dau of No3	7mo	F	1/32			
10931	6 " Charley L 1	Son of No3	3mo	M	1/32			
I.W. 1475	7 Paddock Reuben 58	Father	58	M	I.W.			
	8							
	9							

ENROLLMENT
OF NOS. 1,2,3,4,5 and 6   HEREON
APPROVED BY THE SECRETARY
OF INTERIOR   Feb 4 1903

No.7 formerly husband of Elizabeth
C. Paddock, a Choctaw who died about
1890

No7 Caddo I.T. 5/27/05

17 P.O. Lindsay, I.T.

TRIBAL ENROLLMENT OF PARENTS

	Name of Father	Year	County	Name of Mother	Year	County
1	Reuben Paddock		Non Citz	Eliza Paddock	Dead	Blue
2	" "		" "	" "	"	"
3	" "		" "	" "	"	"
4	" "		" "	" "	"	"
5	George Simmons		non citizen	No3		
6	" "		" "	No3		

7 For child of No2 see NB (Act   OF NOS. Seven   HEREON
8 Mar 3-05) Card #271   APPROVED BY THE SECRETARY   OF INTERIOR   Aug 22 1905
9 No4 on 1896 roll as Annie Paddock
10 No.3 is now the wife of George Simmons, a non citizen. Evidence
of marriage requested this day June 27, 1901. Received and filed July 9, 1901.
11 No5 Enrolled June 27 1901
12 7/23/02 Nos 1,2 and 3 admitted by Act of Choctaw council approved 11/5/88. See Choc D.20
No6 Born Aug 10, 1902. Enrolled Nov. 20, 1902
13 Name of No7 placed hereon June 22d 1905 in accordance with a decision of the
14 Commission of that date holding application was made within time   Date of Application for Enrollment.
prescribed by Act of Congress approved July 1st 1902 (32 Stat. 641)
15 No7 admitted by Act of Choctaw council approved Nov. 5, 1888   Aug 24/99
16 See decision of Commission of June 22, 1905 enrolling No.7

Choctaw By Blood Enrollment Cards 1898-1914

RESIDENCE:	Atoka	COUNTY.					CARD No.
POST OFFICE: Coalgate, I.T.		**Choctaw Nation**			Choctaw Roll (Not Including Freedmen)		FIELD No. 3881

Dawes' Roll No.	NAME	Relationship to Person	AGE	SEX	BLOOD	TRIBAL ENROLLMENT		
						Year	County	No.
10932	1 Huggins, Lula E 27	First Named	24	F	1/16	1896	Tobucksy	5380
10933	2 " Ollie 10	Dau	7	"	1/32	1896	"	5381
10934	3 " Oscar 8	Son	5	M	1/32	1896	"	5382
DEAD.	4 " Edgar DEAD	"	1	"	1/32			
10935	5 " Oliver 2	Son	4mo	M	1/32			
	6							
7/32/02	7 No1 was admitted by Act of Council approved 11/5/88							
	8 See Choctaw D-20							
	9							
	10 ENROLLMENT							
	11 OF NOS. 1,2,3 and 5 HEREON APPROVED BY THE SECRETARY							
	12 OF INTERIOR FEB 4 1903							
	13 No 4 HEREON DISMISSED UNDER							
	14 ORDER OF THE COMMISSION TO THE FIVE							
	15 CIVILIZED TRIBES OF MARCH 31, 1905.							
	16 For child of No1 see NB (Apr 26/06) Card #339							
	17 " " " " " " (Mar 3-05) " #698							

TRIBAL ENROLLMENT OF PARENTS

Name of Father	Year	County	Name of Mother	Year	County
1 E. F. Campbell		Blue	Mollie Campbell	Dead	Non Citz
2 J. J. Huggins		Non Citz	No1		
3 " " "		" "	No1		
4 " " "		" "	No1		
5 " " "		" "	No1		
6					
7 No1 on 1896 roll as Ella Higgins					
8 No2 " 1896 " Ollie "					
9 No3 " 1896 " Osper "					
10 No4 Affidavit of birth to be					
11 supplied:- Received and filed Nov. 2d, 1899					
12 No1 Evidence as to marriage of parents to be supplied:- Filed Nov 2/99					
13 No.4 died September 7, 1899 See statement of father, filed June 6, 1901			#1 to 4		
14 No.5 Enrolled June 6, 1901			Date of Application for Enrollment.		
15 No.4 Proof of death filed Aug 22 1901			Aug 24/99		
16					
17 PO					

281

RESIDENCE:	Blue	COUNTY.							

RESIDENCE: Blue **COUNTY.**
POST OFFICE: Albany, I.T.

Choctaw Nation

Choctaw Roll (Not Including Freedmen)

CARD No.
FIELD No. 3882

Dawes' Roll No.	NAME	Relationship to Person First Named	AGE	SEX	BLOOD	TRIBAL ENROLLMENT		
						Year	County	No.
10936	1 Campbell, Ephraim F 53	First Named	50	M	1/8	1896	Tobucksy	2386
I.W. 143	2 " Lucy 35	Wife	32	F	IW			
10937	3 " William 20	Son	17	M	1/16	1896	Tobucksy	2387
10938	4 " Annie 4	Dau	6mo	F	1/16			
I.W. 1607	5 " Idonia	Wife of No3	19	F	I.W.			
	6							
	7							
	8	ENROLLMENT						
	9	OF NOS. 1, 3 and 4 HEREON APPROVED BY THE SECRETARY						
	10	OF INTERIOR FEB 4 1903						
	11							
	12	ENROLLMENT						
	13	OF NOS. 2 ~~~~ HEREON APPROVED BY THE SECRETARY						
	14	OF INTERIOR JUN 13 1903						
	15	ENROLLMENT						
	16	OF NOS. ~~~~5~~~~ HEREON APPROVED BY THE SECRETARY						
	17	OF INTERIOR FEB 12 1907						

TRIBAL ENROLLMENT OF PARENTS

	Name of Father	Year	County	Name of Mother	Year	County
1	L. J. Campbell	Dead	Non Citz	Ellen Campbell	Dead	Choctaw
2	Joe Bryma		" "		"	Non Citz
3	No1			Mollie Campbell	"	" "
4	No1			No2		
5	Terrel Methvin		Non-Citizen	Mary Methvin		non-citizen

6 7/23/02 Nos 1 and 3 were admitted by Act of Choctaw Council of 11/5/88 See Choc D-20
7   No1 on 1896 roll as Ephraim Campbell   No5 placed hereon, under order of
8   No3 " 1896 " " W^m "   Commissioner of October 10, 1906, holding
      No3 Evidence of marriage of parents   that application was made for her enrollment
9 to be supplied:-   within time provided by Act of Congress
10   No4 Affidavit of birth to be   approved April 26, 1906 (34 Stat. 137)
   supplied:- Filed Nov 2/99
11 No1 has left No2: she does not know his whereabouts 12/22/02
12 For child of Nos 1&2 see NB (Apr 26-06) Card #828
13   " " " No 3 " " (Mar 3-05) " #697
14   " " " Nos 1&2 " " " " " " #1416
15   No3 GRANTED OCT 17 1906   #1 to 4
16   Date of Application for Enrollment.
17 Dougherty I.T. 12/22/03   Aug 24/99

Choctaw By Blood Enrollment Cards 1898-1914

RESIDENCE: Blue   COUNTY. **Choctaw Nation**   **Choctaw Roll**   CARD NO.
POST OFFICE: Wade, I.T.   (Not Including Freedmen)   FIELD NO. 3883

Dawes' Roll No.	NAME	Relationship to Person	AGE	SEX	BLOOD	TRIBAL ENROLLMENT		
						Year	County	No.
10939	1 Fryer, Annie L ²⁸	First Named	25	F	1/4	1896	Blue	2869
10940	2 Carpenter, Georgia M ⁶	Dau	3	"	1/8	1896	"	2870
10941	3 Fryer, Lurinda L ⁴	"	1	"	1/8			
	4							
	5							
	6	ENROLLMENT						
	7	OF NOS. 1 2 and 3 HEREON APPROVED BY THE SECRETARY						
	8	OF INTERIOR FEB 4 1903						
	9							
	10							
	11							
	12							
	13							
	14							
	15							
	16							
	17							

TRIBAL ENROLLMENT OF PARENTS

	Name of Father	Year	County	Name of Mother	Year	County
1	Absalom Brown		Non Citz	Margaret Brown	Dead	Skullyville
2	Geo Carpenter	Dead	" "	No1		
3	Andrew Fryer			No1		
4						
5						
6						
7			No1 on 1896 roll as Annie Lee Carpenter			
8						
9			No3 Affidavit of birth to be			
10			supplied. Recd Oct 7/99			
11			No 2 Admitted as a citizen by blood by Dawes Commission in 1896: Choctaw case #744: No appeal			
12						
13						Date of Application for Enrollment.
14						Aug 24/99
15						
16						
17						

Choctaw By Blood Enrollment Cards 1898-1914

RESIDENCE: Blue
POST OFFICE: Caddo, I.T.
COUNTY. **Choctaw Nation**
Choctaw Roll *(Not Including Freedmen)*
CARD NO.
FIELD NO. 3884

Dawes' Roll No.	NAME		Relationship to Person	AGE	SEX	BLOOD	TRIBAL ENROLLMENT		
							Year	County	No.
10942	1 Puckett, William	25	First Named	22	M	3/8	1896	Blue	10513
10943	2 " Edna C	1	Dau	4mo	F	3/16			
I.W 1007	3 " Liddy	18	Wife	18	F	IW			
	4								
	5								
	6	ENROLLMENT							
	7	OF NOS. 1 and 2 HEREON							
	8	APPROVED BY THE SECRETARY OF INTERIOR FEB 4 1903							
	9								
	10	ENROLLMENT							
	11	OF NOS. ~~~ 3 ~~~ HEREON							
	12	APPROVED BY THE SECRETARY OF INTERIOR OCT 21 1904							
	13								
	14								
	15								
	16								
	17								

TRIBAL ENROLLMENT OF PARENTS

	Name of Father	Year	County	Name of Mother	Year	County
1	Alex Puckett	Dead	Non Citz	Corinne Puckett	Dead	Blue
2	No1			Liddie Pucket[sic]		
3	J C Boehme		noncitizen	Antoine Boehme		noncitizen
4						
5						
6						
7						
8						
9	On 1896 roll as Wm Puckert					
10	No1 is now husband of Liddy Puckett on Choctaw card # #829					
11	No2 born August 14, 1902. enrolled Dec 11, 1902					
12	No3 transferred from Choctaw card D829, August 11, 1904					
13	See decision of July 26, 1904					
14						#1
15	For child of Nos 1&3 see NB (Apr 26-06) Card #810				Date of Application for Enrollment.	Aug 24/99
16	" " " " " " (Mar 3-05) " #993					
17	Blue I.T. 11/19/02					

284

Choctaw By Blood Enrollment Cards 1898-1914

RESIDENCE:	Blue	COUNTY.	Choctaw Nation	Choctaw Roll	CARD No.
POST OFFICE:	Caddo, I.T.			*(Not Including Freedmen)*	FIELD No. 3885

Dawes' Roll No.	NAME		Relationship to Person	AGE	SEX	BLOOD	TRIBAL ENROLLMENT		
							Year	County	No.
10944	1 O'Dea, Mary E	20	First Named	17	F	3/8	1896	Blue	9999
10945	2 " Anna T	19	Sister	16	"	3/8	1896	"	10000
10946	3 " Cora E	16	"	13	"	3/8	1896	"	10001
10947	4 " Katie E	14	"	11	"	3/8	1896	"	10002
10948	5 " Thomas J	12	Bro	9	M	3/8	1896	"	10003
	6								
	7								
	8								
	9								
	10								
	11								
	12								
	13								
	14								
	15								
	16								
	17								

ENROLLMENT
OF NOS. 1-2-3-4 and 5 HEREON
APPROVED BY THE SECRETARY
OF INTERIOR FEB 4 1903

TRIBAL ENROLLMENT OF PARENTS

	Name of Father	Year	County	Name of Mother	Year	County
1	Michael J O'Dea		Non Citz	Corinne E. O'Dea	Dead	Blue
2	" " "		" "	" " "	"	"
3	" " "		" "	" " "	"	"
4	" " "		" "	" " "	"	"
5	" " "		" "	" " "	"	"
6						
7						
8			No5 on 1896 roll as Thos. J. O'Dea			
9						
10						
11						
12						
13					Date of Application for Enrollment.	
14						
15					Aug 24/99	
16						
17						

Choctaw By Blood Enrollment Cards 1898-1914

RESIDENCE:	Blue		
POST OFFICE:	Caddo, I.T.		

COUNTY. **Choctaw Nation**

Choctaw Roll (Not Including Freedmen)

CARD NO. FIELD NO. 3886

Dawes' Roll No.		NAME		Relationship to Person	AGE	SEX	BLOOD	TRIBAL ENROLLMENT		
								Year	County	No.
10949	1	Richards, Cornelia	58	First Named	55	F	1/4	1896	Blue	10948
	2									
	3									
	4									
	5	ENROLLMENT								
	6	OF NOS. 1 HEREON APPROVED BY THE SECRETARY								
	7	OF INTERIOR FEB 4 1903								
	8									
	9									
	10									
	11									
	12									
	13									
	14									
	15									
	16									
	17									

TRIBAL ENROLLMENT OF PARENTS

	Name of Father	Year	County	Name of Mother	Year	County
1	Geo W Harkins	Dead	Towson	Seliney Towson	Dead	Towson
2						
3						
4						
5						
6						
7	No 1 is the wife of William W Richards on Choctaw card #3983.					
8						
9						
10						
11						
12						
13					Date of Application for Enrollment.	
14					Aug 24/99	
15						
16						
17						

Choctaw By Blood Enrollment Cards 1898-1914

RESIDENCE: Blue   COUNTY. **Choctaw Nation**   Choctaw Roll   CARD NO.
POST OFFICE: Caddo, I.T.   *(Not Including Freedmen)*   FIELD NO. 3887

Dawes' Roll No.	NAME	Relationship to Person	AGE	SEX	BLOOD	TRIBAL ENROLLMENT		
						Year	County	No.
I.W. 356	1 Hill, Charles 52	First Named	49	M	IW			
	2							
	3							
	4							
	5							
	6							
	7							
	8							
	9	ENROLLMENT						
	10	OF NOS. 1 HEREON APPROVED BY THE SECRETARY						
	11	OF INTERIOR SEP 12 1903						
	12							
	13							
	14							
	15							
	16							
	17							

TRIBAL ENROLLMENT OF PARENTS

	Name of Father	Year	County	Name of Mother	Year	County
1	Green Hill	Dead	Non Citz	Mary Hill	Dead	Non Citz
2						
3						
4						
5						
6						
7	Admitted by Dawes Com, Case No 1180. No appeal					
8						
9						
10						
11						
12						
13				Date of Application for Enrollment.		
14				Aug 24/99		
15						
16						
17						

Choctaw By Blood Enrollment Cards 1898-1914

RESIDENCE: Jackson   COUNTY.   **Choctaw Nation**   Choctaw Roll   CARD NO.
POST OFFICE: Jackson, I.T.   *(Not Including Freedmen)*   FIELD NO. 5888

Dawes' Roll No.	NAME	Relationship to Person First Named	AGE	SEX	BLOOD	TRIBAL ENROLLMENT Year	County	No.
I.W.357	1 Whittenburg, Lorenzo H (37)	First Named	42	M	IW	1896	Jackson	15185
	2							
	3							
	4							
	5							
	6							
	7							
	8							
	9							
	10							
	11							
	12							
	13							
	14							
	15							
	16							
	17							

ENROLLMENT
OF NOS. 1 HEREON
APPROVED BY THE SECRETARY
OF INTERIOR SEP 12 1903

TRIBAL ENROLLMENT OF PARENTS

Name of Father	Year	County	Name of Mother	Year	County
1 John Whittenburg		Non Citz	Mary Whittenburg		Non Citz
2					
3					
4					
5					
6		On 1896 roll as L. H. Whittenburg			
7					
8		Admitted by Dawes Com, Case No 942 No appeal			
9					
10					
11					
12					
13					
14					Date of Application for Enrollment.
15					Aug 24/99
16					
17					

288

RESIDENCE: Blue   COUNTY.

POST OFFICE: Bok Chito, I.T.

Choctaw Nation

Choctaw Roll [blacked out] NO.

(Not Including Freedmen)   FIELD NO. 3889

Dawes' Roll No.	NAME	Relationship to Person	AGE	SEX	BLOOD	TRIBAL ENROLLMENT Year	County	No.
10950	1 Medell, Susan ²⁴	First Named	21	F	1/2	1893	Blue	779
10951	2 " William O ⁶	Son	2	M	1/4			
10952	3 Medell Lela May ²	Dau	7mo	F	1/4			
I.W. 1008	4 " William ³⁵	Hus.	35	M	I.W.			
	5							
	6							
	7	ENROLLMENT OF NOS. 1, 2 and 3 HEREON APPROVED BY THE SECRETARY OF INTERIOR FEB 4 1903						
	8							
	9							
	10							
	11	ENROLLMENT OF NOS. 4 HEREON APPROVED BY THE SECRETARY OF INTERIOR OCT 21 1904						
	12							
	13							
	14							
	15							
	16							
	17							

TRIBAL ENROLLMENT OF PARENTS

	Name of Father	Year	County	Name of Mother	Year	County
1	Will Labor		Non Citz	Pe-sa-bey	Dead	Nashoba
2	Wᵐ McDell		white man	No 1		
3	Wᵐ Medell		" "	No 1		
4	Erick McDell	D'd	non-citz	Bata McDell		non citz
5						
6						
7						
8	No 1 on 1893 Pay Roll, Page 74, No 779					
9	Blue Co., as Susan Labor					
10						
11	Husband on Card No D362					
12	Correct surname of these people is Medell. See letter of Wᵐ Medell filed 9/24/01					
13	No3 Enrolled Sept 24, 1901				Date of Application for Enrollment.	
14	No4 transferred from Choctaw card #D 360. See Decision of Sept 9, 1904				Aug 24/99	
15					1 & 2	
16						
17	No4 P.O. Bennington IT 11/20/04					

Choctaw By Blood Enrollment Cards 1898-1914

RESIDENCE: Blue COUNTY.	Choctaw Nation				Choctaw Roll CARD NO.		
POST OFFICE: Caddo, I.T.					(Not Including Freedmen) FIELD NO. 3890		

Dawes' Roll No.	NAME	Relationship to Person First Named	AGE	SEX	BLOOD	TRIBAL ENROLLMENT		
						Year	County	No.
I.W. 144	1 Mugler, Francisco C 42	First Named	39	M	IW	1896	Blue	14828
10953	2 " Theodocia 32	Wife	29	F	1/4	1896	"	8776
10954	3 " Delphine 17	Dau	14	"	1/8	1896	"	8777
	4							
	5							
	6	ENROLLMENT OF NOS. 2 and 3 HEREON						
	7	APPROVED BY THE SECRETARY						
	8	OF INTERIOR FEB 4 1903						
	9							
	10	ENROLLMENT OF NOS. 1 HEREON						
	11	APPROVED BY THE SECRETARY						
	12	OF INTERIOR JUN 13 1903						
	13							
	14							
	15							
	16							
	17							

TRIBAL ENROLLMENT OF PARENTS

Name of Father	Year	County	Name of Mother	Year	County
1 H. J. Mugler		Non Citz	Ellen Mugler	Dead	Non Citz
2 Caleb Impson	Dead	Blue	Melina Freeny		Blue
3 No1			No2		
4					
5					
6					
7 No1 on 1896 roll as Francis C Mugler					
8 No3 " 1896 " " Delphene "					
9 No.1 admitted by Dawes Commission in 1896 as an intermarried citizen: Choctaw case #384; no appeal					
10 For child of No.3 see NB (March 3, 1905) #1265					
11					
12					
13					
14				Date of Application for Enrollment.	
15				Aug 24/99	
16					
17					

RESIDENCE:	Red River	COUNTY.	Choctaw Nation		Choctaw Roll	CARD No.	
POST OFFICE:	Harris, I.T.				(Not Including Freedmen)	FIELD No.	3891

Dawes' Roll No.	NAME	Relationship to Person	AGE	SEX	BLOOD	TRIBAL ENROLLMENT		
						Year	County	No.
10955	₁ Tindell Amanda ⁴⁸	First Named	45	F	3/4	1896	Red River	5727
10956	₂ Lewis, Emma ⁹	Dau	6	"	1/2	1896	" "	8049
I.W.671	₃ Tindell Andrew J ³³	Hus	33	M	I.W.			
	4							
	5	ENROLLMENT						
	6	OF NOS. 1 and 2 HEREON APPROVED BY THE SECRETARY						
	7	OF INTERIOR FEB 4 1903						
	8							
	9	ENROLLMENT						
	10	OF NOS. 3 HEREON APPROVED BY THE SECRETARY						
	11	OF INTERIOR MAR 26 1904						
	12							
	13							
	14							
	15							
	16							
	17							

TRIBAL ENROLLMENT OF PARENTS

	Name of Father	Year	County	Name of Mother	Year	County
₁	Isaac Hampton	Dead	Red River	Sheliney Hampton	Dead	Red River
₂	Holman Lewis	"	" "	Mary Lewis	"	Non Citz
₃	Unknown	"	noncitizen	Sarah Tindell	"	noncitizen
4						
5						
6						
7	No3 transferred from Choctaw card D648 January 25, 1904					
8	See decision of January 7, 1904					
9	No1 on 1896 roll as Manda Hampton					
10	No2 " 1896 " " Emma Louis					
11	No2 As to marriage of parents, see testimony of No1					
12	No1 is now the wife of Andrew J Tindell on Choctaw Card #D648. Evidence of					
13	marriage filed Aug 21, 1901, with papers in Choctaw Case #D648					Date of Application for Enrollment.
14						Aug 24/99
15						
16						
17						

291

Choctaw By Blood Enrollment Cards 1898-1914

Dawes' Roll No.	NAME	Relationship to Person First Named	AGE	SEX	BLOOD	TRIBAL ENROLLMENT Year	County	No.
I.W. 358	1 Wilmoth, William M 51	First Named	38	M	IW			
10957	2 " Kizzie 48	Wife	45	F	1/2	1896	Red River	5679
10958	3 Hampton, Isaac D 22	S.Son	19	M	5/8	1896	" "	5680
10959	4 " Willie 17	"	14	"	5/8	1896	" "	5681
10960	5 Heflin, Lena L 10	S.Dau	7	F	1/4	1896	" "	5682
	6							
	7							
	8	ENROLLMENT						
	9	OF NOS. 2,3,4 and 5 HEREON						
	10	APPROVED BY THE SECRETARY OF INTERIOR FEB 4 1903						
	11	ENROLLMENT						
	12	OF NOS. 1 HEREON APPROVED BY THE SECRETARY						
	13	OF INTERIOR SEP 12 1903						
	14							
	15							
	16							
	17							

TRIBAL ENROLLMENT OF PARENTS

	Name of Father	Year	County	Name of Mother	Year	County
1	William Wilmoth	Dead	Non Citz	Mary A Wilmoth		Non Citz
2	Silas Jones	"	Red River	Bessie Jones	Dead	Red River
3	Mike Hampton	"	" "	No2		
4	" "	"	" "	No2		
5	W. H. Heflin		Non Citz	No2		
6						
7						
8						
9						
10	No2 on 1896 roll as Kizzie Heflin					
11						
12	No1 Evidence of marriage to be supplied:- Recd Oct 7/99					
13	For child of No3 see NB (March 3,1905) #1134					Date of Application for Enrollment.
14	Father of No.5 is on Choctaw Card #D686					Aug 24/99
15	Evidence of divorce between Nº2 and her former husband James Costilow, also evidence of divorce between Nº2 and her former					
16	husband W.H. Heflin filed Jany 2, 1903					
17						

292

RESIDENCE:	Blue	COUNTY.						CARD NO.	
POST OFFICE:	Caddo, I.T.		**Choctaw Nation**			Choctaw Roll *(Not Including Freedmen)*		FIELD NO. 3893	

Dawes' Roll No.	NAME	Relationship to Person First Named	AGE	SEX	BLOOD	TRIBAL ENROLLMENT		
						Year	County	No.
1	Smith, Joseph C	Named	39	M	1/8		D	
2	" Gertrude E	Dau	14	F	1/16		D	
3	" Henry D	Son	10	M	1/16		D	
4	" Cleo E	Dau	8	F	1/16		D	
5	" John M	Son	6	M	1/16		D	
6	" Ella	Dau	3	F	1/16		D	
7	" Onice M	Dau	1 mo	F	1/16		DIS	
8	No1 denied by C.C.C.C. as Joseph							
9	J.C. Smith or Jas. J.C. Smith							
10	#7 DISMISSED							
11	NOV 12 1904							
12								
13	See Pet #10, 90 See 33-884							
14	DENIED CITIZENSHIP BY THE CHOCTAW AND							
15								
16	Nos 1,2,3,4,5 and 6 CHICKASAW CITIZENSHIP COURT							
17						Case 107M Oct 20 '04		

TRIBAL ENROLLMENT OF PARENTS

	Name of Father	Year	County	Name of Mother	Year	County
1	W.H.P. Smith	Dead	Non Citz	Mary A Loving		Choctaw
2	No1			Nancy J Smith		Non Citz
3	No1			" " "		" "
4	No1			" " "		" "
5	No1			" " "		" "
6	No1			" " "		" "
7	No.1			" " "		" "
8						
9						
10	No1 Denied in 96 Case #546					
11	Admitted by U.S. Court, U.S Court[sic] Central Dist., Sept 11/97, Case No 71.					
12	As to residence, see testimony of No1					
13	No.7 Enrolled Oct 1st, 1900 For child of No2 see NB (Apr 26 '06) Card #884					
14	Judgment of US Ct admitting Nos 1 to6 incl vacated and set aside by Decree of Choctaw Chickasaw Cit Court Decr 17'02					
15	Nos 1 to 7 incl now in C.C.C.C. Case #107					
16					Date of Application for Enrollment.	Aug 24/99
17						

293

Choctaw By Blood Enrollment Cards 1898-1914

RESIDENCE: Blue	COUNTY.				Choctaw Roll	CARD NO.
POST OFFICE: Caddo, I.T.	**Choctaw Nation**				*(Not Including Freedmen)*	FIELD NO. 3894

Dawes' Roll No.	NAME	Relationship to Person First Named	AGE	SEX	BLOOD	TRIBAL ENROLLMENT		
						Year	County	No.
✓ 1	Smith, Daniel A		29	M	1/8		D	
2								
3								
4								
5								
6								
7								
8								
9								
10								
11								
12								
13								
14								
15								
16								
17								

TRIBAL ENROLLMENT OF PARENTS

	Name of Father	Year	County	Name of Mother	Year	County
1	W.H.P. Smith	Dead	Non Citz	Mary A Loving		Choctaw
2						
3						
4						
5						
6						
7	No1 Denied in 96 Case #546					
8	Admitted by U.S. Court, Central Dist					
9	Sept 11/97, Case No 71. As to residence see his testimony.					
10	Judgment of U.S. Ct admitting No vacated and set aside by Decree of Choctaw Chickasaw Citizenship Court Dec' 17'02					
11	No1 now in C.C.C.C. Case #107					
12						
13						
14						
15				Date of Application for Enrollment.		Aug 24/99
16						
17		See C 134				

DENIED CITIZENSHIP BY THE CHOCTAW AND CHICKASAW CITIZENSHIP COURT

Choctaw By Blood Enrollment Cards 1898-1914

RESIDENCE:	Blue	COUNTY:	**Choctaw Nation**			**Choctaw Roll**	CARD NO.	
POST OFFICE:	Caddo, I.T.					(Not Including Freedmen)	FIELD NO. 3895	

Dawes' Roll No.	NAME	Relationship to Person First Named	AGE	SEX	BLOOD	TRIBAL ENROLLMENT		
						Year	County	No.
* 1	Riddie, Dumas S	Named	44	M	1/8			
* 2	" William E	Son	12	"	1/16			
* 3	" Jennie E	Dau	10	F	1/16			
* 4	" Martha	"	8	"	1/16			
* 5	" Claude D	Son	6	M	1/16			
* 6	" Joe	Dau	4	"	1/16			
7	" Ruby	"	16mo	"	1/16			
8								
9								
	Nos 1 to 6 incl. Denied by C.C.C.C. Mar 21 04							
	No7 (Jurisdiction) Dismissed " " "							
12								
13								
14		DISMISSED						
15		MAY 25 1904						
16								
17								

TRIBAL ENROLLMENT OF PARENTS						
Name of Father	Year	County	Name of Mother	Year	County	
1 Hampton Riddle	Dead	Choctaw	Nancy Riddle	Dead	Non Citz	
2 No1			Jennie Riddle		" "	
3 No1			" "		" "	
4 No1					" "	
5 No1		"	" "		" " Mar 21 04	
6 No1			" "		"	
7 No1			" "		" "	
8						
9						
10						

DENIED CITIZENSHIP BY THE CHOCTAW AND CHICKASAW CITIZENSHIP COURT

No1 to 6 incl denied in 96 Case #686
All but No7 were admitted by U.S.
Court, Central Dist., Aug 30/97. As
to residence and birth of No7, which
occurred March 23/98, see testimony of
No1. Judgment of U.S Court admitting Nos 1 to 6 incl vacated and set aside by Decree of Choctaw Chickasaw Citizenship Court Dec 17/02

Evidence as to marriage of parents
of No7 to be supplied:- Recd Oct 7/99
Nos 1 to 7 inclusive now in C.C.C.C. Case #108

Date of Application for Enrollment.	Aug 24/99

295

Choctaw By Blood Enrollment Cards 1898-1914

RESIDENCE: **Blue**	COUNTY.					Choctaw Roll	CARD NO.	
POST OFFICE: Caddo, I.T.	**Choctaw Nation**					*(Not Including Freedmen)*	FIELD NO. **3896**	

Dawes' Roll No.	NAME	Relationship to Person First Named	AGE	SEX	BLOOD	TRIBAL ENROLLMENT		
						Year	County	No.
* 1	Riddle, James T		30	M	1/8			
2								
3								
4								
5								
6								
7								
8								
9								
10								
11								
12								
13								
14								
15								
16								
17								

TRIBAL ENROLLMENT OF PARENTS

	Name of Father	Year	County	Name of Mother	Year	County
1	Hampton Riddle	Dead	Choctaw	Nancy Riddle	Dead	Non Citz
2						
3						
4						
5						
6						
7						
8						

No1 denied in 96 Case #686

Admitted by U.S. Court, Central
Dist, Aug 30/07, Case No 8. As
to residence, see his testimony.

Judgment of US Court setting No1 aside and set aside by Decree of Choctaw Chickasaw Citizenship Court Dec 17 1902

No1 now in C.C.C.C. Case #108

No1 Denied by C.C.C.C. Case #108 March 2? '04

Is No1 the husband of Mary A Riddle on Choctaw #3810?

Date of Application for Enrollment.

Aug 24/99

Choctaw By Blood Enrollment Cards 1898-1914

RESIDENCE: Blue County
POST OFFICE: Caddo, I.T.
Choctaw Nation
Choctaw Roll
CARD NO.
FIELD NO. 3897

Dawes' Roll No.	NAME		Relationship to Person	AGE	SEX	BLOOD	TRIBAL ENROLLMENT		
							Year	County	No.
10961	1 Freeny, Robert C	52	First Named	49	M	1/8	1896	Blue	4370
I.W. 359	2 " Josephine	34	Wife	35	F	I.W	1896	"	14537
10962	3 Oakes, Mary A	22	Dau	19	"	1/16	1896	"	4371
10963	4 Freeny, Ella B	20	"	17	"	1/16	1896	"	4372
10964	5 " Robert C Jr	18	Son	15	M	1/16	1896	"	4373
10965	6 " Ellis D	16	"	13	"	1/16	1896	"	4374
10966	7 " John W	6	"	3	"	1/16	1896	"	4375
10967	8 " Homer M	4	"	9mo	"	1/16			
10968	9 " Carrie Ida	2	Dau	3mo	F	1/16			
10969	10 Oakes, Thomas Clay	1	Son of No3	1mo	M	3/16			
10970	11 Freeny, Arlington H	1	Son	3mo	"	1/16			

12 No3,4,5&6 drew the Cherokee Strip Payment
13 money in the Cherokee Nation. The mother of
14 above children was a Cherokee, her maiden name
was Mary Beck

ENROLLMENT
OF NOS. 1,3,4,5,6,7,8,9,10 and 11 HEREON
APPROVED BY THE SECRETARY
OF INTERIOR FEB 4 1903

ENROLLMENT
OF NOS. 2 HEREON
APPROVED BY THE SECRETARY
OF INTERIOR SEP 12 1903

TRIBAL ENR

	Name of Father	Year	County				
1	Robert Freeny	Dead	Non Citz				
2	Banter	"	" "	Manda Banter		Non-Citizen	
3	No1			Mary Freeny		Dead	Cherokee
4	No1			" "		"	"
5	No1			" "		"	"
6	No1			" "		"	"
7	No1			No2			
8	No1			No2			
9	No1			No2			
10	Daniel W Oakes	1896	Kiamitia	No3			
11	No1			No2			

12 No1 On 1896 Roll as R.C. Freeney; No3 is now the wife of Daniel W Oakes on Choctaw Card #1467
No2 " 1896 " " Josephine Freeny; Evidence of marriage filed Aug 24 1901 in the papers herein
13 No3 " 1896 " " Mary Freeny; No8 Affidavit of birth to be supplied. Received Oct 7/99
14 No4 " 1896 " " Elle " ; No9 Enrolled Decr 15th 1900
15 No5 " 1896 " " Robert " ; "10 Enrolled Aug 24' 1901
No6 " 1896 " " Walter " ; "11 Born Aug 29 1902 Enrolled Dec 24' 1902
16 No7 " 1896 " " John " ; For child of No3 see NB (Mar 3-05) #572
17 " " " Nos1&2 " " " " #814
For child of No4 see NB (Act Mar 3'05) Card #272.

Date of Application
for Enrollment. Aug 24/99

Choctaw By Blood Enrollment Cards 1898-1914

RESIDENCE:	Blue	COUNTY.				
POST OFFICE:	Folsom, I.T.	**Choctaw Nation**		Choctaw Roll *(Not Including Freedmen)*	CARD NO. FIELD NO. **3898**	

Dawes' Roll No.	NAME	Relationship to Person First Named	AGE	SEX	BLOOD	TRIBAL ENROLLMENT		
						Year	County	No.
10971	1 Pebsworth, James L ²⁶	First Named	23	M	1/16	1893	Blue	981
I.W. 360	2 " Willie A ²⁵	Wife	21	F	I.W			
	3							
	4							
	5	*Further action in connection with allotment to Nos 1&2 suspended under protest of*						
	6	*Attorneys for Choctaw and Chickasaw Nations Jan 23 '04. Protest withdrawn by Attys*						
	7	*Mch 24 1904*						
	8							
	9							
	10	ENROLLMENT						
	11	OF NOS. 1 HEREON						
	12	APPROVED BY THE SECRETARY OF INTERIOR Feb 4 1903						
	13	ENROLLMENT						
	14	OF NOS. 2 HEREON						
	15	APPROVED BY THE SECRETARY OF INTERIOR Sep 12 1903						
	16							
	17							

TRIBAL ENROLLMENT OF PARENTS

	Name of Father	Year	County	Name of Mother	Year	County
1	John Pebsworth	Dead	Non Citz	Mary A Pebsworth	Dead	Blue
2	John Davison	" "		Natt Davison		Non Citz
3						
4						
5						
6						
7			No1 on 1893 Pay Roll, Page 95, No 981, Blue			
8			Co, as Lee Pebsworth.			
9			As to enrollment, see his testimony			
	Nos 1&2 divorced, see copy of decree in jacket NB (Apr 26-06) #449					
10	For child of No1 see NB (Apr 26-06) Card #449					
11						
12						
13						
14						
15				Date of Application for Enrollment.	Aug 24/99	
16						
17						

298

Choctaw By Blood Enrollment Cards 1898-1914

RESIDENCE: Jackson COUNTY. **Choctaw Nation**
POST OFFICE: Bennington, I.T. (Not Including Freedmen) FIELD NO. 3899

Choctaw Roll CARD NO.

Dawes' Roll No.	NAME	Relationship to Person First Named	AGE	SEX	BLOOD	TRIBAL ENROLLMENT		
						Year	County	No.
10972	1 Jones, Jacob ⁵⁴	First Named	51	M	1/2	1896	Jackson	7127
	2							
	3							
	4	ENROLLMENT						
	5	OF NOS. 1 HEREON APPROVED BY THE SECRETARY						
	6	OF INTERIOR FEB 4 1903						
	7							
	8							
	9							
	10							
	11							
	12							
	13							
	14							
	15							
	16							
	17							

TRIBAL ENROLLMENT OF PARENTS

	Name of Father	Year	County	Name of Mother	Year	County
1	Silas Jones	Dead	Red River	Bessie Jones	Dead	Red River
2						
3						
4						
5						
6						
7						
8						
9						
10						
11						
12						
13						
14					Date of Application for Enrollment	
15					Aug 24/99	
16						
17						

299

Choctaw By Blood Enrollment Cards 1898-1914

RESIDENCE: Chickasaw Nation ~~COUNTY~~ Choctaw Nation   Choctaw Roll   CARD NO.
POST OFFICE: Marlow, I.T.   (Not Including Freedmen)   FIELD NO. 3900

Dawes' Roll No.	NAME	Relationship to Person	AGE	SEX	BLOOD	TRIBAL ENROLLMENT		
						Year	County	No.
10973	1 Simpson, Elizabeth H 64	First Named	61	F	1/4	1893	Chick Dist	70
	2							
	3							
	4							
	5	ENROLLMENT						
	6	OF NOS. 1 HEREON APPROVED BY THE SECRETARY						
	7	OF INTERIOR FEB 4 1903						
	8							
	9							
	10							
	11							
	12							
	13							
	14							
	15							
	16							
	17							

TRIBAL ENROLLMENT OF PARENTS

	Name of Father	Year	County	Name of Mother	Year	County
1	Wm LeFlore	Dead	in Mississippi	Martha LeFlore	Dead	Non Citz
2						
3						
4						
5			On 1893 Pay Roll, Page 7, No 70, Chick Dist.			
6			as Elizabeth Brummett			
7						
8			As to marriage of parents, see her			
9			own testimony			
10						
11			Husband on card No D362			
12						
13						
14				Date of Application for Enrollment		
15						Aug 24/99
16						
17						

FREENEY
Melina..................161,162
R C 297
FREENY
Arlington H........................297
Carrie Ida.........................297
Ella B................................297
Elle 297
Ellis D...............................297
Henry................................108
Homer M 297
Ida M 162
Jno W...............................108
John 162,297
John W.......................108,297
Josephine.........................297
Malina..............................162
Mary 297
Melina.........................272,290
R A 108
Robert..............................297
Robert C 297
Robert C, Jr......................297
Walter..............................297
FRY
Allington..........................107
Bessie 107
Billy.................................107
Edmond 107
Emma 107
Ita.....................................107
James...............................107
Jim...................................107
Lena.................................107
Natt..................................107
Pusley 107
Robert..............................107
Vicey 107
FRYER
Adeline 236
Andrew.............................283
Annie L.............................283
Bert..................................236
Edith 236
A J 236
Lurinda L..........................283
Oliver B 236

FULLOMME..........................269
Gibson 269
FULSOM
Katie.................................26
Robert..............................126
Robt 126
GARDNER
Arabella 205,210,275
Arabella C....................206,207
Arabella S 209
Bessie A............................207
Daniel 98
Daniel H 206
Daniel Harris 206
Dona Lee 209
Dona S..............................207
Dora S...............................207
Edward N...........................209
Florence............................176
Green 176,206,207,209,210
Harriet...............................176
Iona...................................209
Jesse G..............................207
Leroy 176
Luther 176
Martin L.............................176
Mary A 210
Mary J...............................98
Mimie 206
Minnie 206
Othena 206
Raymon R..........................98
Robert L.............................207
Robt L...............................207
Rosetta..............................209
Samuel..............................176
Samuel G 176
Willie.................................176
Willington L 207
Wilson 132
GARLAND
Aurilla...............................212
Jack..................................212
James 212
Jim...................................212
John 212
Levi..................................212

Index

www.ingramcontent.com/pod-product-compliance
Lightning Source LLC
Chambersburg PA
CBHW030236030426
42336CB00009B/122